The German-American Radical Press

The Shaping of a Left Political Culture, 1850–1940

EDITED BY

Elliott Shore

Ken Fones-Wolf

James P. Danky

UNIVERSITY OF ILLINOIS PRESS
Urbana and Chicago

© 1992 by the Board of Trustees of the University of Illinois
Manufactured in the United States of America
C 5 4 3 2 1

This book is printed on acid-free paper.

Library of Congress Cataloging-in-Publication Data

The German-American radical press : the shaping of a left political
    culture, 1850–1940 / edited by Elliott Shore, Ken Fones-Wolf, James
    P. Danky.
        p. cm.
    Includes bibliographical references and index.
    ISBN 0-252-01830-3
    1. German-American newspapers—History. 2. German-American
periodicals—History. 3. German Americans—Politics and government.
4. Political culture—United States—History. 5. Radicalism—United
States—History. I. Shore, Elliott, 1951–   . II. Fones-Wolf,
Ken. III. Danky, James Philip, 1947–   .
PN4885.G3G47   1992
071'.3'08931—dc20   91-22855
                                                               CIP

Contents

Acknowledgments

The editors would like to thank their respective institutions for encouraging the work that helped to make this volume possible: the Institute for Advanced Study, Princeton, New Jersey; the University of Massachusetts-Amherst; West Virginia University; and the State Historical Society of Wisconsin. We would also like to thank the Max Kade Institute of the University of Wisconsin, which provided the impetus for a number of the essays in this volume. Special thanks are due to Gail Malmgreen of the Tamiment Library, New York University, for her critical comments on an early version of the manuscript, and to Denise Diamond of the Institute for Advanced Study, for her work in preparing the text for publication. We are especially grateful to Pat Hollahan, of the University of Illinois Press, for improving a manuscript of diverse essays into what we hope the reader will find to be a unified work.

Elliott Shore, Ken Fones-Wolf, and James P. Danky

Introduction

Few communities in America were as intricately connected with their newspapers as were German-American radicals. Wilhelm Weitling, a self-educated tailor who had become a prominent utopian socialist in Germany and who helped to organize the Arbeiterbund and to establish a utopian colony in Communia, Iowa, was one of the first to comment on this phenomenon. Writing in 1850 in the New York radical paper he founded, *Die Republik der Arbeiter,* Weitling said of German-American radicals:

> Everybody wants to put out a little paper, everybody wants to lead an association, everybody wants to start a fund, everybody wants to be a teacher, interpreting everything on his own for the people. Over here is someone who mixes decentralization with socialism, while over there another mixes atheism with reason, and a third person does socialist gymnastics, while the fourth works for decisive progress. The first person wants to create a society for the spirit, the second for mankind, the third for the people, the fourth for the workers, one for singers, another for tailors, for gymnasts, for refugees, and so forth. And a hundred others also want all of this, but each with a little difference.[1]

As Weitling's comments suggest, by 1850 there were myriad variations in the German-American radical scene. Indeed, they had been apparent for almost a generation. Political refugees who arrived in the 1830s helped to revitalize the press in the German-American communities where they found refuge, whether it was the famous Philadelphia paper *Alte und Neue Welt,* the *Freiheitsfreund* in Chambersburg, the *Weltbürger* in Cincinnati, or Philadelphia's *Der Freisinnige.* Working-class immigrants in the 1840s established their own papers, beginning

1

with what was probably the first truly German worker's paper published in the United States—*Der Adoptivbürger*, edited by Georg Dietz in Philadelphia in 1845, which was followed closely by *Der Volks-Tribun* in 1846 in New York City.[2] In these early years it would have been quite difficult to classify the German papers politically because of the enormous impact that would follow the series of revolutions in Europe in 1848 and the subsequent addition of 48ers to the staffs of established papers. The prominence of radical sentiments is clear in a contemporary history of the Germans in America written in 1855, which stated flatly that the most important papers in America were the *Deutsche Schnellpost* of New York, followed closely by the *Anzeiger des Westens* of St. Louis.[3] The *Schnellpost* was famous for publishing correspondence from the emerging socialist movement in Germany, as well as being linked to the movement in France, and the *Anzeiger* was the imaginative paper published by the 48er Heinrich Börnstein, important to both the European and American radical movements (see Rowan's essay in this volume). These papers were of course not without their critics, some (like Weitling) sympathetic, but others more caustic, such as a recent immigrant who complained to his father about the paper he enclosed (almost certainly the *Schnellpost*): "You'll see that it is an indifferently edited paper that is entirely one-sided and overflowing with exaggerated liberal ideas." Yet even critics had to admit that the papers were influential.[4]

These early papers were the forerunners of a press which was to be large and important for about a century. To put together an anthology that covers the entire spectrum of the German-American radical press would be a daunting project. Instead, what this anthology has attempted to do is to offer some thematic essays which provide a broad-based view of the complexity and richness of this press. Similarly, our definition of radical is broad, including everything that Wilhelm Weitling discussed and more, from free thought to socialism, from working people's papers to the *Turner*, from anarchists to feminists. Unfortunately, we do not have contributions on all of these variations. We do not specifically discuss the *Turner* papers, nor do we look at the work of Karl Heinzen and Johann Most, to mention two important editors. But we do hope to provide in these essays a long-overdue addition to what we know about the importance of the German-language radical press, to indicate its significance in a century of American history. And we point, in Moses Rischin's Envoi, to some unanswered questions and some directions that future research might take. What we have highlighted here is the period from 1870 to 1910, when the social democratic press was at its height, and we have chosen to do so because these anarchist, socialist, and trade-union papers, unlike those of the 48ers, have been virtually neglected. This is a step toward redressing that imbalance.

The tendency toward political differences to which Weitling alluded was, of course, hardly restricted to what could be called the radical press of the nineteenth and twentieth centuries. The first prominent German-American newspaper dynasty, that of the Christopher Sauer family, clashed in its *Germantauner Zeitung* and *Pennsylvanische Staats Courier* with the prorevolutionary Heinrich Miller, editor of the *Pennsylvanischer Staatsbote*.[5] Religious differences, length of stay in America, and points of origin in Germany all helped fuel the desire for diversity among the German-American community from its very inception. In Milwaukee, perhaps the archetypical German-American city, the importance and diversity of the press was apparent almost from the birth of the city. The first German journal appeared in 1844 and half of the new papers issued in the 1850s—fifteen of thirty—were in German, including several radical ones: *Grad'Aus, Humanist,* and a feminist radical monthly edited by Franziska Anneke, *Frauenzeitung.*[6]

When viewed in comparison with the other foreign-language papers in the United States, the extent of the German-American press in general, and its large radical subsection in particular, is little short of astonishing. From about 1880 to the turn of the century, at least two-thirds of all foreign-language newspapers in the country were in German. In 1890, for example, there were more than one thousand German newspapers published in America, and only 278 other foreign-language papers (eighty-four of which were Scandinavian).[7] One reason for the huge number of papers is that, except for the Irish, the Germans were the largest immigrant group to come to the United States. Four million German-speaking immigrants arrived in the second half of the nineteenth century. And, to give just Chicago as an example, in 1900 two-thirds of these were still in working-class immigrant households.[8] The German press in nineteenth-century America was such a strong force in certain states that it successfully lobbied for laws mandating the publication of official notices in German. In Pennsylvania, the German press even had its own organization in the 1860s and 1870s.[9] And German-American printers formed their own union, Deutsch-Amerikanische Typographia, which flourished from the 1870s through World War II.[10]

The percentage of German-language radical papers as a total of the whole was also significant. The key research in this field has been done by the Labor Migration Project and Labor Newspaper Preservation Project at the University of Bremen (see Hoerder's essay in this volume for more detail). The absolute numbers of papers increased from the 1840s to the early 1890s, and there were many more German-language and Nordic-language radical and working-class papers than for any other language group. The project estimates a total of about 240 German and 160 Northern European labor and radical periodicals in the period from the 1840s to the 1940s. From the 1840s to the 1860s, more than 60 papers were established by radical 48ers, utopian socialists, and workers' clubs. The golden period was from 1870 to 1902, when more than 120 periodicals were founded, including citywide labor papers, union papers, and papers of socialist and anarchist groups. From 1902 to 1920, the project found, German-American radicals were reading the English-language radical press, and so only 20 new papers were born. In the 1930s and 1940s, there was a new upsurge of the German-language radical press, by refugees from Germany and German-American antifascists.[11]

The work included here builds upon four distinct phases in the writing of the history of the German-American radical press. The first features the memoirs of participants and early histories that appeared in the first German-American historical journals, such as *Der Deutsche Pionier, Americana Germanica,* and the *Deutsch-Amerikanische Geschichtsblätter,* on which much of the later historical work has been based. This was followed closely by investigations, such as William Frederic Kamman's *Socialism in German-American Literature* (1917) and Adolph Eduard Zucker's *Robert Reitzel* (1917), which were largely descriptive and fairly sympathetic to the radical past they described.

The third phase followed swiftly on the heels of World War I. Robert E. Park, who had been secretary to Booker T. Washington, wrote *The Immigrant Press and Its Control* (1922), commissioned by the Carnegie Corporation of New York and published in a series of Americanization studies, which was motivated by a concept Park helped to develop: assimilationism.[12] Park asserted two primary things about the foreign-language press in general, and the radical press specifically, that continued to shape the field until the 1960s, and was instrumental in the debate that emerged in the 1920s about the concept of ethnicity in the social sciences. He argued that the ethnic press in general was a transitional phenomenon which, at its best, helped to ease the process of assimilation, preserving the ethnic heritage of the group in its first generation as it counseled its members on how to become Americans. At its worst, however, in its radical manifestation, the immigrant press, and specifically its German element, struggled against the current in American life, misleading and slowing down the natural tendency toward acculturation.

This view of the press was considerably softened in the still standard work of Carl Wittke, who, after World War II, wrote in the accepted "Americanizing" vein that Park had done so much to establish—reading a teleological pattern back into the German-American press tradition. Wittke also valued those publications whose language and literary tastes tended toward the elite tradition in German culture, especially when he was writing about the radical press. Biographer of two of the foremost 48er radicals, Karl Heinzen (*Against the Current* [1945]) and Wilhelm Weitling (*The Utopian Communist* [1950]), Wittke was sympathetic to an important portion of the radical past of German-America, but still he tried to fit that past into a framework, not of his own making, which dominated American radical scholarship in the 1950s and early 1960s. The prevailing model, which appears also in the radical historiography of Howard Quint and David Shannon, tried to incorporate the radicalism of the pre-World War I socialists into a consensus mode, arguing (in Wittke's case) that the absence of press censorship in the United States gave the German radicals a freedom which was liberating but which ultimately failed to make headway in America. Wittke's work strongly evokes the German-American press in general and the radical press in particular, despite the constraints under which he worked.

The current trend, begun in the 1960s, is characterized by the ground-breaking work of Hartmut Keil and Dirk Hoerder. Unlike Wittke, who looked at only thirty German-American newspapers in compiling his general history and three in his chapter on the radical press, Hoerder, assisted by Christiane Harzig in Bremen and by specialists all over Europe and North America, has unearthed and described hundreds of German-American radical papers, as well as the radical press of the other European language groups in America. Extending and deepening the monumental bibliographical work of Karl Arndt and May Olson, Hoerder, working with files of newspapers held in both the United States and Europe, has used this material to go beyond the questions that Park and Wittke asked by looking closely at the contents of the German-American radical press. Likewise, in their work on Chicago, Keil and John Jentz made the ideas and words of those Americans whose working-class movements spoke another language accessible for the first time to American historians who do not use other than English-language sources.

They have uncovered the same rich diversity that Weitling knew, and to an extent despaired of, in 1850. Instead of seeing in the general ethnic press the march to the melting pot and in the maintenance of cultural identity a sentimental longing for a world that was beyond their reach, the new generation of ethnic historians is looking at the words and actions of the radical German-American men and women in the context of their times. They are finding a rich pattern that belies the prescriptive approach of the preceding generation of historians. Through Dirk Hoerder and Christiane Harzig's *Immigrant Labor Press in North America* (3 volumes, 1987–88); Carol Poore's *German-American Socialist Literature 1865–1900* (1982); Keil and Jentz's *German Worker's Culture in the United States 1850 to 1920* (1988); Dirk Hoerder and Thomas Weber's *Glimpses of the German-American Radical Press* (1985); Steven Rowan's *Germans for a Free Missouri: Translations from the St. Louis Radical Press, 1857–1862*; and Ulrike Heider's *Der Arme Teufel: Robert Reitzel, von Vormärz zum Haymarket* (1986), a more fully developed historical view of the German-American radical past is emerging.[13]

This anthology is a contribution to that effort. Earlier versions of about half of these essays came out of a conference on the German-American press held under the auspices of the Max Kade Institute at the State Historical Society of Wisconsin, in the fall of 1987. For this volume, those essays were considerably revised and expanded, and additional pieces by Carol Poore, Bruce Nelson, and Richard Oestreicher were commissioned. An earlier version of John Jentz's essay was read at the American Historical Association's 1988 conference. In his concluding essay, Moses Rischin, who helped to strengthen a number of the essays through his comments at the conference, explores further avenues for research in the field.

Alternatives to the standard reading of assimilation are offered here, together with more sensitive readings of the nature of German-American radicalism. Hartmut Keil starts with Wittke's assertion that the 48ers boosted a waning press tradition by applying the same pattern to the next generation of German-American radical immigrants, most notably the socialist and trade-union refugees from the newly founded German state, a group that has never been extensively studied before. Using life stories, painstakingly re-created largely on the basis of material made accessible through Dirk Hoerder's bibliographical project, Keil makes a first approximation of a collective biography which sheds light on social, cultural, and economic standing. The work of these new exiles for the radical press reveals an important dimension in German-American ethnic identity, for they brought a revitalized language and culture to a community that was losing its first generation of native speakers. Ironically, the radical press "claimed to be the true heirs of the German high cultural tradition, whereas in their opinion German-American middle-class papers had given in to mass popular tastes and lower standards, especially when it came to writing German and propagating German classical literature" (Keil, p. 26).

Ken Fones-Wolf and Elliott Shore directly confront one of the hardy perennials of ethnic history—the move to assimilation—by looking at two periods of labor unrest in Philadelphia through the medium of both the Republican and Democratic German-American dailies and the one avowedly labor and radical paper. What they find seriously undermines received wisdom about group unity and assimilation in the large German working-class community of Philadelphia in the 1870s and 1880s. Instead of heeding calls for communal solidarity in the 1870s, German working-class leaders began to call on their fellow workers to learn English in order to desert the German-American press in favor of the city's more sympathetic English-language paper. Yet less than a generation later, German-American radical workers turned away from the larger goals of a united working-class movement, seeking instead to reinforce intra-ethnic group solidarity for more immediate goals.

Nowhere is the complexity of the German-American radical past articulated more clearly than in the women's page of the *New Yorker Volkszeitung* (*NYVZ*). Ruth Seifert's research carefully re-creates the positions taken by such leaders as Meta Stern and Johanna Greie-Cramer. Where Wittke assigns one paragraph in his work to two women journalists,[14] Seifert opens up a world in which women pose the difficult questions that the German-American socialist men were not ready to try to answer. Although ostensibly a part of the "Sunday supplement" that would offer women instruction in socialism by providing orthodox propositions for them to learn, the women's page, unlike similar pages in newspapers in Germany, quickly became a forum for the discussion of a wide range of issues relating to women—a forum in which the orthodox position did not prevail. Seifert shows how suffrage, to take one of many issues, pointed up the contradictions of male-dominated German-American socialism.

The views held by the *NYVZ* were significant not only for German-American women but for all American socialists, women and men. As Paul Buhle shows, the *NYVZ*, a daily for fifty-four years and a weekly for twelve more, was the standard American Marxist newspaper. In its pages, the practical positions of, and the possibilities for, an American Marxism were played out, anchored in an ethnic community from which it drew support. Buhle reveals that the *NYVZ* and its editor, Ludwig Lore, were independent and sensitive to variations in both Marxist theory and American life, reminding us of the promise that American socialism held out and the dilemmas it posed.

Much of the richness of German-American socialism is missed

through a narrowly political reading of the *NYVZ*, and of the radical press in general. The *NYVZ* published such writers as Covington Hall and Miriam Allen DeFord and sponsored a yearly calendar which prospered as long as the daily newspaper. The *Pionier* calendar, in a long historical tradition dating from the invention of printing, aimed to provide a popular cultural framework for the year in the German-American home. Filled with stories, sketches, art reproductions, humor, and political writing, this fifty-year success story in radical publishing showed what an alternative culture looked like. Carol Poore samples some of the diversity of that culture, which rendered political such acts as interior decorating and choices for popular reading. Perhaps more than any other of the publications of the radical press, the *Pionier* calendar shows the modern reader what it meant for a household to be both German-American and socialist.

The nature of the business practices of these papers brings another part of the German-American radical experience into focus by demonstrating how the German ethnic community dealt with the lack of capital for developing its newspapers. In Chicago, as Bruce Nelson shows, all of the radical publications were issued by publishing societies, with Germans of various radical affiliations banding together to buy stock and running the noncommercial papers on a cooperative basis. One such group, the Socialist Publishing Society, defined its mission as the "education and intellectual improvement of its members through the fostering of moral culture, history, political economy, statistics, philosophy, and other subjects, by means of regular meetings, debates, lectures and addresses, pamphlets, newspapers, periodicals and publications" (Nelson, p. 90). With Chicago's German working class split in ways similar to Philadelphia's and New York's, by religion, place of birth in Germany, and generational differences among the immigrants, these newspapers and their publishing groups united people of common backgrounds, often grouped by neighborhood, and provided a subcontext for the labor history of Chicago's German working-class "community."[15]

Individual radicals made contributions to the literary and cultural landscape of American letters that have only begun to be recovered and that bring into sharp focus the dilemma of ethnic identity: whether to remain a separate language group or to embrace assimilation. One figure, Robert Reitzel, is justly described by Richard Oestreicher as probably "the most lively and imaginative, certainly the most irreverent, literary voice of nineteenth-century American Germania" (p. 147). Reitzel, the poet, literary critic, essayist, and radical proponent of sexual emancipation, feminism, homosexual rights, and individual freedom, published *Der arme Teufel* in Detroit in the 1880s and 1890s. His publication was so popular among Germans of all classes that it spawned Arme Teufel clubs in Toledo, Pittsburgh, St. Louis, and Cincinnati. Tireless in his defense of the Haymarket martyrs, this eloquent humanist provided yet another notion of what it was possible to think in the period, in many ways anticipating political and social developments from the Progressive Era through the Movement of the 1960s. With subscribers drawn mostly from the middle class, Reitzel sought to revive interest in the German classics while promoting causes that were supposed to be anathema to the very same middle class which welcomed his words.

What Reitzel was for the generation of radical humanists late in the century, Franz Schmidt had been for the freethinking community in St. Louis ten years before the Civil War. As Steven Rowan makes clear, his stongly anticlerical *Freie Blätter* pointed up one of the most important problems for the German-American radical: the question of religion. The German-American community had, since its inception in the late seventeenth century, centered much of its life around religion. Schmidt's anticlericalism was a radical response to the threat posed to independent thought by religions dominated by their clergy. To satisfy the need to associate, as religions of all kinds did for their adherents, Schmidt set up the Verein Freier Männer where the like-minded of St. Louis could meet every other Sunday.

Josef Jodlbauer, even more obscure than Franz Schmidt, in some ways completes a cycle for the German-American radical press. Where Schmidt's optimism and Reitzel's determined humanism kept them fighting for independent thought in nineteenth-century America, Jodlbauer, who came to the United States in 1910 and was forced back to Austria in 1923, had few illusions about the possibility of radical change in the life of his adopted country. Dirk Hoerder uses the case of Jodlbauer to illustrate his contentions that radical immigrants knew what they were leaving and had no illusions about what they might find, and that the perceptions of American political institutions found in the radical labor press were never refuted. As John Jentz shows, these political perceptions had already transformed German-American radicalism at the time of the Civil War. As the German-American community was being built, its interaction with American electoral politics became the battleground where ethnic ties and radical politics clashed.

One of the largest German-American radical newspapers in the nineteenth century, *Der Vorbote*, published in Chicago, argued that "the history of the labor movement is simultaneously the history of the labor press" (Nelson, p. 81). While this may be a slight exaggeration, the sentiment is understandable, given the importance of the press to the German-American community. Aside from the obvious usefulness of the radical press for the history of radicalism in America, it is also essential, as Hoerder shows, as a means of opening up the question of the "unmarked category," in this case the view of America in the press itself. The radical press and its editors show strikingly that the daily paper was not the only possible way for contemporaries to look at current events.

Kampfblätter was what German immigrant workers called their newspapers, which were aimed at supporting the struggle—*Kampf*—for a better life.[16] This volume is a contribution to the study of those women and men who made it their life to attempt to create a better world. They often saw their battle simply as one pitting good against evil, in stark terms, as are recalled in these lines from the 1903 Jubilee edition of the *NYVZ*. The capitalist press is described as swimming with the tide, supporting and supported by the status quo. "Against that [i.e., the capitalist press], comes a worker-newspaper, always like a Cinderella to the world and just like the Saviour of Christendom, she is so lowly . . . almost literally born in a stable, and a wretched manger is her cradle." But this worker press is not just a Cinderella; "her inner substance is a proud, warlike Amazon," someone "true and trustworthy, born of the people," to whom alone she is loyal and for whom she helps to create "new, strong life."[17] This characterization, romantic and self-congratulatory, spoke of the constant yearning to right the wrongs of the world. The use of female imagery is just one evidence of the nostalgic and romantic that would soon be challenged. But it was in the tradition of a press then more than a half-century old. That dream, of the triumph of the good, was the hope of the 48ers as it would be the hope of the antifascist press of the 1930s and 1940s.

A *Revolutionsfest*, held in New York on March 25, 1848, featured fourteen speakers, four different languages, and a daylong parade down Broadway. The prevailing sentiment spoke of the revolutionary flag of the German 48ers: "When the black-red-and-gold flutters proudly beside the Star Spangled Banner, and the spirit of George Washington watches over them both, then Germans on both sides of the Atlantic will cry in their hearts, God bless Germany."[18] Somehow it seems appropriate that this volume, which reinvokes the spirit of these men and women of vision, principle, and hope, was completed in the autumn of 1990, when German reunification began. Perhaps the spirit which is here recalled will serve as a harbinger to another century.

NOTES

1. *Republik der Arbeiter*, 1850, pp. 180ff., as quoted in William Frederic Kamman, *Socialism in German American Literature*, p. 20. This translation, and all others in this volume, are by the authors of the individual articles, unless otherwise noted. On Weitling himself, see Carl Wittke, *Utopian Communist*; Ernst Schraepler, *Handwerkerbünde und Arbeitervereine 1830–1853*; and Robert E. Cazden, *Social History of the German Book Trade in America*, pp. 627–37.

2. Hermann Schlüter, *Die Anfänge der deutschen Arbeiterbewegung in Amerika* [1907], p. 19; Cazden, *Social History of the German Book Trade in America*, pp. 621–22.

3. Franz Loeher, *Geschichte und Zustände der Deutschen in Amerika*, p. 456.

4. Letter from Alfred Benecke in New York to his father, July 11, 1845, as reprinted in *"Amerika ist ein freies Land,"* p. 181. Internal evidence suggests that he was talking about the *Schnellpost*.

5. On the early German-American press, see Carl Wittke, *German Language Press in America*, chap. 1. The major source of past critical work on the history of the press is volume 3 of Karl J. R. Arndt and May E. Olson, *German Language Press of the Americas*. It reprints standard work from the nineteenth and the first half of the twentieth centuries. Cazden's momumental work, cited in n. 1, contains a long section on German radicalism and social utopias which provides a comprehensive empirical basis to look at the radical periodical press prior to the Civil War.

6. Kathleen Conzen, *Immigrant Milwaukee*, pp. 184–88.

7. Robert E. Park, *Immigrant Press and Its Control*, p. 318.

8. Klaus J. Bade, *Vom Auswanderungsland zum Einwanderungsland?* and Hartmut Keil, "German Immigrant Workers in Nineteenth Century America," p. 193.

9. Marion L. Huffines, "Language-Maintenance Efforts among German Immigrants and Their Descendants," p. 243.

10. *Immigrant Labor Press in North America*, vol. 3, p. 505.

11. Dirk Hoerder and Christiane Harzig, *"Why Did You Come?"—Proletarian Mass Migration*, pp. 51–61. Frank Luther Mott's standard work, *American Journalism*, counted a total of 133 German papers by 1850; that number doubled by the end of the decade. The entire foreign-language press doubled from 1872 to 1892, but the total press tripled; thus the foreign-language press fell behind as a percentage of the total. Foreign-language press strength in the United States peaked in 1914, with 1000 newpapers and 300 periodicals, of which 40 percent were in German. Of the papers, 140 were dailies with a total aggregate circulation of 2.6 million (Mott, pp. 317, 493, 730).

12. See Michael Omi and Howard Winant, *Racial Formation in the United States*, p. 15.

13. For a more complete listing of these works, see nn. 1 and 2 of Keil's essay in this volume.

14. Wittke mentions two women journalists as "curiosities"—Amalie

Introduction

Struve and Mathilde Franziska Anneke (*German Language Press in America*, pp. 101–2).

15. Keil, "German Immigrant Workers in Nineteenth Century America," p. 198.

16. Hoerder and Harzig, *"Why Did You Come?"* p. 64.

17. *NYVZ* Jubiläums-Beilage, 1878–1903, Feb. 21, 1903, as reprinted in *Glimpses of the German-American Radical Press*, pp. 42–43.

18. Carl Wittke, *Refugees of Revolution*, p. 33.

I

The Radical Editors

Hartmut Keil

A Profile of Editors of the German-American Radical Press, 1850–1910

Paradoxically, the state of our knowledge of the German-American radical press is both substantial and limited. With respect to the radical tradition of the 48ers, a considerable body of interpretative literature has been available for some time.[1] Carl Wittke devoted almost one-third of *The German-Language Press in America,* published in 1957, to the revitalizing effects of those intellectuals and journalists who had been involved in revolutionary activities in one way or other and who, after emigrating to the United States, founded papers or joined the editorial staffs of existing ones.[2] Likewise, A. E. Zucker in his "Biographical Dictionary of the Forty-Eighters" published important biographical data on prominent individuals who served on German-American papers in some capacity; his list of the professions of the persons he included in his dictionary is led by the category "journalist."[3] However, by way of example these works also show what a limited notion of German-American radical journalism the received view has had: Since it concentrated on this group of radical democrats, it was also confined to a relatively short time period, basically to the dozen years before the Civil War. The important social democratic, socialist, anarchist, and trade-union publications founded in the last third of the nineteenth century by newly arriving German immigrants, so different from the earlier group in socioeconomic as well as in political terms, have been almost completely neglected. Thus, Wittke conceded a scant six pages to those papers, and he did not even seem to be aware of the substantial number of German-language trade-union publications. Only in recent years has the post-Civil War radical press received the

Hartmut Keil

attention it rightly deserves; however, a comprehensive interpretation has yet to be written.[4]

This essay will concentrate on the German-American radical press for the period from the Civil War to World War I, using the findings on the 48er radical journalists and press for comparative purposes. It is based on the following hypotheses: Wittke's argument of the juvenescence of the German-American press in the wake of the 48er arrivals can also be applied to the later radical journalism of socialist and anarchist persuasion. Although grounded in a different social and institutional setting, and therefore quickly adapting to a changing American journalistic landscape and addressing a new clientele, these new radical papers again helped raise linguistic and cultural standards that had been weakened as a result of social, cultural, and language adaptation. The post-Civil War radical press, like its predecessor, was able to serve this invigorating function because of the transfer of experience, skills, and ideology by editors many of whom had professional experience before emigrating. This transfer was decisive not only in the initial phase of founding a paper but also at a later stage when a paper's orientation gradually began to shift according to the changed interests of its readership. The German-American radical press of the post-Civil War period retained its vitality so long as it was able to replenish its editorial staff with immigrating journalists. It began to face serious trouble when the gap widened between an audience more and more assimilated into American mainstream culture and an editorial staff nurtured in German (high) culture.

A methodological note is in order at this point. A study of the personal backgrounds and career patterns of editors and journalists seems to me a useful approach to confirm (or refute) the claim made here that these individuals played a central role in the development, direction, appearance, and quality of the papers. Did individual career patterns display similarities that allow for making generalizations? The approach of this essay is therefore that of collective biography. However, biographical data for a substantial number of editors are (still) incomplete; they are available for prominent editors and journalists only and are thus not comprehensive enough to make a careful statistical analysis. More detailed information is available for only some forty editors, whereas many more were active during the time period considered here (see Appendix).[5] Despite these evident limitations, a characteristic pattern emerges from the available data, which justifies sketching a profile of these editors and journalists.

Institutional Setting

First it is necessary to describe the institutional setting in which the post-Civil War press operated. A major change had taken place in comparison with the German-American newspaper scene of the 1850s. Newspapers and journals then were either profit-oriented enterprises run according to market dictates and therefore adapting to commercial as well as political pressures or the creations of idealistic individuals inspired by humanitarian, cultural, and political convictions who sacrificed their (and often their families') time, money, and health for their zealous work. Such personal journalism succumbed to the crass materialism of Gilded-Age America. Only Karl Heinzen was able to continue his *Pionier* until 1879 with the help of his wife and the financial assistance of friends. After Heinzen's paper merged with the *Freidenker*, Robert Reitzel's *Der arme Teufel*, launched in 1884, proved to be the sole exception to the rule that papers reflecting the personal opinions of their editors had become outmoded.

The radical press that emerged after the Civil War was closely linked to the German-American labor movement and its various organizations. It also had to operate in highly competitive surroundings and accordingly had to adapt to commercial and market considerations by increasingly opening its pages to advertisements and by satisfying the needs of its readers for general information in competition with middle-class German-American dailies as well as English-language papers. But it could never have survived on a purely competitive basis without the special organizational frame on which it was usually founded, i.e., the cooperative association, and without the support of labor organizations and their members.

Obviously, newspaper associations founded in Germany by the Social Democracy set the precedent for this organizational structure. Section 1 of the International Workingmen's Association (IWA) passed statutes for the *Arbeiterzeitung* in 1873 which provided for membership control of the paper through an administrative committee and a board of supervision elected by the members.[6] The founding of the Social Democratic Labor party of North America in 1874 was accompanied by the establishment of a paper, the *Social-Demokrat*, which was owned by the party. The Social Democratic Printing Association, founded at the same time, was a stock company which party members could join by acquiring shares of $5 each.[7] The example copied in this case is obvious: It was that of the publishing house and print shop of the *Social-Demokrat*, the paper of the General German Workingmen's Association. Members of the Labor party of Illinois requested the statutes of the Berlin and Leipzig cooperative publishing houses in 1875 in order to follow these precedents when establishing a cooperative association for the Chicago *Vorbote*.[8] More typical, however, were local papers not controlled by a party but jointly owned by trade unions, by mutual benefit or other societies, or by individual party and trade-union members who had founded a cooperative publishing association.

The example of the *Milwaukee'r Socialist* may serve to show the typical steps taken when founding a labor paper. The Milwaukee section of the IWA was able to publish the paper beginning on November 1, 1875, "with little means at its disposal," because comrade Joseph Brucker "selflessly contributed his print equipment." About one year later plans materialized to found a publishing association in order to become independent of other publishers. Although the German-American Typographical Union No. 10 had only thirty members in Milwaukee at the time, it was confident, despite warnings to the contrary, that this was the right course; for "the establishments of our German colleagues in Berlin, Munich, Frankfurt, Leipzig, Chemnitz, Crimmitschau etc. give the best proof that such [publishing associations] can exist, if managed on an expert basis." In this case, too, shares of five dollars each were issued. The printing house eventually began operations on February 1, 1877. In addition to the *Milwaukee'r Socialist* it set and printed the weekly *Vorwärts* as well as the English-language *Social Democrat*, and the *Emancipator* of Cincinnati, and it also took on job printing. The associational form guaranteed the democratic management and control of the company.[9]

In spite of confident expectations, the publishing association floundered and failed in the summer of 1877 because of personal antagonisms, the low circulation of the *Milwaukee'r Socialist*, wages for the typesetters and printers that were lower than those paid by capitalistic enterprises, and competition by two other publishing associations in Chicago and St. Louis. The Socialist Printing Company in Milwaukee bought the association in order to save the paper, but one year later it was discontinued and the company dissolved. The example demonstrates that in the United States, as in Germany, "in several cases local organs were founded rashly, without the necessary financial and personal prerequisites and without the necessary minimum number of subscribers."[10]

In those cases where solid preparations were made, as in Chicago and New York, papers were put on a lasting, if financially shaky, basis. The *Chicagoer Arbeiter-Zeitung* succeeded because it was preceded by the weekly *Vorbote*, which tried out various organizational forms and secured a permanent circle of readers, and because it appeared on a triweekly basis for two years before it was turned into a daily in the spring of 1879. Members (and in later years trade unions also) were guaranteed adequate participation in the Socialistic Publishing Society, a nonprofit association.[11] The *New Yorker Volkszeitung* (*NYVZ*), on the other hand, was to appear as a daily from the very beginning, and various preparations had to be made to ensure its success: In addition to founding the Socialistic Cooperative Publishing Association and selling shares to party and union members, members solicited subscriptions several weeks before publication began. In fact, 278 members of the Socialist Labor party systematically canvassed city wards, precincts, and blocks in New York and Brooklyn until some four thousand persons had subscribed to the paper.[12] Not surprisingly, however, its appearance negatively affected the party paper, *Arbeiterstimme*, also published in New York. The latter quickly lost so many subscribers that it had to fold up.[13]

Remarks by the experienced editor Carl Hirsch, characterizing the condition of the social democratic press in Germany in the 1870s, are even more appropriate for the American situation. He observed, "It is a fact that the majority of our local papers to this day can only be maintained because of great circumspection and willingness to make personal sacrifices. Most party members do not know of the sacrifices in terms of money, time and energy demanded by our party press since its emergence."[14] Since in the United States institutional bases for a radical labor press did not survive the Civil War and had to be created anew afterwards, the contributions of many members and the use of the associational or shareholding model after the German example was the only available alternative which, despite many drawbacks and disappointments, led to the founding of permanent high-quality newspapers.

Backgrounds and Career Patterns

Describing the origins and the ten-year history of the *NYVZ* in 1888, Alexander Jonas, the paper's editor-in-chief, observed: "There never was, and still isn't up to this day, an abundance of persons who thoroughly understand the theory of modern socialism, who know how to present it in clear and graphic ways and who besides—or rather primarily—are journalists."[15] While the German-American radical press needed experienced journalists, especially during the period of its enormous expansion in the 1870s and 1880s, it could not readily draw upon a reserve of persons with an adequate professional back-

Hartmut Keil

ground. It thus had to rely on the social democratic movement in Germany for recruits. For example, in 1875 Jacob Winnen asked the German party for help in finding a competent replacement for the *Vorbote*'s editor, Conrad Conzett, explaining that the paper's board "cannot come by anybody in the United States trained in social science matters and prominent enough to satisfy our needs." Winnen continued: "We don't know of any other way to solve the problem but to turn to you and ask you to help us out of this dilemma, if at all possible. . . . Perhaps a party member with prior experience in the party press who would make for a capable editor might be willing to emigrate, if he found immediate and certain employment."[16] How successful was the German-American radical press in attracting editors and journalists from Germany?

Many persons who took over responsibility for a paper in the United States obviously had some previous experience in journalism in Germany, although not necessarily as chief editors. Gustav Lyser, for example, had been an assistant editor for social democratic papers in Chemnitz and Braunschweig before coming to New York at the age of thirty-three and assuming the editorship of the *Social-Demokrat*, the organ of the Social Democratic party of North America, in 1874. Thirty years later, when he entered the United States at the age of thirty, Heinrich Bartel could also look back on ten years of journalistic experience on the editorial staffs of the *Freiheit* and *Volkswille* in northern Bohemia.[17] The low median age upon immigration (thirty-two) of this group of journalists is a clear indication that they were usually in mid-career, that is, they had already been adherents of social democracy for ten to fifteen years and were well on their way to more responsible positions within the movement, which they attained not in Germany but in the United States.

Some of them were already quite prominent. Their reasons for emigrating were persecution and the precariousness of their economic status. Thus Julius Vahlteich, former secretary to Ferdinand Lassalle, social democratic delegate to the Imperial Diet, and editor of the party's local paper *Chemnitzer Freie Presse*, emigrated in 1881, as did the venerable Friedrich Wilhelm Fritzsche, also a member of the Diet, president of the German Cigarmakers Union, and editor of its weekly paper. Both had toured the United States on an official visit in the spring of 1881. Paul Grottkau, prominent labor leader from Berlin, editor of the organ of the Bricklayers Union and of the *Berliner Freie Presse*, barely escaped the Prussian police in 1878, when they tried to arrest him once again. The gifted writer and orator immediately found employment on the staff of the *Chicagoer Arbeiter-Zeitung* and

20

Vorbote.[18] In a few cases German-American papers offered their chief editorial position to experienced German editors, as in the case of the *Social-Demokrat* (*Arbeiterstimme*). August Otto-Walster came to New York from Dresden at the request of the paper's owner, the Social Democratic Labor party of North America.[19] The more prominent émigrés were older than the average: Joseph Dietzgen and Fritzsche were already beyond their mid-fifties, Vahlteich and Otto-Walster were both forty-two.

Most sizeable was that group of journalists who sought refuge because of various kinds of political persecution. Notorious in this respect was the period of antisocialist legislation from 1878 to 1890.[20] However, even before that law went into effect, several journalists left after having been harassed or repeatedly jailed, like Grottkau, Rudolf Starke from Basel (1870), and Jacob Franz from Munich (1878). After October 1878, the German social democratic press, and along with it the whole infrastructure of the party's communication network, was completely destroyed. Editors and printers lost their means of livelihood and many were banned from their hometowns. A large number of persecuted or exiled socialists who had been involved in some capacity in publishing and distributing social democratic papers emigrated to the United States, among them journalists who sought to continue their careers there (Hasselmann, Vahlteich, Lossau, Hepner, Christensen, Ibsen, Stoehr, Keitel, Milke, Most, Rosenberg, Werner, Reimer, Schlüter). In the face of a limited number of jobs, it was difficult for them to gain a foothold. Vahlteich, for example, had to resort to his old shoemaker's trade in New York. Only after he moved to Chicago did he find employment with a middle-class paper, before taking on the editorship of the short-lived *Illinois Volkszeitung* (and later of other papers). Hasselmann opened a saloon in New York; the paper which he founded several years later failed after six months. Most of them did finally find a niche in the German-American labor press, and some became very successful editors, like Johann Most (*Freiheit*), Adolph Hepner (*St. Louis Tageblatt*) and Hermann Schlüter (*NYVZ*). Others were quickly forgotten, however, after continuing their journalistic career for only a short time. Jens Christensen had to give up his position as editor of the *Chicagoer Arbeiter-Zeitung* after a year and a half; he died in the poorhouse in New York.

Among German-American editors there was another group—those who were under twenty-five when they immigrated and who first entered the profession in the United States, like August Spies, Michael Schwab, and Robert Schilling. They were a relatively small minority; out of thirty-four persons whose age at immigration is known, only seven were under twenty-five. It may not be a coincidence that among them were found two printers (Conzett, Fischer) and one bookbinder (Schwab). These trades, connected as they were with publishing, had been the traditional resources for labor journalists from artisan and craft ranks. Other workers more advanced in their life cycles when entering the United States had already made this career move in Germany (Franz, Lyser, Most), while for these younger people, becoming an editor still lay ahead.

A slim majority of editors had working-class backgrounds. They were the self-educated who had learned a craft like cabinetmaking (Speyer), shoemaking (Vahlteich), tanning (Dietzgen), tailoring (Carl and Starke), or weaving, who helped organize their respective trades or a labor party and assumed positions of responsibility in the process, and who founded, or gradually took over the editorship of, labor papers. This was strongest among printers and bookbinders, one dozen of whom could be identified. On the other hand, there was a strong minority of intellectuals among these labor journalists, most of them apparently of middle-class background. They had studied at German universities (Berger, Christensen, Douai, Drescher, Hasselmann, Heinzen, Hepner, Jonas, Lore, Otto-Walster, Reitzel, Rosenberg, Schewitsch, Landsberg). Not all of them can be said to have really belonged to the labor movement. As Jonas pointed out, when the *NYVZ* was launched some professional journalists who were not socialists had to be hired for lack of capable party members, and he himself had to learn from experience how to publish a daily labor paper. Sometimes recourse had to be taken to sympathizing liberals; thus the lawyer Dr. Wilhelm Landsberg became the first editor of the *New Yorker Arbeiter-Union*, before Dr. Adolf Douai replaced him; and when Grottkau was forced out of the editorship of the *Chicagoer Arbeiter-Zeitung* and *Vorbote* in 1880, Dr. Liebig took over. He apparently proved inadequate for the job, and Grottkau was reinstituted.

Thus there was a certain heterogeneity of backgrounds, especially when including editors of both trade-union publications and socialist as well as other radical dailies and weeklies. But there were no clear-cut boundaries between these different types of papers when it came to their editorial staffs; moves from one paper to another were readily made. Karl Ibsen (*Deutsch-Amerikanische Bäckerzeitung, Clevelander Volksfreund*), Robert Degen (*Deutsch-Amerikanische Bäckerzeitung, NYVZ*), and Jacob Franz (*Philadelphia Tageblatt, NYVZ, Brauerzeitung*) consecutively worked for both socialist dailies and trade-union papers. Even more important, however, was the convergence of experience in the United States, because of the need to fulfill several important functions through the editorial position. The labor paper was such a central institution in the labor movement that whoever held the editorship not only dominated public opinion but had other leadership functions as well: as union and party organizer and representative and as speaker during demonstrations, strikes, and other important public events. Also typical was a high degree of geographical and job mobility, partly because of the precarious financial standing of many radical papers, and partly because of personnel changes in the movement and ideological shifts in the papers' editorial policies. Thus editors did not make easy and uninterrupted transitions from one job to the next, but were often unemployed for several months and sometimes had to make a living in between through other means. And they certainly did not gather riches. Jens L. Christensen may have been an exception in that he died in a poorhouse. But all of them were overworked and received relatively low pay. Jonas quoted the following salaries for the editorial staff of the NYVZ during its first two-and-a-half years in the late 1870s, while the paper was in the red: "A. Douai $16.00 per week, Alex. Jonas $14.00, R. Degen $12.00, J. Schaefer $11.00 and J. Holler $11.00. For comparative purposes let me add that the average wage of a typesetter for one week (six days' work) was then about $16.00, that of a foreman $25.00."[21]

Comparing these radical journalists who arrived later to the 48er generation yields some remarkable similarities as well as differences. Both groups contained a high percentage of experienced journalists with some kind of university training. While hardly any of the earlier immigrants left Germany of their own free will, many, but not all, of the socialists also were forced out of their home country. Missing among the latter is the category of intellectuals who were inexperienced in journalism but entered the profession in the United States as a last resort. In order to be accepted in the emerging German-American labor movement, individuals had to be soundly grounded in it; they had to be willing to make the personal sacrifices that were apparently a prerequisite for the job; thus in the flowering period of the German-American labor press outsiders were an exception. In later years, because of an increasing shortage of qualified editors—after 1890 these preferred to remain in Germany where the Social Democracy and its press became important social and political factors—the German-American labor press sometimes had to turn to other expedients. Although information is still scarce, there are indications that older editors who in Germany might have been succeeded by a younger generation were unable to retire in the United States because no one else was there to take over. Julius Vahlteich was in his sixties when he accepted a position with the *NYVZ;* he helped out at the *Chicagoer Arbeiter-Zeitung* when he was already seventy years old, and he worked for the paper almost until his death in 1915 at the age of seventy-six.[22] This is just one example demonstrating that the ranks of the guardians of German cultural traditions were thinning out.

Cultural Traditions and Adaptations

Editors of the post-Civil War German-American radical press were steeped in the German social democratic tradition and in many ways served as its most important agents of transfer and preservation. This cannot equally be claimed for freethinking and Turner journals, although their editors also immigrated. Individuals like Carl Hermann Boppe of the *Freidenker* and Reitzel continued the 48er liberal democratic tradition, often in increasing contrast and opposition to their readers, who became more conservative as time passed. The labor press also counted some of its able journalists from among the ranks of these 48er radicals, the most prominent being Adolf Douai, who eventually turned into a social democrat. More often the liberals (e.g., Dr. Ernst Schmidt, Friedrich Adolph Sorge, Dr. Georg Stiebeling) pursued careers other than journalism, while regularly contributing essays, stories, and scholarly articles to journals and the labor papers' Sunday editions.

The youthful German-American movement badly needed journalists with both organizational experience and knowledge of the workings of labor institutions in general and of the press as the major means of communication. Therefore the transfer of personnel was as important as copying the organizational structure of German labor institutions. However, continuity did not mean that the German-American side was always the beneficiary. These journalists also served important functions for their European comrades, since the papers they edited in the United States were read by fellow editors in Europe and extensively copied for European readership. Thus the editors of the *Sozial-Demokrat* in Zurich received all German-language labor papers from the United States and quoted them at length or summarized significant articles and information, just as the *NYVZ* and socialist dailies in other American cities did with the European labor papers. This mutual exchange reinforced ideological agreement on both sides of the Atlantic and helped Europeans to judge American developments on the basis of sound information. In addition, German-Americans served as foreign correspondents for German labor organs, providing firsthand accounts of specific events as well as overall analysis, as did prominent German socialists who had been hired by German-American labor papers to report on German and European events. Sometimes journalists returned to Germany after working for German-American papers. After having published and edited the Chicago *Vorbote* and *Arbeiter-Zeitung* for several years, Conrad Conzett (like Hermann Schlüter, who had returned from Chicago during the depression of the 1870s) contributed his considerable knowledge to publishing the *Sozial-Demokrat* and a Swiss labor paper. Schlüter later went back to the United States, eventually becoming editor-in-chief of the *NYVZ*.[23] Especially after the antisocialist law had been repealed in Germany in 1890, other individuals also returned there and continued working for the labor press (Otto Reimer, Sergius Schewitsch, Otto-Walster, Hepner, Biedenkapp). Thus, the trans-Atlantic job mobility of labor journalists and editors, as well as mutual visits, helped keep up the flow of information in this geographically extensive network.

But German-American labor papers were eventually forced to change their appearance and contents. They faced tough competition from the German-language middle-class press and were threatened with a declining readership, initially because of the lures of upward mobility and the actual growth of the middle class and later because of the increasing numerical preponderance of the second generation, which tended to turn from German-language to English-language publications (a development that affected middle-class papers equally). The papers' ethnic character became more pronounced and visible when the membership of ethnic associations had to be humored as a considerable part of the papers' readership. Mass consumerism, which took off at the beginning of the twentieth century, took its toll on all ethnic subcultures, and made the mass press more desirable to all classes of readers.

All of this could perhaps still be harmonized with the original purposes of these papers. It was especially the decline of the first and the growth of the second generation, though, that threatened the very existence of the radical (as well as the middle-class) press and its editors. The concern they voiced over this issue was quite ambivalent. As convinced socialists they argued and fought for the Americanization of the movement with all consequences that such an attitude entailed. Thus they deplored the lack of English-language labor papers and other socialist literature and actively tried to help remedy this situation. Pamphlets written in German by some of the more prominent journalists for agitational purposes were also translated by them into English, and English-language papers were funded by German socialists and edited and printed in the offices of German publishers.[24] At the same time editors understood one of their major tasks to be the preservation of the German language and German culture. They claimed to be the true heirs of the German high cultural tradition, whereas in their opinion German-American middle-class papers had given in to mass popular tastes and lower standards, especially when it came to writing German and propagating German classical literature.[25]

The conflict between the preservation of language and culture on the one hand and adaptation to American life and the English language on the other was easily solved in the case of German-language trade-union publications, because here first priority was given to union organization. Therefore all these papers except the *Deutsch-Amerikanische Buchdrucker-Zeitung* made the transition to English sometime between the mid-1880s and World War I, usually by first appearing as a bilingual publication before completely abandoning German pages. Editors of socialist dailies were keenly aware of the changing and declining social base of their readership. Because of its dual marginal status, that is, its ethnic as well as its ideologically "alien" character, the socialist daily press suffered more from this development than the middle-class press, even before events during World War I forced it into a quick decline. Taking up a discussion that had been going on for a generation, Robert Reitzel in 1890 predicted the fate of German cultural tradition, and by implication that (as he saw it) of its foremost guardians, the editors of the radical press, when he pessimistically (or should we rather say realistically?) observed, "This much is certain: German-American culture, brought over by immigrants in their flesh and blood, like their Lessing and Feuerbach and Börne, will die with us, who have lost their homeland and are strangers in their own house."[26]

NOTES

1. Here reference is made only to the most important works, since practically no analysis of the 48ers has ignored the role of the press: Carl Wittke, *German Language Press in America;* Wittke, *Refugees of Revolution;* Wittke, *Against the Current;* Wittke, *Utopian Communist;* Adolf Eduard Zucker, ed., *The Forty-Eighters;* Ernst Bruncken, *German Political Refugees;* Robert E. Cazden, *Social History of the German Book Trade in America;* Eitel W. Dobert, *Deutsche Demokraten in Amerika;* Karl Obermann, *Joseph Weydemeyer; Germans for a Free Missouri;* Hermann Schlüter, *Die Anfänge der deutschen Arbeiterbewegung in Amerika* [1907] and "Die Anfänge der deutschen Arbeiterbewegung in New York und ihre Presse" [1903], pp. 8–12. For further bibliographical information see Karl J. R. Arndt and May E. Olson, *German-American Newspapers and Periodicals;* Don Heinrich Tolzman, *German-Americana.*

2. Wittke, *German Language Press in America*, chaps. 4 to 7.

3. Zucker, *Forty-Eighters*, pp. 269–357; the list is on p. 270.

4. *Glimpses of the German-American Radical Press*; Renate Kiesewetter, "Institution der deutsch-amerikanischen Arbeiterpresse in Chicago"; Elisabeth Pitzer, "Bürgerliche Presse und Arbeiterpresse im Wandel"; Ulrike Heider, *Der arme Teufel: Robert Reitzel vom Vormärz zum Haymarket*. So far, however, these radical papers have mostly been used for information on the respective radical movements and have not been analyzed as papers; cf. Carol Poore, *German-American Socialist Literature; Deutsch-amerikanische sozialistische Literatur; German Workers in Industrial Chicago;* Keil, ed., "Chicago-Projekt: Lebensweise und Kultur der deutschen Arbeiterschaft Chicagos"; Keil, ed., *Deutsche Arbeiterkultur in Chicago von 1850 bis zum Ersten Weltkrieg: Eine Anthologie* (Ostfildern, 1984), English translation published as *German Workers in Chicago: A Documentary History of Working-Class Culture from 1850 to World War I;* and *German Workers' Culture in the United States*.

5. I owe special thanks to Dirk Hoerder and Christiane Harzig, editors of *The Immigrant Labor Press in North America,* who generously made their work available to me in manuscript form, including detailed biographical information on about forty editors and journalists as well as data on when these persons worked for which paper. I also want to express my debt to Anne Spier, who compiled much of this biographical material. Without it (as well as without Arndt and Olson's bibliography) I would have been unable to compile the list of journalists (see Appendix). Further data were collected in connection with my own research, especially for my habilitation thesis, see n. 20.

6. "Konstitution des Verwaltungsrathes der 'Arbeiter-Zeitung,'" Papers of the International Workingmen's Association, Reel 1, misc., State Historical Society of Wisconsin.

7. *Vorbote*, July 18, 1874.

8. Jacob Winnen, letter "An den Ausschuss der sozialistischen Arbeiterpartei Deutschlands," Dec. 21, 1875, file 200/4/836, Institute for Marxism-Leninism, Moscow.

9. *Milwaukee'r Socialist,* Nov. 1, 1876; *Deutsch-Amerikanische Buchdrucker-Zeitung,* Aug. 1, Oct. 15, Nov. 1 and 15, Dec. 15, 1876, May 1, 1877.

10. Dieter Fricke, *Deutsche Arbeiterbewegung,* pp. 373f.

11. For a detailed analysis of the organizational structure of the *Vorbote* and the *Chicagoer Arbeiter-Zeitung* see Kiesewetter, "Institution der deutsch-amerikanischen Arbeiterpresse in Chicago."

12. *New Yorker Volkszeitung* (*NYVZ*), 10th anniversary issue, Jan. 28, 1888.

13. Sozialistische Arbeiterpartei von Nord-Amerika, *Offizielles Protokoll der 3. National-Konvention,* p. 10.

14. Carl Hirsch, *Die Parteipresse,* p. 3; quoted in Fricke, *Deutsche Arbeiterbewegung,* pp. 374f.

15. Alexander Jonas, "Wie die 'N.Y. Volkszeitung' entstand," *NYVZ*, 10th anniversary edition, repr. in 25th anniversary edition, p. 15.

16. Winnen, letter "An den Ausschuss," Dec. 21, 1875.

17. See Heinz Ickstadt and Hartmut Keil, "A Forgotten Piece of Working-Class Literature: Gustav Lyser's Satire of the Hewitt Hearing of 1878"; " 'Unrealistische' Genossen: I. Heinrich Bartel," *Solidarität* 41, no. 7, 178–28; no. 9, 165–66; no. 10, 183–84.

18. See Hartmut Keil, "German Immigrant Working Class of Chicago."

19. August Otto-Walster, letter to Karl Marx, undated (written before Nov. 13, 1874), and letter to Marx, Nov. 13, 1874, Marx-Engels papers, D 3606 and D 3607, International Institute of Social History, Amsterdam; letter to Wilhelm Liebknecht, Feb. 23, 1875, file 200/4/743, Institute for Marxism-Leninism, Moscow.

20. Dirk Hoerder and Hartmut Keil, "The American Case and German Social Democracy"; Hartmut Keil, "Deutsche sozialistische Einwanderer in den USA."

21. Jonas, "Wie die 'N.Y. Volkszeitung' entstand," p. 15.

22. These observations apply also to Theodor Cuno, Joseph Dietzgen, Hermann Schlüter, and Alexander Jonas.

23. See Hoerder and Keil, "The American Case and German Social Democracy."

24. See Hartmut Keil, "German Working-Class Radicalism."

25. For examples see Keil, ed., *Deutsche Arbeiterkultur in Chicago*, pp. 393–401.

26. Robert Reitzel, "Fremd im eigenen Hause," *Der arme Teufel*, Jan. 18, 1890.

II

From 48er Radicalism to a Working-Class Press

The era of the Civil War marked an important time of transition for German-American radicalism. While there were earlier examples of radical German-language newspapers in the United States, émigrés from the failed German revolution of 1848 dominated the German-American radical community's institution-building in the 1850s. The radicalism of the 48ers, however, was rooted in artisan republicanism and free thought; concern for democracy and anticlericalism predominated, not distress over a system of class exploitation through capitalist wage labor.

The experiences and rhetoric of the Civil War transformed German-American radicalism and its press. The 48ers played an important role in introducing concepts of free labor and antislavery to the German-American working class, but the onerous and uneven burdens placed on workers by the war gave the call for free soil and free labor a hollow ring. In the process, German workers began building their own community institutions and developing different conceptions about their political and economic interests. The emergence of a labor movement in cities like Chicago and Philadelphia called into question the basic tenets of 48er radicalism.

In the immediate postwar years, the leadership of the German-American radical press changed hands. Many 48ers joined sides with ethnic power brokers and immigrant community business leaders, while German-American labor activists created their own distinctive radical newspapers. The shift of the radical press from its role in ethnic community-building to one of building a mass-based, working-class movement was never complete, however. In many cities, like Philadelphia, German-American radicals continued the complex process of interweaving class and ethnicity.

Steven Rowan

Franz Schmidt and the *Freie Blätter* of St. Louis, 1851–53

At the end of March 1853, a foreigner was carried to his grave in Matanzas, Cuba, to the tolling of church bells and the chanting of a priest. To an informed onlooker it must have seemed a cruel joke that the man being buried in Caribbean soil had been a vocal enemy not only of Catholicism but of all religions.[1] Franz Schmidt's departure from this earth had the pathetic qualities of a scene out of an overheated anticlerical novel of the 1850s.

The brief and stormy life of Franz Schmidt has yet to find its chronicler, but at least its provocative outlines are clear.[2] Born in Nieder-Saltzbrunn in Upper Silesia on November 28, 1818, Schmidt came to radical politics out of religious commitment, and there are indications that he remained essentially a religious thinker to the end of his life. Born and raised in the multiethnic province of Silesia, the former seminarian Schmidt set himself apart from most German radicals through his ability to sympathize with the Polish national revival as well as with the interests of exploited workers, so much so that in 1845 he was designated by Prussian officials as a dangerous adherent to the Polish cause as well as a communist.[3] After a period as a private teacher in the household of a Polish nationalist nobleman in the Prussian-ruled Grand Duchy of Posen (Poznan), Schmidt accepted a position in Löwenberg in Lower Silesia as a preacher for the burgeoning German-Catholic (Deutschkatholisch) movement, which was emerging as a major force in Silesia under the leadership of Johannes Ronge. The Silesian weavers' revolt of 1844 had caused many to pose basic critical questions about the existing political and economic system, and the rationalist German-Catholic movement addressed some of these questions of social and political enlightenment under the guise of a "modern Christianity." Schmidt had already been a member of a Silesian socialist group since the start of 1844, and belonged to the German-Catholic movement from its beginning.

In a period when Prussian authorities were reluctant to suppress plausible religious movements, political agitation could proceed through German-Catholic parishes, but this approach eventually became too limited for many of the participants, who soon evolved into political revolutionaries or cultural freethinkers. Ronge, for example, would become a leading member of the democratic exile leadership in London after 1849.[4] While working in the German-Catholic movement, Schmidt also served as the principal link between the small but active band of Silesian socialists and the leadership of the League of Communists (Bund der Kommunisten) in Brussels.[5] Whether as a preacher in the German-Catholic movement, which he tried to push in a socialist direction, or as a correspondent in reformist journals in Breslau and western Germany, Franz Schmidt was an important voice on the left in Silesia.[6] By 1846 at the latest, he was corresponding directly with the leaders of the communist league, whose secretary, Wilhelm Wolff, was a fellow Silesian and an old friend.[7] His association with proletarian socialists was remarkable since, like most socialists in Silesia at the time, he followed the so-called true socialism, an idealistic petit bourgeois socialist ideology espoused by Karl Gruen, Moses Hess, and their followers. This approach was denigrated by the followers of proletarian socialism, most notably by Marx and Engels in the *German Ideology* of 1846 and the *Communist Manifesto* of 1848.[8]

Following the popular upheavals of March 1848, Schmidt was elected to the National Assembly, which commenced its sessions at the Paulskirche in Frankfurt in May of that year. There Schmidt (commonly known as Schmidt of Löwenberg to distinguish him from others of his common surname) became one of the most vocal of the radicals gathered in the so-called Donnersberg party, and he won particular notoriety on July 25 by denouncing the Prussian government's cynical misrepresentation of the actual ethnic composition of Posen, which he knew by personal experience to be largely Polish rather than German.[9] Here Schmidt was taking a brave stand indeed against German nationalist chauvinism, a conviction found at all points in the political spectrum from left to right. In October Schmidt was threatened with bodily harm by a conservative during a session of the assembly.[10] Later, when the left split at Frankfurt over the offer of the imperial crown to the king of Prussia, Schmidt sided with the more radical members who favored a constitutional state without a hereditary monarch.[11]

By March of 1849, Schmidt was writing directly to Karl Marx, and by 1850 his friend Wilhelm Wolff was able to describe Schmidt to Marx as "to be regarded as one of us" even though he "had not been initiated" into the inner group of the league. Wolff urged that Schmidt be given missions to perform when he arrived in America in 1850, where he was headed once his exile in Zurich, due to the general expulsion of German radicals after 1848, proved untenable.[12] Schmidt, using the code name Theseus, continued to write to Wolff and other members of the league leadership while living in St. Louis. These letters are preserved in the manuscript collections of the Institute for Marxism-Leninism in Berlin and in the Central Party Archives in Moscow.[13]

Once in St. Louis, Franz Schmidt and his wife established a school for girls, and Schmidt even invited Wilhelm Wolff to come to St. Louis to join the faculty of his "Young Ladies' Academy" at Fifth and Elm. This school was certainly a success in attracting the elite of St. Louis German freethinker society, including girls from the Anheuser and Taussig families.[14] But it appears that Marx and Engels had only a vague notion of what Schmidt was up to after his arrival in St. Louis. As Engels wrote from Manchester to Joseph Weydemeyer in New York at the end of February 1852: "Schmidt of Löwenberg is waging crusades against the Jesuits in the area of St. Louis, and in this enterprise he has allied himself with that former swindler and agent of [French Interior Minister Charles-Marie Tanneguy] Duchâtel, Mr. Börnstein of Paris memory. What else he is doing I have not a clue."[15]

What he was about in St. Louis, besides teaching school, was editing a newspaper under the aegis of Heinrich Börnstein (Henry Börnstein), a man who had as many enemies as the lovable Schmidt had friends. Heinrich Börnstein's life was both long and well recorded.[16] Born in Hamburg in 1805, he moved at an early age with his parents to his father's native Galizia, where he was raised. After a stint in the Austrian army, Börnstein made a career in the theater, where he also demonstrated considerable talents as a theatrical manager and a writer of popular plays. Arriving in Paris in the first flush of its Bohemian period in the 1840s, he specialized in the translation of French plays for performance in German-speaking Europe, though he also began a secondary career as a journalist. In 1844 he launched a cultural weekly called *Vorwärts! Pariser Signale aus Kunst, Wissenschaft, Theater, Musik und geselligem Leben*. Rather early in the publication of this cultural weekly, however, Börnstein made a sudden lurch to the left by taking on a cohort of noted German emigrant radicals. These included the poet Heinrich Heine along with most of the contributors to the short-lived *Deutsch-Französische Jahrbücher*,[17] among them Karl Marx,

Steven Rowan

Friedrich Engels, Arnold Ruge, and Karl Ludwig Bernays.[18] In early
1845 the journal was suppressed by French authorities. Börnstein later
helped to organize the Paris German Legion to aid the German 1848
revolution, which did not improve the regard in which Marx and his
following held him—as hopelessly petit bourgeois in his politics and
utterly untrustworthy as a person. He left France in early 1849 after
the election of Louis Napoléon as president of France, to join Bernays,
who had already gone to St. Louis.

No bedraggled refugee, Börnstein brought with him twenty-two
chests filled with every imaginable item necessary for a civilized life.
After an interlude in the Swiss community of Highland, Illinois, as a
pharmacist and allopathic physician, Börnstein was called to St. Louis
in early 1850 to assume the editorship of the *Anzeiger des Westens*, and
although he proclaimed himself to be a public educator only interested
in elevating the cultural level of the immigrant community, he soon
earned a reputation as an anti-Catholic agitator.[19] To boost circulation
of the *Anzeiger* and to promote an alliance between American nativists
and German radicals, he undertook to write and publish a sensational
anti-Jesuit serial novel entitled *The Mysteries of St. Louis, Or, The Jesuits
on the Prairie des Noyers, A Western Tale*.[20] It was dedicated to former
United States senator Thomas Hart Benton, who would be Börnstein's
candidate for the House of Representatives in 1852. This potboiler
would go through many editions in German and would also be translated into French, English, and Czech.[21] Börnstein later claimed that
the novel was the foundation for a career in Missouri which would
flourish until he broke with the Frémont radicals in 1862, a political
decision which precipitated the collapse of his St. Louis businesses
in 1863, while he was in Bremen serving as United States consul. He
never returned to America, and he died in Austria in 1892.

While Börnstein was still publishing the first parts of *The Mysteries,*
on March 18, 1851, Franz Schmidt launched his own weekly, *Freie Blätter,* published by Börnstein's printing company. The *Freie Blätter* is our
major source of information on what freethinker St. Louis was doing
in the early 1850s, and for a while it was considered one of the leading
freethinker publications in German North America.[22] It would continue publication until March 5, 1853, shortly before its editor's death
from tuberculosis in Matanzas, Cuba, where he had gone in a futile
effort to regain his health.[23]

Schmidt prefaced the first issue of the weekly, subtitled *Ein Organ
für religiöse Erklärung,* with a forthright statement of first principles, a
"Creed" of eight points which affirmed belief in an eternal material
nature operating without external agencies, a possible multiplicity of

34

inhabited planets, and the preeminent dignity of mankind as the apex of nature. Consequently, there could be no higher crime than to degrade human dignity. The creed said further that humanity had been called to order and harmony, not to perpetual conflict, but that history consisted of the progressive struggle of mankind against oppression, with the ultimate goal of order, harmony, and freedom to be realized only in the future. Christianity, which at one time had been an advance over earlier belief-systems, was outmoded, and the Bible, upon which Christianity rested, was a dubious and partisan document. Lastly, the nineteenth century was the time of mankind's final liberation.[24] This progressive vision of the process of nature was utopian rather than Marxist, and the shrinking away from serious politics which would characterize Schmidt's St. Louis years is already visible. Still, this "Creed" kept him in trouble with pious St. Louis for the rest of his life there.

Also at the beginning of the first issue of the journal, Schmidt declared that the presence of a constitution and binding laws approved by the people was not the essence of freedom but only its precondition. True liberation required genuine freedom of thought, which grew out of being freed from the domination of clergy and other dictators. Instead of freedom of religion, people needed a religion of freedom. The *Freie Blätter*, for its part, would avoid personalities and parties and instead "let principle struggle with principle, ideal with ideal, philosophy with philosophy." Above all, there were to be no personal attacks.[25] This philosophy seems to have struck a chord; the immediate success of the weekly is reflected in the fact that the press run was raised from one thousand to fifteen hundred copies, and that a condensed reprint of the first eight numbers was soon issued.[26] There is every indication that the journal had a wide circulation, even if it would never be a financial success.

The *Freie Blätter* subjected its St. Louis environment to a sharp critique, especially when it reflected the spirit of its companion organization, the Verein Freier Männer,[27] always from the starting point of anticlericalism. The absence of formal censorship in America, for example, did not appear to Schmidt automatically to result in free expression, since overwhelming public pressure for conformity achieved the same results as a centralized censorship, sometimes with greater ruthlessness and efficiency. Self-censored minds thus made a police state superfluous.[28] Religious institutions in America were seen as primary organs of social discipline and hence of self-censorship. Such an argument also shows that the articles in the *Freie Blätter* were aimed at a more literate audience than that which followed the daily press, so that readers were expected to work through rather technical essays on electricity or exposés of arcane religious fraud through the ages. Although editorially distinct, the *Freie Blätter* was produced from the same building as the *Anzeiger,* and the close ties between the two journals were never a secret. The *Anzeiger* concentrated on garden-variety anticlericalism, but the *Freie Blätter* handled those items which were too hot even for the scandalmonger Börnstein to set in type, engaging in anti-Christian polemics and the lampooning of Christian scriptures. The paper even denounced the Thanksgiving Day proclamation of the governor of Missouri on one occasion.[29]

The result was that the paper engaged in head-to-head confrontations with clerical writers in the Catholic *Sonntagsblatt* or the *Tages-Chronik,* but the most violent wars were reserved for the Lutheran leader C. F. W. Walther, editor of *Der Lutheraner,* and his followers.[30] In one such dispute, a seminarian from Concordia Seminary published an anonymous pamphlet denouncing the "Fleshly Religion of the Free Men."[31] When all other arguments failed, Schmidt denigrated the pamphlet's author as a mere Stephanite, the dregs of the German emigration and a scandal to all decent moral men, adding that the Old Lutherans were a moral sump which stank even worse than the St. Louis levee on a hot day.[32] Such censoriousness moved even the intellectual leader of the older Missouri immigration, Friedrich Münch, to voice his misgivings about the stridently anti-Christian tone of much of the paper. Schmidt replied to this firmly, though with more courtesy than he could usually muster when dealing with a critic.[33] He was, after all, addressing one who was already a noted member of the rationalist community.

Beginning at the end of 1851, Schmidt began to give exposure to the writings of Karl Heinzen.[34] An old enemy of the Marxists,[35] and the German-American heir of the "true socialists" of ancient memory, he was for a long time the chief writer and speaker of the left in German-America, and his militant refusal to go along with the ordinary political process justified Carl Wittke's title of the biography of Heinzen, *Against the Current.*[36] Most pointedly, Schmidt launched this campaign with a critique by Heinzen of the writings of Friedrich Münch (under his pen name of Far West), featuring Heinzen's "Letters to a Reasonable Man" as responses to Münch's "Letters to a Pious Man."[37] In the middle of the next year, however, Heinzen became a major contributor with protocols of speeches made in a major lecture tour which included stops in Hermann, Missouri, and St. Louis.[38] Heinzen's final series for *Freie Blätter* parallels Schmidt's and the paper's own development, reflecting both his earlier polemic with Münch and the more exclusively religious stress of Schmidt's last days, "To a Pious Man." [39]

Within ten days after the first publication of the *Freie Blätter*, a new organization was launched which came to be intimately tied to it, for good or ill. In his memoirs, Börnstein recalled that he had received a note from a young German freethinker named Brossart who claimed that he was being held prisoner in the Jesuit house (the Saint Stanislaus Seminary—today a museum of the Jesuit Order) in Florissant.[40] Börnstein claimed that he dissuaded a German mass meeting from launching a raid on the Jesuits by proposing the creation of a "Verein freier Männer" on March 28, 1851. In actual fact, the Brossart episode was already over at least a week before the gathering in question, though the atmosphere of agitation certainly contributed to the sense of urgency which possessed the German freethinkers.[41] The first meeting of this new association appointed a committee, which included Schmidt and Börnstein, to draw up a statement of purposes, a statement which proclaimed a love of the true spirit of American liberty while warning of the threat to that liberty from clerical religion. During the deliberations, a participant specifically lauded both the *Anzeiger des Westens* and the *Freie Blätter* for furthering the cause of free thought.[42] On May 12 the assembled members of the Verein elected Schmidt as president and Börnstein corresponding secretary, and it was decided to hold meetings on Sundays alternately in north and south St. Louis, since there was no convenient place to meet in the central area, where few Germans resided.[43] Schmidt was reelected president in November, at which time a formal association of the Verein with the *Freie Blätter* was approved by the membership.[44] Despite internal dissent over the cost of building two school buildings (founded in July 1851) and other difficulties over common finances,[45] Schmidt was elected yet again as president in April 1852, with his friend Carl Muegge as vice president.[46] It is thus proper that his posthumous portrait shows him as president of the Verein Freier Männer of St. Louis.

Although Börnstein did not hold a regular position as a major officer with the Verein after the first few months, he continued to be regarded by English-speaking outsiders as the evil genius behind what was taken to be a conspiracy against all good morals.[47] The mouthpiece of the St. Louis Whig establishment, the *Missouri Republican*, could see little good in what it called "The Association of Free Men." After rejecting the notion that a gathering of even four to five hundred men could be taken to represent a diverse German population of about thirty thousand, the *Republican* suggested that the group was all too obviously a claque for the *Anzeiger des Westens*, the *Freie Blät-ter*, and Heinrich Wilhelm Gempp's *German American*. It was not clear whether the gathering was more for "Socialism, Red Republicanism or Infidelity," since the association supported all of them at once. In any case, the "Free Men" obviously were anti-Whig in their local politics, and that helped place them beyond the pale.[48] The intimate connection of the *Freie Blätter* and the *Anzeiger* (both published by the *Anzeiger*, together with the bilingual *German American* and the French *Moniteur de l'Ouest*)[49] was given particularly dramatic visual form reported by a horrified *Republican:*

> The society of Free Men is a society whose leading spirit is Boernstein, whose organs are the Freie Blätter and the Anzeiger; whose liberty is free-dom from restraint; whose business is to war against all religion. Those who wish to see their aims and objects shadowed forth on paper, can do so by stepping into a beer-house in the city. There they will see posted up in a conspicuous place an engraving, in which the world is seen rolling through space—the continent north America being uppermost. Standing alone in the midst of this continent, and "monarch of all he surveys," a figure (per-haps Boernstein,) with a standard in his hand, from the top of which floats as banners the Freie Blätter and Anzeiger, while grim figures, intended to represent Catholicism, Presbyterianism, and all other religions, with Satan and the Bible in the midst, are flying in terror before him into the region of outer darkness.[50]

Despite opposition from outside, the *Freie Blätter* seems to have functioned quietly if not smoothly in its role as the official organ of the Verein from July 1851 until late April 1852, when internal dissent over the financial management of the Verein became public.[51] At a spe-cial meeting on July 30, Börnstein, who had just recently been elected to the school committee, and Schmidt confronted the Verein with a bill of complaints about its failure to provide financial support to the *Freie Blätter*. Börnstein also rejected what he described as a false re-port on audits of the southern Freimänner-Schule.[52] On August 10, in another special meeting of the Verein, Schmidt presented the report of the majority of the school committee, which revealed that the dis-putes over financing the schools had not been laid to rest.[53] The losing side in this dispute, a full thirty-two members, soon brought a petition against Schmidt and other officers and members for violating the con-stitution of the association.[54] The upshot of this confrontation was that Schmidt and Börnstein broke the formal ties between the *Freie Blätter* and the association, so that all mention of the Verein disappeared from the masthead of the paper after September 11, 1852. Börnstein and Schmidt made a joint announcement that members of the Verein had never lived up to their commitment to provide monetary support for the paper, and that the two of them had each lost over one thousand dollars keeping the journal going.

This public divorce of the *Freie Blätter* from the Verein went hand in hand with the organization's progressive disintegration. Although an investigation cleared Schmidt and Börnstein, as well as two other officers, of charges of mismanaging society funds, the formal tie between the paper and the association would never be restored.[55] In fact, in October the dissidents in the association, led by Martin Nau and Peter Pellizzaro, obtained a court order to seize control of the two school buildings.[56] In a bitter reprise of the conflict, Schmidt argued that it all arose from his and Börnstein's refusal to countenance political partisanship by the association in 1851, particularly the "National Reform" movement and the German revolutionary national loan. Schmidt darkly hinted that some of the accusers did not have their private lives entirely in order and were given to mistreating dogs and small children.[57] (Börnstein led a meeting in the northern schoolhouse on October 10 to choose a new head teacher for one of the schools after the previous one had been removed for unspecified moral failings.)[58] After the organization was refounded, with a new constitution and bylaws, the general assembly of the Verein elected Franz Schmidt as president yet again, with Muegge as vice president. Several officers and members of the dissident group were formally expelled.[59]

Schmidt and Börnstein had thus ostensibly rejected efforts to turn the Verein into a politically partisan group, despite the fact that Börnstein was concurrently deeply involved in getting both Germans and Americans of proper persuasions elected to public office. Members of the association occasionally marched at public demonstrations, most notably at a commemoration for the failure of a putsch in Cuba in early autumn of 1851. The English-language papers observed with distaste that the procession had taken place on a Sunday.[60] In July 1852, however, a request that the Verein participate in the commemorative procession for Henry Clay was grudgingly accepted lest it offend the (English-speaking) public, but it was agreed that such activities were not a good idea in the future.[61]

In the aftermath of the crisis of late 1852, the group appeared to lose much of its tone. The two schools established in 1851–52 were still operating at the end of 1852, although soon the buildings would be redeveloped as public schools after the Verein itself dissolved.[62] By the mid-1850s the dramatic society established by Börnstein in conjunction with the Verein had found a new home at the Freie Gemeinde of North St. Louis, a similar freethinker organization that survived the immigration period as a center of neighborhood life and continued to flourish into the twentieth century.[63]

One of the most significant episodes of the period in which the *Freie Blätter* had served as the mouthpiece of the Verein was its brief support for an English-speaking socialist group. In mid-1851 formal cooperation between the Verein and the English-speaking group called the Social Reformers had been ushered in by exchanges of greetings,[64] but by the autumn this connection had grown to include the publication in the *Freie Blätter* of a series of tracts in English, followed by German translations, which advocated reforms to reverse the overconcentration of wealth in the hands of the few.[65] These articles meticulously examined the structure and volatility of property-holding in St. Louis, demanded an expansion of workers' cooperatives and restriction of the use of professional lawyers in public courts, and discussed the need for sexual equality, education for women, and the liberalization of marriage laws. In letters to the journal, other members of the Social Reform Association attacked the readiness of the clergy to defend capital and reject self-help by labor. The publication of articles by the Social Reformers went together with the experiment of using the Verein schools as centers of tricultural progressive education, bringing together Anglo-American, German, and French-speaking Creole children.[66] The Verein declared itself ready to provide the columns of its paper to the Social Reformers until they could afford to publish their own journal.[67] This episode of progressive political agitation was relatively short-lived, however; it appears that Schmidt published these daring and revealing articles only at the request of the Verein.

When Börnstein and Schmidt gave up the pretense of acting as the organ of the Verein, such essays as those of the Social Reformers ceased at once. On his own, Schmidt appeared to prefer to discuss the wonders of modern science, questions of pedagogy (notably the ideas of Jacetot and Froebel), and the stupidities of revealed religion. The shortage of adequate textbooks based on freethinker principles moved Schmidt to publish materials in the *Freie Blätter* which could be used in schools. In fact, such discussion of a rational pedagogy based on nonsectarian principles would be revived after the American Civil War by the so-called St. Louis Movement, a gathering of German and American devotees of Hegelian and transcendentalist thought around Henry Brockmeyer. Both the refounder of the St. Louis public schools, William Torrey Harris, and Susan Blow, who introduced the Froebel principles to the first public school kindergarten, were unconsciously following a path first explored in St. Louis by Franz Schmidt.

Articles later in 1852 also tended to focus on the peculiar doctrinal concerns of rationalism, including articles by Karl Lüdeking, a protégé of Schmidt who would become the guiding spirit of the Freie Gemeinde of North St. Louis into the 1880s and would represent all the Free Congregations of the United States at an international assembly of freethinkers in Naples in 1870.[68]

The "cultural" stress of the *Freie Blätter* caused it serenely to ignore current political events, so that Börnstein's abortive demands in 1851 for a German political party in St. Louis which would demand parity for German office-holders were left unmentioned,[69] as was the epoch-making struggle in 1851 and 1852 for Benton Democracy, which for the first time established Free-Soil principles as a winning formula in Missouri.[70] (This in turn would lay the groundwork for the Missouri Republican party, the chief political instrument of the overthrow of the Missouri state government in 1861.) None of these matters would ever surface in the *Freie Blätter*.

In the *Freie Blätter* of January 15, 1853, an article by Börnstein reprinted from the *Anzeiger des Westens* bade Franz Schmidt farewell on the morrow of his departure for Matanzas, Cuba, to spend the winter. Schmidt's tuberculosis had been plaguing him for years, so much so that he had hesitated to accept an invitation to present the keynote address at the dedication of the hall of the Freie Gemeinde von Nord-St. Louis in July 1851, due to his chronic poor health.[71] Now Börnstein formally took over editing the *Freie Blätter* during Schmidt's absence, and Schmidt's wife assumed leadership of his girls' school.[72] Thereafter, until its last number on March 5, 1853 (vol. 2, no. 51), the paper simply reprinted materials from other freethinker journals.

A week after the appearance of the last issue of the *Freie Blätter*, the weekly *Anzeiger* printed the first installment of a promised series of letters from Schmidt, who was then serving as a sort of overseas correspondent in Cuba. The first three letters described his harrowingly difficult winter journey down the Mississippi by riverboat and from New Orleans to Havana by ship, finally reaching his goal in Matanzas by carriage. There he had settled in for a "sugar-juice cure" of his illness in the plantation house of acquaintances (Plagge and Biranyi, both old friends of Carl Muegge) who managed a sugar refinery for a German owner. His account communicated a personal warmth and humor which all too seldom animated his published St. Louis writings but which had won him many loyal friends through the years. At one point he began to complain about the heavy Spanish duties on imported goods, but caught himself in mid-thought and wrote, "But stop—no politics!"[73]

On April 17, 1853, the *Anzeiger des Westens* was headed by a notice edged in black announcing that Schmidt had succumbed to his tuber-culosis in the morning hours of March 29, 1853. Although his state of health had seemed to improve somewhat in the warmth of the Cuban winter, his mind had lost its edge. On the night before his death, Börn-stein wrote, Schmidt had been possessed by the conviction that his wife was on her way to visit him, and he had attempted to dress to go to meet her. It was only with difficulty that he was dissuaded from his notion, and he returned to his bed and died quietly about 5 A.M. Börn-stein, genuinely moved for once in his life, mourned his lost friend as an "enthusiastic German Republican, one of the most decisive rep-resentatives of the people on the left in the Frankfurt Paulskirche, an unshaken fighter for truth and light."[74]

Almost a month later, in a letter dated April 12, the absurd con-clusion to this story was recounted: Spanish officials had threatened Schmidt's friends with dire consequences if they did not pay for a full Catholic funeral for the dead German. His body would otherwise have been thrown into a ditch in the manner reserved for atheists and here-tics, or delivered to the tender mercies of the police. Thus "that most unshakeable and yet lovable atheist, the most dangerous foe of catholi-cism, the editor of the *Freie Blätter*, the flaming German radical" was laid to rest to the strains of the *Dies irae*. His clothes, watch, rings, and papers fell to the *Alcalde*, since Schmidt was a foreigner dying alone in a far land. His wife and children received nothing.[75]

The largely complete file[76] of the *Freie Blätter* preserved at the St. Louis Public Library constitutes a valuable resource for our under-standing of the tensions and contradictions within progressive emi-grant circles in the American Midwest in the period before the rise of the militant nativism of the mid-1850s. Although this group engaged in virtually pro forma polemics with Catholics and Lutherans, they appear to have become the best of enemies. The true trouble was to be found within the circle of the freethinkers, since there were those who saw "enlightenment" in strictly cultural and "spiritual" terms, while others were seeking to make it an instrument for changing the very bases of human existence. With the exception of their brief, obviously reluctant, opening to the Social Reform Association, Börnstein and Schmidt appear to have been uncomfortable with any serious ques-tioning of the existing social and economic system. Whatever politi-cally radical convictions either Börnstein or Schmidt might once have harbored tended to fade in the face of concrete American conditions. As for Franz Schmidt, the former Silesian preacher returned to his first loves of rationalism, ethics, and education in his brief sojourn on the banks of the Mississippi. His premature death in Cuba left a gap in the ranks of German-America which was never to be filled.

NOTES

1. *Anzeiger des Westens*, weekly edition, vol. 18, no. 28, May 14, 1853, p. 4, letter dated Apr. 12 from Matanzas.

2. I want to thank Prof. Dr. Walter Schmidt, formerly Director of the Zentralinstitut für Geschichte bei der Akademie der Wissenschaften der DDR, Berlin, for his helpful criticism of an earlier version of this paper, and for his kindness in sending me materials not readily available to me in St. Louis.

3. Walter Schmidt, *Wilhelm Wolff: Sein Weg*, pp. 123–24, n. 12, report of the Posen district president to the Interior Ministry, May 1, 1845.

4. *Lexikon für Theologie und Kirche*, 2d ed., 3:279, 9:38. Walter Schmidt, *Wilhelm Wolff: Kampfgefährte*, p. 31: "The German Catholic movement played a special role in almost all of the letters [from Franz Schmidt to Wolff]. This movement was a specifically religious form of the bourgeois opposition against the ruling conditions in Vormärz, which had found an outlet in Silesia and also was disseminated widely here" [trans. eds.]. On Ronge, see Karl Marx and Friedrich Engels, "Die grossen Männer des Exils," *Werke*, 8:233–333, esp. pp. 306–7.

5. Schmidt, *Wolff: Sein Weg*, p. 226.

6. Schmidt, *Wolff: Sein Weg*, pp. 187–88.

7. Schmidt, *Wolff: Sein Weg*, esp. pp. 119, 123–24, 187–89, 288–89; and *Wolff: Kampfgefährte*, p. 22.

8. Schmidt, *Wolff: Sein Weg*, pp. 183–87. On "true socialism," see Friedrich Engels, "Zwei Aufsätze über die 'wahren' Sozialisten," in Marx and Engels, *Werke*, 4:205–90; and Karl Marx and Friedrich Engels, "Manifest der Kommunistischen Partei," *Werke*, 4:485–88; Karl Marx and Friedrich Engels, *The German Ideology*, pp. 79–193.

9. Günther Hildebrandt, *Die Paulskirche in der Revolution*, pp. 120–21 (Hildebrandt erroneously gives Schmidt's age as only twenty-three in 1848 [p. 47], but he was born in 1818); for Friedrich Engels's comment on Schmidt's speech, see Marx and Engels, *Werke*, 5:350.

10. Hildebrandt, *Die Paulskirche in der Revolution*, p. 169.

11. Hildebrandt, *Die Paulskirche in der Revolution*, p. 256.

12. Schmidt, *Wolff: Kampfgefährte*, pp. 226, 252.

13. Schmidt, *Wolff: Kampfgefährte*, pp. 252, 263 and notes on letters of "Theseus" to Wolff of Dec. 16 and 28, 1850, see *Zeitgenossen von Marx und Engels*, which demonstrates that "Theseus" was Franz Schmidt. One letter from Schmidt to Wolff (Dec. 28, 1850) is reproduced in *Land ohne Nachtigall. Deutsche Immigranten in Amerika, 1777–1886*, ed. Rolf Weber, pp. 159–68, 436–37.

14. See *Freie Blätter*, vol. 1, no. 40, Dec. 13, 1851, p. 317, program of Öffent-

liche Schulprüfung for Dec. 23, 1851, including mention of students Lilly Anheuser, the heiress of the Anheuser Brewery and later wife of Adolphus Busch, as well as Minna Taussig.

15. Engels to Joseph Weydemeyer, Feb. 27, 1852, in Marx and Engels, *Werke*, 28:500. On Duchâtel, see Marx and Engels, *Werke*, 8:691.

16. Besides the published materials cited in the literature, there are about fifty letters, poems, and manuscripts listed concerning Börnstein in the Archiv der Stadt Wien. See also Robert E. Cazden, *Social History of the German Book Trade in America*, p. 221.

17. For a complete reprint of this volume, see Arnold Ruge and Karl Marx, *Deutsch-französische Jahrbücher;* see the condescending remarks in Heinrich Börnstein, *Fünfundsiebzig Jahre*, 1:349: "I mention this only because nowadays hardly any examples of this literary curiosity can be rummaged up, and much of the content still is of value" [trans. eds.].

18. *Vorwärts*, Unveränderter Neudruck; see the detailed preface by Walter Schmidt.

19. Erich P. Hofacker, *German Literature as Reflected in the German-Language Press*, on the publication program of Börnstein. See Steven Rowan, "Cultural Program of Heinrich Börnstein."

20. *Anzeiger des Westens*, vol. 16, no. 100, Feb. 16, 1851, first installment of *Die Geheimnisse von St. Louis*, last excerpt was no. 206, June 20, 1851. See Cazden, *Social History of the German Book Trade in America*, pp. 391–92. The English translation of the book was by Friedrich Münch. A modern edition is available, edited by Steven Rowan and Elizabeth Sims (Henry Boernstein, *The Mysteries of St. Louis.*)

21. Patricia Herminghouse, "Radicalism and the 'Great Cause,' " largely on *The Mysteries of St. Louis*. For other references to Börnstein, see esp. *Germans for a Free Missouri*, pp. 37–41, and Alfred Vagts, "Heinrich Boernstein, Ex- and Repatriate"; generally, one should always look at George Hellmuth Kellner, *German Element on the Urban Frontier*. As if to prove that bigotry knows no country, one of the central scenes of *The Mysteries*, in which the superiors of the Jesuits meet at midnight on Bloody Island in the Mississippi River to plot the overthrow of the American republic, might have been the ultimate model for the infamous anti-Semitic *Protocols of the Elders of Zion*. The model for the *Protocols* which Norman Cohn has fingered (the chapter "In the Jewish Cemetery of Prague" of the novel *Biarritz* [1868], by Hermann Goedsche, whose pen name was Sir John Retcliffe) would not be published until almost two decades later (Norman Cohn, *Warrant for Genocide*, pp. 32–40). It is altogether probable that Goedsche was familiar with Börnstein's work.

22. Robert Cazden, *A Social History of the German Book Trade in America*, p. 290, n. 100.

23. St. Louis Public Library, main branch, *Freie Blätter*, Mar. 18, 1851–Mar. 5, 1853. The bound copy has a lithographic portrait of Schmidt (drawn by Theodore Anders, lithographed by A. M. McLean of St. Louis) glued in as

a frontispiece with his vital dates: born Nieder Saltzbrunn, Nov. 28, 1818, died Matanzas, Cuba, Mar. 29, 1853.

24. *Freie Blätter,* vol. 1, Mar. 18, 1851; also reprint, pp. 1–2.

25. *Freie Blätter,* reprint, p. 1, "The *Freie Blätter* . . . would on its part eagerly attempt to hold itself aloof from battles over specific individuals and factions, preferring to pit principle against principle, and worldview versus worldview."

26. *Freie Blätter,* reprint, p. 1, mentions that the reprint is "in small type, and that except for the title, advertisements and small casual notices, it comprises the entire reading matter of the sold-out issues" [trans. eds.].

27. *Freie Blätter,* vol. 1, no. 9, May 10, 1851, p. 71.

28. *Freie Blätter,* reprint, p. 12, responding to an attack on the *Anzeiger des Westens* by the *Missouri Republican.*

29. *Freie Blätter,* vol. 1, no. 36, Nov. 15, 1851, pp. 287–88.

30. For reference to Franz Schmidt and the *Freie Blätter,* see *Der Lutheraner,* vol. 7, no. 16, Apr. 1, 1851, pp. 124–25; no. 17, Apr. 15, 1851, pp. 134–35; no. 18, Apr. 29, 1851, pp. 139–40; no. 21, June 10, 1851, pp. 163–65; no. 25, Aug. 5, 1851, pp. 193–98 (lead article by C. F. W. Walther), p. 200; no. 26, Aug. 19, 1851, pp. 205–6; vol. 8, no. 7, Nov. 25, 1851, p. 55; finally a brief gloat over the internal troubles of the Verein recorded in the *Freie Blätter,* vol. 8, no. 3, Sept. 28, 1852, p. 23.

31. A copy of this pamphlet could not be located at the Concordia Historical Society, Clayton, Missouri. For further bibliographic information see Cazden, *Social History of the German Book Trade in America,* p. 541, n. 125.

32. *Freie Blätter,* vol. 1, no. 20, July 26, 1851, pp. 158–59.

33. *Freie Blätter,* vol. 1, no. 32, Oct. 18, 1851, p. 253, letter by F. M. (=Friedrich Münch): "Ich bin kein Knecht des Christenthums, aber die von dessen Stifter verkündeten Wahrheiten sind mir doch nicht weniger werthvoll, als ob sie Bako [Sir Francis Bacon] oder Shakespeare verkündigt hatten." ["I am no slave to Christianity, but the truths proclaimed by its founder are no less valuable to me than if they had been proclaimed by Bacon or Shakespeare."] Reply *Freie Blätter,* vol. 1, no. 33, Oct. 25, 1851, p. 257, article signed by Franz Schmidt.

34. The affinity of Börnstein for Heinzen had already been noted over a year and a half earlier by the ever-watchful *Missouri Republican,* vol. 30, no. 112, May 12, 1851, in a letter from an anonymous German entitled "The Anzeiger and the N. Y. Schnellpost." The letter declared that since Börnstein's total takeover of the *Anzeiger,* he had been using Heinzen's articles extensively. Heinzen, "a rank abolitionist" was called "an infinitely better writer." The difference between them was that Börnstein was much more covert about his opinions, and he used Heinzen as a front to get his own radical views in print.

35. See, for example, Friedrich Engels, "Die Kommunisten und Karl Heinzen," in Marx and Engels, *Werke,* 4:209–24; Karl Marx, "Die moralisierende Kritik und die kritisierende Moral: Beitrag zur Deutschen Kulturgeschichte gegen Karl Heinzen von Karl Marx," in Marx and Engels, *Werke,* 4:331–59, and

Karl Marx and Friedrich Engels, "Die grossen Männer des Exils," in Marx and Engels, *Werke*, 8:282–87.

36. Carl Wittke, *Against the Current*.

37. *Freie Blätter*, vol. 1, no. 39, Dec. 6, 1851, pp. 308–10; no. 40, Dec. 13, 1851, p. 318.

38. *Freie Blätter*, vol. 2, no. 13, June 5, 1852, pp. 99, 103 [Philadelphia]; no. 22, Aug. 7, 1852, pp. 170–71; no. 23, Aug. 14, 1852, pp. 178–79; no. 24, Aug. 21, 1852, pp. 185–87 [Hermann, Mo.]; no. 25, Aug. 28, 1852, pp. 193–96 [St. Louis]; no. 26, Sept. 4, 1852, pp. 201–4 [Chicago]; no. 27, Sept. 11, 1852, pp. 209–11.

39. *Freie Blätter* vol. 2, no. 42, Dec. 25, 1852, pp. 319–21; no. 43, Jan. 8, 1853, pp. 338–39; no. 45 [should be 44], Jan. 15, 1853, pp. 343–45.

40. See *Missouri Republican*, daily edition, vol. 30, no. 65, Mar. 18, 1851; no. 66, Mar. 20; no. 67, Mar. 21.

41. For the Brossart events, see *Anzeiger des Westens*, daily edition, vol. 16, no. 123, Mar. 15, 1851, first clear description of story, with reference to publication in previous edition (article not found); no. 124, Mar. 16, efforts to win Brossart's release with a court order; no. 125, Mar. 18, doubts begin to set in about the story ("The question now is, whether Mr. Peter Brossart is a swindler or a lunatic"); no. 127, Mar. 20, statement that Brossart had probably been hired by persons unknown to stir up trouble and discredit Börnstein.

42. Heinrich Börnstein, *Fünfundsiebzig Jahre*, 2:106–8; *Anzeiger des Westens*, vol. 16, no. 136, Mar. 30, 1851; account of the first meeting in *Freie Blätter*, reprint, pp. 19–20.

43. *Freie Blätter*, vol. 1, no. 10, May 17, 1851, p. 79.

44. *Freie Blätter*, vol. 1, no. 35, Nov. 8, 1851, report of meeting of Nov. 2.

45. *Freie Blätter*, vol. 1, no. 22, July 9, 1851, advertisement on last page. The school for the south was at the corner of Seventh and Hickory, that for the north at Sixteenth and Wash.

46. *Freie Blätter*, vol. 2, no. 9, May 8, 1852, report of meeting of Apr. 28.

47. *Missouri Republican*, vol. 30, no. 194a, Sept. 19, 1851, declared the Free Men were not free, "they are completely under the control of Boernstein as the serfs of Russia under the Autocrat."

48. *Missouri Republican*, vol. 30, no. 78, Apr. 2, 1851, p. 2; other, more precise, growth figures are to be found in the *Anzeiger des Westens*, daily edition, vol. 16, no. 185, May 26, 1851: on Apr. 15, at first organization, 55 members; on Apr. 18, 111 members; by May 5, 200 members; and by May 26, 306 members.

49. *Anzeiger des Westens*, daily edition, vol. 16, no. 176, May 16, 1851, p. 3, advertisement for "Deutsche, englische und französische Buchdruckerei des Anzeigers des Westens, Eigenthümer: H. Börnstein und H. W. Gempp." Gempp and Börnstein had bought out the interests of Arthur Olshausen in April 1851 (*Missouri Republican*, daily edition, vol. 30, no. 96, Apr. 23, 1851). Gempp (born Dec. 26, 1798, in St. Louis since 1836) died on May 31, 1851; see *Anzeiger des Westens*, vol. 16, no. 190, June 1, 1851; and Börnstein became the sole owner of the company after buying out Gempp's widow.

50. *Missouri Republican,* vol. 30, no. 194, Sept. 19, 1851, p. 2.

51. *Freie Blätter,* vol. 2, no. 7, Apr. 24, 1852.

52. *Freie Blätter,* vol. 2, no. 22, Aug. 7, 1852, p. 171, report of special meeting of July 30.

53. *Freie Blätter,* vol. 2, no. 23, p. 179, Aug. 14, 1852, report of special meeting of 10 Aug. 10.

54. *Freie Blätter,* vol. 2, no. 27, Sept. 11, 1852, p. 211, report of special meeting of Aug. 31, 1852; pp. 214–15, a "Concordia-Klubb [*sic*] der freien Männer" was briefly formed on Sept. 8 to isolate the protesters.

55. *Freie Blätter,* vol. 2, no. 30, Oct. 2, 1852, pp. 233–35.

56. *Freie Blätter,* vol. 2, no. 32, Oct. 16, 1852, p. 249. Despite the seizure, both buildings were back in the hands of the Verein in a matter of a few days.

57. *Freie Blätter,* vol. 2, no. 32, Oct. 16, 1852, pp. 249–50: "Both endeavors hindered the Verein from the *purity of its original intention:* education and spiritual enlightenment" [trans. eds.; emphasis in original].

58. *Freie Blätter,* vol. 2, no. 32, Oct. 16, 1852, p. 251, report of special meeting of Oct. 10.

59. *Freie Blätter,* vol. 2, no. 33, Oct. 23, 1852, pp. 260–61, new constitution; p. 263, report of meeting of Oct. 16.

60. *Missouri Republican,* daily edition, vol. 30, no. 204, Sept. 1, 1851; also no. 206, Sept. 3, 1851.

61. *Freie Blätter,* vol. 2, no. 19, July 17, 1852, p. 147.

62. *Freie Blätter,* vol. 2, no. 42, Dec. 25, 1852.

63. E. D. Kargau, *St. Louis in Früheren Jahren,* pp. 286–93, for the entire narrative on the Freie Gemeinde, which confused the origins of the Freie Gemeinde with that of the Verein Freier Männer. Kargau believed that Franz Schmidt had been a founder of the Freie Gemeinde, and even that the Freie Gemeinde had grown out of the Verein Freier Männer, though the Freie Gemeinde was in fact half a year older. For the records of the Freie Gemeinde, see Western Historical Manuscripts Collection, University of Missouri-St. Louis, collection 37, Protocols of the *Freie Gemeinde von Nord-St. Louis,* p. 5, Protokoll I, Nov. 6, 1850 (first meeting); see also the caustic comment on the establishment of the Freie Gemeinde by *Der Lutheraner,* vol. 7, no. 10, Jan. 7, 1851, pp. 75–77. There is a response to an article of the *Freie Blätter* calling for a national conference of Freie Gemeinden in the Freie Gemeinde Protocols, p. 18, Protokoll VIII, July 13, 1851.

64. *Freie Blätter,* vol. 1, no. 19, July 19, 1851, p. 151, notice of meeting of the Verein of July 18, mentioning the visit of Dr. T. Moore, city councilman of the Second Ward and the naming of committees to explore possible future cooperation.

65. *Freie Blätter,* vol. 1, no. 30, Oct. 4, 1851, pp. 233–34, and subsequent issues.

66. *Freie Blätter,* vol. 2, no. 19, July 17, 1852, p. 147, "Report on the last investigation of the St. Louis independent confessional high school for boys and young men."

67. *Freie Blätter*, vol. 1, no. 31, Oct. 11, 1851, p. 247.

68. Kargau, *St. Louis in Früheren Jahren*, pp. 288–93.

69. *Missouri Republican*, daily edition, vol. 30, no. 187, Aug. 8, 1851, and following.

70. *St. Louis Evening News*, daily edition, vol. 1, no. 92, Aug. 4, 1852, reporting results of the Aug. 2 election, showed that Thomas Hart Benton won over the Whig candidate heavily in the German-dominated wards, while carrying the total congressional district by a mere five hundred votes. Although Börnstein's boast that the total electorate for Benton was German was certainly overstated, the Germans probably gave him the margin of victory in an extremely close race.

71. Western Historical Manuscripts Collection, University of Missouri-St. Louis, collection 37, folder 1: Freie Gemeinde Protocols, p. 21, Protokoll IX, July 20, 1851: "Herr Franz Schmidt hatte die Einladung, eine Festrede zu halten, angenommen, wenn seine jetzt leidende Gesundheit es dann erlauben werde." [Mr. Franz Schmidt had accepted the invitation to give the main speech, if his then poor health would permit it.] [trans. eds.]

72. *Freie Blätter*, vol. 2, no. 44, Jan. 15, 1853, p. 343; *Anzeiger des Westens*, weekly edition, vol. 18, no. 12, Jan. 12, 1853: "Die Redaktion der 'Freien Blätter' wird während Schmidts Abwesenheit von uns geführt werden—und was Schmidts so schön blühende Mädchenschule betrifft, so werden fähige Lehrer und Frau Schmidt selbst die Anstalt in demselben Geiste und Sinne fortführen, bis Schmidt uns und seinen Schülerinnen wiedergegeben ist." [The editing of the *Freie Blätter* will be taken on by us during Schmidt's absence. And as far as Schmidt's thriving Girls' School is concerned, capable teachers and Mrs. Schmidt herself will carry on the leadership of the institution in the same spirit until Schmidt is returned to us and his school girls.] [trans. eds.]

73. *Anzeiger des Westens*, vol. 18, no. 19, Mar. 12, 1853, p. 1, letters dated Jan. 31, Feb. 2, Feb. 4.

74. *Anzeiger des Westens*, weekly edition, Apr. 23, 1853, article dated Apr. 17. Börnstein promised a detailed obituary, which I have not been able to find.

75. *Anzeiger des Westens*, weekly edition, vol. 18, no. 28, May 14, 1853, p. 4, letter dated Apr. 12.

76. The volume is missing vol. 1, nos. 2–7 (which are largely covered by the reprint), 12–14, 18, 24–26, 48–50; vol. 2, nos. 6, 14, 17(a), 18, 20–21, 36–37, 40.

John B. Jentz

The 48ers and the Politics of the German Labor Movement in Chicago during the Civil War Era: Community Formation and the Rise of a Labor Press

During the Civil War a vital interethnic labor movement emerged in Chicago, as in other major northern cities. The Chicago movement combined Irish, German, British, and native-born workers in numerous unions and created a city central body that published its own labor paper. After the war this labor movement made Chicago the center of a national campaign for the eight-hour day. Although the eight-hour movement failed after the defeat of a massive strike in May 1867, organized labor regrouped and even expanded in some industries afterwards. Yet after 1867 there were really two organized movements, one German- and the other English-speaking. By 1869 each had its own city central organization of constituent unions as well as its own labor paper—the *Workingman's Advocate* and *Der Deutsche Arbeiter*. By the early 1870s—and for different reasons—both of these city central organizations had disbanded, while their member unions were considerably weakened. The first era of Chicago labor history had ended, and a new one would begin with the onset of the depression of the 1870s.

This paper examines the first era of Chicago labor history from the perspective of German workers and the 48ers who usually spoke for them in the public arena. Its goal is to shed new light on the complex interrelationship of class and ethnicity in American labor history, particularly by tying the history of German workers to the evolution of their ethnic group and its politics. Basically it argues that during the 1850s and 1860s Germans in Chicago—workers included—were preoccupied with building the social, cultural, and economic institutions of their community. These institutions included not only churches and ethnic clubs but also manufacturing enterprises, labor organizations, and newspapers. During this period 48ers led German labor politically, while the actual organization of unions and benefit societies was done by German craftsmen, often in cooperation with skilled workers from other ethnic groups.

The ability of the 48ers to lead German workers politically rested in large measure on the authority they derived from their critical role in defining German-American ethnicity and founding the key institutions of German Chicago. Newspapers, and particularly the *Illinois Staats-Zeitung*, were critically important to the 48ers in this role because the papers served as vehicles for defining ethnic identity, articulating common concerns, and mobilizing the group politically in defense of its interests. In this period these interests were threatened with peculiar force by nativist and temperance movements. When the period of community formation ended, so too did much of the political authority of the radical 48ers over German workers. The end of the period was marked by the founding of German-language newspapers rivaling the *Staats-Zeitung*, including labor's *Der Deutsche Arbeiter*.

German 48ers, German Workers, and the Origins of the Chicago Republican Party

The leadership of the 48ers in defining German-American ethnicity amidst the nativist and temperance agitation of the 1850s is well known. Chicago too had its short-lived Know-Nothing political victory in 1855; and its German community mobilized in opposition, with inspired leadership provided by 48ers. Between 1853 and 1856—when Know-Nothing activity was at its peak—48ers took over the *Illinois Staats-Zeitung*, making it into a major daily; and they helped to organize the central secular institutions of the German community—the Turner society; the men's choir; the German Society, an immigrant aid organization; and German House, a central meeting hall. Although the 48ers had considerable aid from others, they played a catalytic role because of their energy, organizational skills, and cultural achievements, as well as the opportunities of the moment: the nativists had created an unease among all Germans, who looked for the leadership that the 48ers provided. In this crisis of the mid-1850s the secularity of the 48ers aided them in their claim to found institutions—such as German House—open to all Germans and not identified with any one religious or political group. To the extent that the 48ers advocated free thought and the policies of the emerging Republican party this claim proved suspect. Also well known to students of German-American history is the role the 48ers played in leading a substantial German element—including a significant group of German craftsmen—into the new Republican party.[1] This German constituency helped make the Republican party competitive in a city that had been overwhelmingly Democratic.

Less well known is the 48ers' attitude toward labor while they were doing so much to shape German-American ethnicity and politics. The left-wing of 48er opinion was expressed at a national meeting organized by Karl Heinzen in Louisville during March 1854. Nativism was rampant in the land; and the Kansas-Nebraska Act had just been passed, making the extension of slavery into the territories the central political question of the moment. The result of this meeting was the "Louisville Platform," which provided a controversial touchstone for German-American politics during the Civil War era.[2] The Louisville platform divided the 48er radicals from their more moderate brethren by its advocacy of racial and sexual equality, as well as by its tone of dissatisfaction with American political institutions which did not live up to the ideals expressed in the Declaration of Independence. Although the issues of slavery and nativism were the central ones, the platform also had a section on "measures for the welfare of the people" in which it addressed the condition of labor.[3]

There were two fundamental presuppositions of this section of the platform—first, that labor and capital were antagonistic and, second, that laboring for a capitalist was a temporary necessity taken up because labor lacked sufficient capital to engage in its own enterprise. Both ideas were also current in American labor circles during the Jacksonian era; and the ideology of the Republican party, which was to emerge in a few years, assumed that wage labor was not meant to be a permanent station in life.[4] The Louisville platform took a distinctive turn, however, in recommending state intervention to aid labor in its contest with capital if a "just agreement" could not be reached. As the "arbitrator of all contending interests," the state should mediate the claims of both parties, setting a minimum wage equal to the value of labor and a maximum workday of ten hours. The state should also aid associations of working men with credit banks and government contracts. These labor planks of the Louisville platform must be understood, however, within the context of its overarching goal, which was to provide a political program behind which all Germans could unite under 48er leadership. Although the radicalism of the program doomed this endeavor from the start, both the platform and

the larger enterprise of creating a left-leaning German political movement in American politics remained significant for the history of labor,
particularly in Illinois.

Labor was also on the program of a subsequent meeting in 1854
held in Peoria, Illinois. It was designed to build local support for the
political agenda enunciated in Louisville. The initiative for the Peoria
meeting came from the political circle around the Chicago-based *Illinois Staats-Zeitung*, which hoped to form an umbrella organization of
liberal associations and Free Men's organizations from throughout the
state.[5] The support of the group around the *Staats-Zeitung* for the Louisville platform illustrates the strong presence of radical 48ers in Chicago
and helps explain their effort to speak to labor, and especially to the
city's constituency of radical craftsmen. The political program adopted
at Peoria was similar to the Louisville platform, placing slavery first on
the list of priorities but also advocating religious freedom, free high
schools, the ten-hour day for laborers, and easier suffrage require-
ments.[6] A permanent organization was set up, based at the *Illinois
Staats-Zeitung* and composed almost entirely of members of its radical
circle of 48ers. When the leadership council of this organization met in
July 1854, five Chicago associations were represented, three of them
recently founded and dominated by 48ers—the Turners, a liberal singing society, and the local "Free Men's" association. The other two were
the associations of carpenters and tailors.[7]

Recently formed craft associations with benevolent features, the carpenters' and the tailors' associations were the two most significant
German labor organizations then in the city.[8] Their presence illustrates
the popularity among craftsmen of the radical republicanism originat-
ing in the 1848 Revolution.[9] The actions of the July meeting in Chicago
included an appeal to this labor constituency in its call for a stronger
organization of the "free societies." The meeting called for workers in
the plants of Chicago and other cities to organize themselves and then
unite in a larger organization.[10] In an acknowledgment of the independent position of labor within German Chicago, the workers were not
asked simply to join the umbrella organization of "Free Associations
of Illinois, but rather to cooperate with it." This call to workers was
a recognition of labor organizational activity that had taken place in
Chicago in 1853 and 1854, when several crafts had witnessed disputes
over prices paid to journeymen.[11] In April of 1854, for example, the
German tailors, in association with workers of other nationalities, had
formulated a price list which was accepted by most of their employers
and formed the basis of labor relations in the trade until 1862.[12] Contemporary with similar and more substantial activity in other cities,

this labor organizing in Chicago did not produce a set of unions with a core of German journeymen but rather the craft associations of the carpenters and tailors.[13]

In the mid-1850s the most significant facts about German labor in Chicago were that it had several distinct and substantial organizations and that its needs were recognized and integrated into the politics of the 48ers, particularly through the efforts of the city's strong 48er left. The participation of German labor in German liberal and radical politics meant that the history of the 48ers related directly to the city's German-American labor history. Yet the 48ers' most important agenda was not the sustenance of labor, not even the destruction of slavery, but rather the creation of a German presence in American politics under their leadership. Radicals were more inclined than liberals to advocate a distinct party that would promote goals such as those expressed in the Louisville platform. Liberal and moderate 48ers were more inclined to make their presence felt within the Republican coalition. In the late 1850s, however, these tendencies were submerged by the overwhelming significance of the antislavery issue for all 48ers and by the necessities of organizing a strong local Republican party.[14]

Chicago's 48ers had a chance to demonstrate their leadership during the crisis of unemployment created by the Panic of 1857. When, like other national groups, the Germans met in November to organize their relief committees, the editor of the *National Demokrat*, Chicago's German-language Democratic paper, made a challenging and politically volatile proposal: he urged that a committee of five laborers call on the city council and demand work or bread.[15] This proposal was similar to demands posed by workers in eastern cities to their city governments during the economic crisis.[16] In Chicago the proposal for bread or work became a partisan as well as an ethnic issue because it was to be presented to the city's first Republican city council on the initiative of a foreign-language Democratic newspaper.

The editor of the *Demokrat* was challenged in the November German meeting by Hermann Kreismann. He was a member of the 48er circle at the *Staats-Zeitung* who had just been appointed city clerk by Chicago's first Republican mayor.[17] His appointment was one indication of his politics, more moderate than those of some of his colleagues. Appealing to American legal traditions, Kreismann said that the city government had no authority to provide work or relief. Unlike the European despotisms they had fled, the government here "does not interfere by unequal taxation, unjust laws and the establishment of favored classes, in times of prosperity," and thus "it cannot be expected to act as the nursing mother in times of distress."[18] Appealing to German ethnic pride, he acknowledged that something had to be done and called on his countrymen to take care of their own through voluntary associations. In this way the already high reputation of the Germans among the Americans would increase even more. Kreismann won this verbal duel, and the demand for work or bread was not made to the city council by representatives of the German meeting.

The implications of Kreismann's victory were several and profound. First of all, a 48er himself, he effectively asserted the leadership of the 48ers over Chicago's German workers. The existing German craft organizations of the tailors and cabinetmakers already sympathized with the 48ers. Yet this meeting represented a broader constituency, not necessarily organized into labor institutions but conscious of labor's needs in a time of economic crisis. The fact that Kreismann could determine the outcome of this meeting illustrated the broad influence of the 48ers even among unorganized workingmen. When the Chicago labor movement did emerge in 1863 and 1864, its most prominent German political leader was Edward Schlaeger, another 48er, although Schlaeger was a radical and Kreismann a moderate. The result of the November 1857 German meeting also had significant ideological implications. Asserting a responsibility for the state in determining the relations of capital and labor, the Louisville platform could have provided ample rationale for demanding work or bread from the city government.[19] Since he was a moderate, it is no surprise that Kreismann failed to use this means to assert state responsibility for the unemployed, but the city's radical 48ers did not either. At this time the exigencies of forming a stable local Republican party took precedence over ideology. The emergence of Schlaeger as a spokesman for labor during the Civil War can be seen as a return of Chicago's radical 48ers to their original position.

Yet, Kreismann's victory aside, something positive had to be done to relieve distress during the winter of 1857; and the 48ers took action within the limits set by their Republican commitments. Rejecting an open political appeal to the Common Council, the 48ers helped German craftsmen found the Arbeiterverein, a social and mutual benefit organization. The Arbeiterverein was founded within a week of the November meeting called to discuss relief. Combined with the relief efforts of the German Society, the founding of the Arbeiterverein constituted German Chicago's main organized response to the crisis caused by the Panic of 1857.[20] Patterned after similar groups then developing in Germany, the Chicago Arbeiterverein was the most important German labor organization for the next ten, very critical, years.[21] Its importance, however, transcended its German roots, for it was Chicago's first effective labor organization that united workers across craft lines. Through the Arbeiterverein Chicago's 48ers asserted their leadership over the politics of the city's first German labor movement. The Republican cast they gave to these politics helped insure that the public presence of Germans in Chicago's first labor movement—which had a Democratic coloring—was less than the extent of German participation warranted. At the same time the Arbeiterverein's emphasis on self-help and voluntarism paved the way for future cooperation with the associations of Anglo-American workingmen.

German Labor during the Civil War and Subsequent Eight-Hour Movement

On the eve of the Civil War there were not more than ten labor organizations in Chicago. Apart from the Typographical Union (founded in 1852), the Iron Molders Union (founded in 1857), and the Machinists and Blacksmiths' Union (founded in 1859), they were all ethnically affiliated benevolent societies. A sharp rise in consumer prices during the early war years, combined with a growing labor shortage, quickly transformed this situation. By 1864 Chicago newspapers reported thirteen strikes, three more than the total during the previous three years. Out of this conflict came fifteen new unions.[22] For the most part, they were stronger than the temporary, makeshift associations which had been the norm in previous years. Most important, the new unions were multiethnic, the first time in the city's history there had been a broad movement among workers that transcended divisions among nationalities. When, for example, the journeymen coopers held a ball as part of their effort to found an association, their organizing committee was composed of Irish and Germans. During a strike in 1864, the tailors' union met at German House to hear speeches in English and German and then elect its officers, Lawrence Shea and Edward Henderson.[23] During a strike in 1864 the position of the overwhelmingly German bakers was represented within the new Trades Assembly by men named Dooley, Burke, and Shay.[24] These leadership choices reflected the unfamiliarity of recently arrived German workers with the language and politics of a foreign land. Overall Chicago's Civil War union movement was led by English-speaking immigrants—British and Irish workers—whose knowledge of both the English language and American political culture gave them an advantage.[25] This leadership also helped give Chicago's first labor movement its Democratic political coloring.

While German unionists had been active in the labor movement from the beginning, significant political leadership for German labor awaited a split among the city's German Republicans over the Frémont candidacy for president in 1864. Although in 1856 the 48ers as a group had been drawn to Frémont, his candidacy in 1864 in opposition to Lincoln divided them into radical and moderate factions. In Chicago the Frémont people were drawn predominantly from the Social Arbeiterverein, a branch of the central Arbeiterverein based in Chicago's heavily working-class Tenth Ward. In late May 1864 the Social Arbeiterverein contributed two of three delegates from the Chicago Arbeiterverein to the pro-Frémont Cleveland convention, which not only broke from the Republican party but also noted the increasing conflict between capital and labor.

The sending of representatives to the Cleveland convention from the Chicago Arbeiterverein split the organization. The more radical group kept the name Arbeiterverein, while the moderates formed an exclusively educational organization.[26] As the Frémont candidacy became increasingly hopeless, the radicals in the Arbeiterverein turned toward the city's labor movement. At an August 1864 meeting of the Arbeiterverein, speakers stressed that while politicians divided the people, trade unions "would unite all nationalities, natives and Irishmen and German."[27] In September the Arbeiterverein sent five delegates to the Trades Assembly which had been formed in the spring. Edward Schlaeger, one of the 48er radicals, abandoned his recently founded anti-Republican paper, the *Union,* and contributed instead a German-language supplement to the newly formed *Workingman's Advocate.*[28] Within its own pages, therefore, the *Advocate* illustrated the interethnic character of the new labor movement. These moves by the Frémonters and Schlaeger, who was also one of them, indicated an alienation from the mainstream Republican party among radical 48ers that aided their participation in the larger English-speaking labor movement.

These radical 48ers in the Arbeiterverein helped keep German labor in Chicago within the English-speaking labor movement after the Civil War. Schlaeger, for example, represented the Chicago Arbeiterverein at the annual convention of the National Labor Union in 1866, where he argued for an independent political initiative by labor.[29] The Arbeiterverein actively supported the movement for the eight-hour day, although it saw cooperation as the only permanent solution to the labor question; and German unionists were a substantial part of the parade in support of the eight-hour day and the subsequent strike in May 1867.[30]

The role of the Frémont faction of the 48ers in providing leadership to German labor in the mid-1860s can be understood in the light of both the Louisville platform and contemporary developments in Germany. In turning to labor the Frémonters who remained in the Arbeiterverein represented a revival of the social import of the Louisville platform. Their concern with the "social question" was particularly apparent in the statements issued by several meetings held in preparation for the Cleveland convention of 1864.[31] It is unclear from the existing evidence whether, following the Louisville statement, the radicals in the Arbeiterverein also supported state intervention to adjust the relation between labor and capital, as well as to provide support for labor institutions. Nevertheless, it is likely that the Arbeiterverein supported state aid for the cooperatives, which it saw as the permanent solution to the labor question.

In a larger perspective, the radicals in the Arbeiterverein can be seen within the spectrum of liberal to left opinion in contemporary Germany as defined by historians Shlomo Na'aman and Toni Offermann.[32] One can distinguish between liberals and democrats on the German left, the dividing line between the two drawn over the question of whether political change was sufficient to reform society or whether some kind of fundamental social change was needed as well. Democrats, as opposed to liberals, advocated social as well as political change. In turn the democrats divided into "blue" and "red" groups, with the blues more moderate and the reds tending toward Lassallean or Marxist positions. The Arbeiterverein radicals in Chicago were blue democrats who split from their more moderate liberal associates in the German wing of the Republican party, then allied themselves with labor, but stayed within the tradition of labor reform. Their advocacy of fundamental social change, but not revolution, underlay their cooperation with the British and Irish leaders of the Chicago labor movement. Within a few years of the great eight-hour strike of 1867, however, Chicago's blue democrats were replaced by Lassallean red democrats, men such as Carl Klings, who occupied key leadership positions in the new German city central body and in the editorship of its labor paper, *Der Deutsche Arbeiter*. This change in the leadership of German labor in Chicago was symbolized by Edward Schlaeger's return to Germany in early 1872.[33]

Two Labor Movements and the End of an Era

These leadership changes at the top of the German labor movement in Chicago should be understood within the context of the maturation of the Chicago German community, not simply as part of the ideological history of the left. The red democrats like Klings were not simply more radical than the Arbeiterverein group, they were new to a city whose scale and complexity made it substantially different from the booming but modest-sized commercial center that the 48ers like Schlaeger entered in the early 1850s. Chicago's population grew from 30,000 to 300,000 in the twenty years after 1850, and by 1870 it had a significant manufacturing economy. At the same time, class divisions were emerging which would become starkly apparent during the depression of the mid-1870s. Before then ethnic ties were stronger than class conflict, but the class divisions that were developing within German Chicago helped create the conditions for the formation of Chicago's first German labor movement.

By the end of the 1860s the initial tasks of institution building and cultural self-definition, in which 48ers of all shades of opinion had played a prominent role, had been largely accomplished. By then Chicago Germans had a new sense of confidence and legitimacy based on their participation in the Civil War; and the public issues of the era had shifted from slavery and secession—upon which the 48ers provided such important leadership—to reconstruction and the labor question. This paper stresses the economic side of the formation of the Chicago German community, mainly because this aspect of ethnic community building is less well known than the founding of ethnic cultural and social institutions. The development of a large, prosperous, and class-divided German community marked the end of the community formation period.

During the 1860s Chicago experienced a manufacturing boom that began to diversify its predominantly commercial economy. Although in 1870 Chicago's manufacturing economy was still smaller than Cincinnati's, the scale and sophistication of its firms ranked with its rival. Even though, for example, the size of Chicago's manufacturing work force was only 70 percent of Cincinnati's, a higher proportion of Chicago's workers labored in firms with more than fifty employees.[34] German entrepreneurs contributed substantially to this manufacturing expansion. In 1870 they actually owned a slightly larger percentage— 37.9—of all manufacturing firms than the native-born, although the businesses of the native-born were considerably larger.[35] Nonetheless, no other foreign-born group could match the German strength in the manufacturing economy.

German manufacturers dominated several branches of industry. They constituted over half of the businesses and hired over half of the workers in the production of tobacco products, alcoholic beverages, and furniture.[36] They also had a substantial presence in other branches of industry—food-processing (not meat-packing), slaughterhouse by-products, wearing apparel, light metal fabrication, carriages and wagons, construction, and building materials.[37] For the history of German labor in Chicago the most important fact was that German manufacturers employed a substantial proportion of their countrymen. In Chicago a German-American labor movement could develop within a German-American world. The strength of this ethnic world gave German workers in several branches of industry the power to sustain their own institutions within a labor movement still predominantly led by Irish, British, and American craftsmen.

By the late 1860s Chicago's 50,000 Germans were stratified along class lines, and German manufacturers constituted a powerful segment of German-American leadership.[38] Their rise is best illustrated by the purchase of the *Illinois Staats-Zeitung*, the bastion of 48er influence, by Anton Hesing, a political boss and manufacturing entrepreneur. Although Hesing's interests were mainly political, he owned Chicago's second-largest planing mill in 1870. Thus it is no surprise that for political as well as economic reasons Hesing was the favorite enemy of Carl Klings, in his capacity as labor editor and radical politician. The founding in 1869 of Klings's *Der Deutsche Arbeiter* is the best example of the emerging class divisions in German Chicago. As the organ of the recently formed German-language city central labor organization, the paper printed on its masthead the names of the constituent unions and labor groups that made up the organization—they included unions and associations of bakers, building carpenters, bricklayers, masons, blacksmiths, shoemakers, furniture workers, and wagonmakers plus the Union veterans.[39] The industries in which labor organized had significant numbers of German entrepreneurs, and together these businessmen and the workers they employed created a strong German presence in the Chicago manufacturing economy.

By the late 1860s Germans in Chicago had built a diversified ethnic community in which the talents of the 48ers were no longer sorely needed. The organization of an independent German labor movement in 1868 represented more than an assertion of ethnic pride among workers who had previously deferred to English-speaking immigrants; it was also a recognition that class questions divided German workers from both their American and their German employers. Nowhere was this division more evident than in the development of Chicago's diverse German press. During the Civil War era the *Illinois Staats-Zeitung* could legitimately claim to be the voice of German Chicago, as its primarily Democratic competitors came and went. The founding of *Der Deutsche Arbeiter* was a forecast of the future. By the mid-1870s Chicago had not only a labor press that would sustain itself into the twenti-

John B. Jentz

eth century but also several substantial German dailies which could compete with the former organ of Chicago's 48ers.

NOTES

An earlier version of this essay was presented on December 29, 1988, at the annual meeting of the American Historical Association in Cincinnati. Research for the essay was supported in part by a grant from the Research Division of the National Endowment for the Humanities.

1. The best sources on this political history are James Manning Bergquist, "Political Attitudes of the German Immigrant in Illinois," and Bruce C. Levine, "Free Soil, Free Labor, and *Freimänner.*"

2. Bergquist, "Political Attitudes of the German Immigrant in Illinois," pp. 147–48; Carl Wittke, *Refugees of Revolution,* pp. 163–65, 184–88; Adolf Eduard Zucker, ed., *The Forty-Eighters,* pp. 173–75.

3. John P. Sanderson, *Republican Landmarks,* pp. 221–22.

4. Eric Foner, *Free Soil, Free Labor, Free Men,* pp. 16–17.

5. Bergquist, "Political Attitudes of the German Immigrant in Illinois," pp. 148–49.

6. Bergquist, "Political Attitudes of the German Immigrant in Illinois," p. 150.

7. *Freeport Deutscher Anzeiger,* July 28, 1854, p. 2.

8. Bessie Louise Pierce, *From Town to City,* p. 166. Both organizations were incorporated by the state in 1855, probably to help them function as benevolent societies.

9. See Levine, "Free Soil, Free Men, and *Freimänner,*" as well as his "In the Spirit of 1848."

10. *Freeport Deutscher Anzeiger,* July 28, 1854, p. 2.

11. Carl Abbott, *Boosters and Businessmen,* p. 25; Pierce, *From Town to City,* pp. 160, 165 (n. 66), 166.

12. *Illinois Staats-Zeitung,* Oct. 2, 1862, p. 4.

13. On a substantial contemporary labor movement in New York City see Charles Iver Bernstein, "New York City Draft Riots," p. 269.

14. A nativist upsurge usually prompted the German 48ers to start organizing for a distinct German political voice, if not an independent party. Similarly, the less the German 48ers were integrated into the Republican party in their localities the more they longed for their own organization. Since they were less integrated in the East than in the West, the eastern 48ers most often advocated striking out on their own, as was the case, for example, in German discussions preparatory to the Republican convention in 1860. The Frémont candidacy was the most obvious representation of the 48ers' desire for their own distinct voice in American political circles. See Bergquist, "Political Attitudes of the German Immigrant in Illinois," pp. 107–10, 180–81, 293–99; Jörg Nagler, *Frémont contra Lincoln,* pp. 119–59.

15. *Chicago Tribune*, Nov. 16, 1857, p. 1. The meeting was attended by three to four hundred people.

16. Amy Bridges, *City in the Republic*, pp. 116–18.

17. Bergquist, "Political Attitudes of the German Immigrant in Illinois," pp. 245–46.

18. *Chicago Tribune*, Nov. 16, 1857, p. 1.

19. Sanderson, *Republican Landmarks*, p. 221.

20. *German Workers in Chicago*, p. 36.

21. Although these German associations were repressed along with the rest of the labor movement after the counterrevolution, there was a revival of labor institutions in the German-speaking world during the late 1850s and early 1860s; Dieter Dowe, "Einleitung," in his *Bibliographie zur Geschichte der deutschen Arbeiterbewegung*, p. 63.

22. These conclusions are based on a reading of the daily *Chicago Tribune*, from 1861 through 1864; see especially March through April 1864; also the *Illinois Staats-Zeitung*, Jan. 24, 1861, and Apr. 6, 1864.

23. *Chicago Tribune*, Apr. 5, 1864; *Illinois Staats-Zeitung*, Jan. 24, 1861; Apr. 6, 1864.

24. *Illinois Staats-Zeitung*, June 9, 1864.

25. The diversity of the leadership comes into clearer focus when we analyze a list of one hundred union leaders of twenty-eight different unions in 1864. As measured by the ethnicity of surname, 40 percent of all leaders were Anglo-American, 31 percent German, and 27 percent Irish. When birthplace was used instead of surname, the percentages were similar.

26. *Illinois Staats-Zeitung*, May 26 and June 10, 12, 13, 23, and 29, 1864.

27. *Chicago Times*, Aug. 19, 1864.

28. *Chicago Times*, Aug. 19, 1864; *Workingman's Advocate*, Sept. 17, 1864.

29. John R. Commons et al., *Documentary History of American Industrial Society*, 9:128.

30. *German Workers in Chicago*, pp. 254–57.

31. Nagler, *Frémont contra Lincoln*, pp. 154, 208–9.

32. Shlomo Na'aman, *Demokratische und soziale Impulse in der Frühgeschichte der deutschen Arbeiterbewegung*, pp. 9–10; Toni Offermann, *Arbeiterbewegung und liberales Bürgertum*, pp. 26–34.

33. Actually Schlaeger's withdrawal from active leadership of the labor movement probably began when he took a position as assistant editor of the *Illinois Staats-Zeitung* in April 1868; *Illinois Staats-Zeitung*, Jan. 20, 1872.

34. Federal manuscript manufacturing census for Chicago, 1870; Steven J. Ross, *Workers on the Edge*, p. 80. In Chicago 53.6 percent of the manufacturing work force labored in firms with more than fifty workers, compared to 49.4 percent in Cincinnati. (The figure for Cincinnati actually refers to firms with fifty or more, not more than fifty.)

35. Federal manuscript manufacturing census for Chicago, 1870. Thus the American firms employed two-thirds of the manufacturing work force, compared to over one-fifth employed by the German-owned businesses.

John B. Jentz

36. Figures on German manufacturing firms in this paragraph were derived from the federal manuscript manufacturing census for Chicago, 1870.

37. These were branches of industry in which Germans owned at least 20, but less than 50, percent of all firms.

38. Edward Bubnys has found that wealth among Chicago's Germans in 1870 was significantly more evenly distributed than among other national groups in the city, including the native-born. (See Edward Bubnys, "Nativity and the Distribution of Wealth," pp. 101–9.) For several reasons I do not take this to mean, however, that class divisions were not emerging among them. In part the more equitable distribution of wealth found by Bubnys likely resulted from a greater German predisposition to invest surplus income in real estate, a finding derived from a study I did of property holding among Chicago's national groups in 1860. Real estate ownership was more likely to appear in the census returns, if only because it was more difficult to conceal. Thus the distinctive German distribution of wealth probably is more visible because of the Germans' propensity for investing in a form of wealth that was better reported.

Yet I would not dismiss Bubnys's findings as simply an anomaly of the sources he used or the German investment predispositions. Germans in Chicago did profit considerably from the economic boom of the 1860s, and the figures on German manufacturers given in this paper are one indication of that fact. The boom helped produce the German entrepreneurs whose increasing presence and self-consciousness contributed to emergent class divisions in their ethnic community. Another indication of German prosperity in the 1860s is the distinctive distribution of wealth found by Bubnys. Skilled workers in particular earned more, even when they were unable to become small entrepreneurs like so many of their countrymen. Yet these same skilled workers were experiencing most directly the transformation of production through mechanization, division of labor, and increase in firm size that was at the root of so much of the nineteenth-century labor movement. It is a commonplace of labor history that skilled workers—of whom Germans constituted a high proportion—were at the core of nineteenth-century labor organizing. It was this type of German worker who organized in the branches of industry where German entrepreneurs also prospered; it was this type of worker who founded the German city central body and subscribed to *Der Deutsche Arbeiter*.

39. The name of the German city central body was the Deutsche-Arbeiter-Central-Schutz-und-Unterstützungs-Verein. The furniture workers were included on the masthead as the United Carpenters.

Ken Fones-Wolf and Elliott Shore

The German Press and Working-Class Politics in Gilded-Age Philadelphia

Ever since the rise of industrialization in the United States, observers have sought to explain why working-class militancy—so potent at the workplace—has rarely been transmitted to politics. Of course, answers range from roast beef (i.e., the standard of living) to professional mass electioneering and include many variations.[1] No area has posed more of a challenge, however, than the conflicting messages of ethnicity and class. Working-class formation in America was a complex and tedious process which partially consisted of sifting through immigrant and indigenous radical cultures for an idiom of class expression. Most wage earners had an outlook shaped by a roughly equal attachment to their participation in an ethnic, racial, or religious community and to their experience as workers in an industrial economy. Dynamic and uneven capitalist development further complicated those loyalties. For instance, the experience of an Irish-Catholic weaver differed greatly from that of an Irish-Catholic machinist. Nevertheless, as ethnicity fragmented workers, class fractured immigrant communities.[2]

The immigrant press reflected the complexity of competing loyalties. In many instances, the ethnic press could encourage group solidarity through language, schools, ties to the homeland, and even social, economic, or cultural initiatives in urban politics. In other cases, ethnic newspapers assisted the assimilation or accommodation of upwardly mobile immigrants by instructing and modifying ethnic culture to blend into America's acquisitive, individualistic values. Less frequently, Irish and German newspapers championed an assimilation of a different sort—one rooted in working-class solidarity. Newspapers like the *Irish World* or the *New Yorker Volkszeitung* maintained important ties to the largely wage-earning ethnic community while advocating class solutions to the unequal distribution of wealth and power in the United States.[3]

Consequently, we cannot talk about the impact of the German-language press on working-class politics as if it was monolithic. In Gilded Age Philadelphia, there were German newspapers of all three varieties, all tugging at the loyalties of the German-American working class. This paper will look at the role those newspapers played at two periods of widespread labor conflict—the 1872 eight-hour strikes and labor's great uprising of 1886—and explore the complex intersection of ethnicity and working-class formation. In 1872 when no pro-labor German-language newspaper existed in Philadelphia, the press actually functioned to break down ethnic solidarity in favor of class unity. By 1885, a radical pro-labor German paper existed. However, its ideological stance helped fragment working-class political initiatives. Perhaps these episodes can suggest some of the difficulties in transposing labor militancy into class politics.

A significant German presence in Philadelphia stretched back into the colonial era. The city's industrial base, with its bewildering variety of job opportunities, made it a desirable location for German immigrants well into the nineteenth century. Although Germans were outnumbered by the Irish by more than two to one in 1850, German immigration actually grew at a faster rate over the next three decades. If nearly three of every ten Philadelphians were either first- or second-generation Irish by 1880, two more were German. More important, Germans came better prepared to control many of the more highly paid crafts comprising the city's occupational market. Particularly in the light consumer-goods industries—shoes, bakery products, clothing, textiles, and furniture—Germans often dominated or at least matched the native-born population.[4]

German immigrants too, came better prepared for participation in working-class activism, especially since the labor movement grew from among many of the crafts in which Germans were disproportionately represented. More than just an artisanal background was necessary to fashion a movement, however. Germans had also absorbed a political consciousness forged in the labor unrest of the 1830s and the revolution of 1848 and nourished in the various republican and radical programs of such artisans as Berlin craftsman Stefan Born. In the 1850s, Philadelphia attracted numerous German immigrants who immediately set out to revive their revolutionary republicanism and anticlerical rationalism in their new home.[5]

Throughout the decade leading up to the Civil War, German immigrants fused their ideological traditions to the free-labor political culture of Northern industrial workers. In 1850, led by socialist tailor Wilhelm Weitling, German-American artisans convened a Workingmen's Congress in Philadelphia which adopted the slogan "equal rights and duties." Meanwhile, German craftsmen and their families built an associational network around fraternal orders, building and loan societies, recreational organizations, and political clubs. Especially in the Turnvereine, plebeian organizations devoted to physical fitness, workers developed political notions about the "slave power," linking their dislike for Southern agrarians to their earlier conflict with the Prussian landed aristocracy. Although Germans split on their opposition to slavery, those associated with the working class "assumed leadership roles in the political and military mobilization" against the South, according to historian Bruce Levine. From the passage of the Kansas-Nebraska Act through the conclusion of the Civil War, German immigrants' "equal rights" ideas attached them to a political culture galvanizing Northern workingmen around the Union cause.[6]

The German-language press in Philadelphia divided over the issue of slavery. The *Freie Presse* took up free labor and equal rights, asserting that it would be advantageous to Northern workingmen. The *Demokrat*, on the other hand, clung to its suspicion of state intervention and centralized government. Ironically, the *Demokrat* was edited by ex-48ers, who one would expect to be more sympathetic to the cause of free labor, but they had also witnessed the power of a centralized state. Meanwhile, Friedrich Thomas, editor of the *Freie Presse*, was a liberal, a freethinker who had emigrated in 1837 and had not experienced the politics of 1848. He adopted the full Republican platform of free labor, a more active state, and high tariffs in the interest of German-American craftsmen.[7] In the postwar era, however, both papers lost contact with the immigrant working class. As new middle-class leaders came to dominate the German community's institutions, they offered the politics of ethnic brokerage to a community increasingly divided along class lines. Meanwhile, old 48ers who had risen to prosperity, like pianomaker Wilhelm Candidus, adopted a more conservative political line.[8]

After the Civil War, German workers felt the dual pinch of declining real wages and the transformation of the labor process. Wages failed to keep pace with war-induced inflation at the same time that employers began to industrialize German-dominated crafts through technological advances and the division of labor.[9] As standards of living worsened,

German workers began to abandon Republican and Democratic solutions and revive the labor movement. There, they benefited from their connection to the free-labor, equal-rights traditions of the native-born working class.

Indeed, antislavery arguments played a critical role in the formation of the postbellum labor movement. The masthead of the Philadelphia labor weekly, *Fincher's Trades Review,* which read "Eight Hours: A Legal Day's Work for Freemen," must have resonated for German workers witnessing the erosion of their artisanal independence. Similarly, Philadelphia labor leader William Sylvis, head of both the molder's union and the National Labor Union, asserted: "The late war resulted in the building up of the most infamous monied aristocracy on the face of the earth. This monied power is fast eating up the substance of the people."[10] By 1870, German workers in Philadelphia had reestablished strong unions in the metal, building, woodworking, and clothing trades in cooperation with English, Irish, and native-born workers. They also created a forceful political lobby and established both English and German branches of the socialist International Workingmen's Association (IWA) in the city.[11]

No issue captured the imagination of the labor movement like the eight-hour workday. Proposed as a class issue by a self-educated machinist, Ira Steward, the demand united German and American workers in the traditions of republicanism and equal rights. Steward wrote that the "anti-slavery idea was that every man had the right to go and come at will. The Labor movement asks how much this abstract [right] is actually worth, without the power to exercise it."[12] In the aftermath of the Civil War, workers in Pennsylvania and six other states pressured state legislatures to pass eight-hour laws, but they were riddled with loopholes and largely ineffective. Nevertheless, the issue transcended ethnic particularities, providing the cause for the first major postwar labor confrontation.

Although the eight-hour issue owed much to the American political culture of free labor, it was the German-American working class that pressed the confrontation in 1872. Frustrated by employer avoidance of the law, German-dominated craft unions in Chicago, New York, and Philadelphia decided to enforce the law through strikes. As early as October 1871, German-American carpenters and furniture workers began building support among their English-speaking counterparts for a movement to limit the hours of labor. By February 1872, H. B. Van Tronk and Frederick Weissman had already made plans for a strike and visited the English section of the IWA to enlist its backing.[13] Following the inauguration of German-led eight-hour strikes in New York and Chicago in May, Philadelphia unionists announced their intention to strike on June 10. At Turner Hall on June 9, Weissman and Anton Koberlein told one thousand furniture workers that they were entitled to the "results of their labor."[14]

The origins of the strike demonstrated the commanding influence of German workers; more than four thousand left their shops on June 11, of whom three thousand were in the German-dominated furniture industry. Shortly thereafter, they were joined by German bakers, leather workers, and brewers. The English-language dailies noted that meetings were held in German halls and that they typically adjourned to nearby beer gardens where there was "an unusual indulgence in the beverage of 'der Faderland'[sic]," prompting German rowdiness.[15]

Within a week, however, the eight-hour agitation had spread beyond the ethnic community. Commentators could no longer simply attribute the conflict to German radicalism when the campaign was joined by English ship carpenters, native-born craftsmen in the garment trades, and Irish and English building trades workers. Moreover, the leadership was becoming increasingly mixed. Damon Kilgore, a pro-labor Irish lawyer, the Scottish Mr. McKentaugh, and James L. Wright, a native-born garment cutter, became popular speakers at strike meetings, and labor organizers sought out people who spoke both German and English. Similarly, strike rhetoric showed the influence of American constitutionalism and free-labor republicanism. William Derrick, a carpenter, pointed to the eight-hour law and demanded that employers act like "law-abiding citizens"; McKentaugh wanted workers to demonstrate "the manliness to come forward and demand their rights"; and French-born carpenter Victor Drury read from Boston eight-hour leader Ira Steward's resolutions: "the lords of the loom and the lords of the lash are natural allies in the conflict between Freedom and Slavery." At meetings, woodworkers placed their banners on both sides of the American flag.[16]

The eight-hour agitation pulled apart the German community just at the point when ethnic leaders were trying to unite immigrants from southern and northern Germany into a single group.[17] Particularly because the strike originated in the furniture industry, where Germans were employers as well as workers, division was inevitable. But the actions of the strikers and employers suggest that class perspectives quickly overwhelmed ethnic unity. When the strike began, workers left their tools, which they still owned, on the shop benches, to reserve their places, expecting the strike to be soon resolved. In short, the workers acted in the manner of traditional artisans. German employers, however, had formed an association which turned a deaf ear to strike demands. They had already begun transforming the industry through the use of power, new machinery, and the division of labor. By 1872, they could count on being able to replace craftsmen with semiskilled labor. Demonstrating that capital and labor no longer bargained from positions of equal power, employer association president D. B. Slifer said he would close his establishment until September rather than capitulate to the eight-hour movement. Just a week later, employers threatened to throw their workers' tools into the street.[18]

Class tensions quickly surfaced during the strike. On June 17, ethnic leader Edward Spoehn spoke against the strike at a meeting in Turner Hall, but was shouted down. The following day, a fight broke out at a German picnic, leading to the arrest of seven men.[19] Strike leader H. B. Van Tronk's rhetoric took on a more class-conscious tone: "the workingman," he claimed, "was being treated like a commodity, which was contrary to man's being a human being." He added that employers were robbing workers of "surplus labor." This Marxian language blended into the strikers' use of American republican traditions of "citizenship."[20]

Opponents of the strike, however, employed the same fealty to citizenship in the "great republic of the west," demonstrating the various uses of that idea.[21] Wilhelm Candidus, the ex-radical who by 1872 was a leader of the German community, demanded to address a strike meeting as a worker, a man, and "a free, American citizen." He accused the strikers of "un-American" behavior and encouraged them to meet with their employers "far from the beer barrel." In his amazing speech, Candidus told the strikers that their enemy was big capital, not their local employers, and warned them not to be led by "demagogues and greenhorns." Candidus's German speech drew a mixed reaction, but when asked by reporters to translate his remarks into English, he began with a denunciation of the strike in New York which had raised "the red flag of the Commune." At this point the strikers, who had been willing to grant Candidus a hearing, erupted with shouts of "throw him out" and "beat him to death," nearly causing a riot over the way he misrepresented his remarks for the English-language press.[22]

Candidus's speech demonstrated the complex role played by German community leaders, a role magnified by the German press. Indeed, much of the strikers' hostility was directed at the pro-employer ethnic press. Both the *Demokrat* and the *Freie Presse* opposed the strikes as damaging to wage earners as well as employers. Eight-hour leaders thus advised Germans to learn English so they could read papers like the *Public Ledger* or the *Age*, which were more favorable to the movement. Such denunciation of the German-language press drew applause from the strikers but alarmed German editors. The *Freie Presse*, for instance, lampooned the suggestion that workers read the *Age*, which had "shown how indifferent and even contemptible of Germans" it was during the Franco-Prussian War. Candidus added that the strikers' praise of the English-language press showed that they had not read it, for "you have been derided in their reports and attacked in their lead articles." The German press also mocked the Irish and Scottish accents of Kilgore and McKentaugh.[23]

Despite the class fissures in Philadelphia's German-America, the strike did not succeed. By June 24, workers realized they were ill prepared for the type of extended conflict necessary to overcome willful employers pursuing class interests. The fact that the employers dominated the ethnic community and its press also made it difficult to draw on ethnic resources to sustain the strike. Finally, city officials played an important role in the strike's failure by arresting organizers on suspicious charges.[24] Nevertheless, German-American workers had reached outside their community and joined with English and Irish immigrant and native-born wage earners to establish a formidable eight-hour league through which they expected to pursue the issue when conditions were more favorable. There was also discussion of an independent labor party to wean German workers away from divisive ethnic politics. Unfortunately, the Panic of 1873 and the ensuing depression postponed those initiatives for more than a decade.

The seemingly episodic nature of the agitation, however, should not hide the important changes occurring in the city's German community. Within a decade, sons of German furniture workers were abandoning their fathers' trade, leaving declining handicraft trades to new, less-skilled immigrants. Moreover, the alliances forged by German-American workers in 1872 formed the basis for a greater activism in the 1880s. If Germanness was blurring differences between southern and northern immigrants, new experiences at the workplace were splintering the group in other ways. Indeed, the *Freie Presse* shifted from its anti-labor position in the late 1870s and was actually considered a pro-socialist paper in the 1880s.[25]

The events of 1872 should also encourage us to reevaluate the role of the German-language press. In many ways, the German-American editors pursued conflicting purposes. They asserted the economic interests of German manufacturers, suggesting they believed in upward mobility as a group assimilation strategy. Yet, at the same time, they stressed a common Germanness when arguing against the mobilization, *and assimilation*, of German workers into a class movement. Working-class experience, however, left many Germans immune to the entreaties of the ethnic press. Alliances with non-German workers, appeals to American political traditions, and support from the English-language press appeared to hold out more possibilities than submission to the interests of ethnic community elites. In the long run, the German-language press had to speak to the class perspectives of a growing majority of the group if it was to maintain its important role in the ethnic community.

In the decade following the depression of 1873, the German-American working class increased its importance in Philadelphia. Although still outnumbered by about three to two by the Irish, Germans were spread more evenly throughout the industrial base, particularly as rural-born, unskilled Germans flocked to America in the 1870s and 1880s. They maintained strength in handicraft trades, but expanded disproportionately in the heavy industrial sectors like metalworking and metalmaking. More importantly, while heavily concentrated in ostensibly skilled occupations, they were frequently in industries experiencing the greatest transformation, like shoes or metals, or in trades increasingly prone to sweatshop conditions, like baking, garment-making, or butchering. Thus, German workers attempted to maintain craft occupations in situations where skill mattered less and less, an explosive mix in shaping working-class consciousness.[26] Germans in Philadelphia were experiencing industrialization as an erosion of their skilled status, yet they were still armed with the traditions of craft organization.

At the same time, many German immigrants of the 1870s were coming to America steeped in forms of European Marxism and related forms of anarchism, as well as radical politics. They implanted the debates between politically oriented Lassalleans and economically oriented Marxists into the American labor movement, particularly since they were among the most active and politically aware trade unionists.[27] The leadership of the Philadelphia section of the Social Democratic Workingmen's party, for instance, demonstrates the importance of the German element. Of the fifteen most active members of the SDWP, nine had German names; two were machinists, four more were shoe and leather workers, the remaining three were middle-class allies. The section sponsored debates, public meetings, and pamphlets to spread its message. When the dramatic railroad strikes occurred in 1877, these German socialists led the propaganda effort on behalf of labor, claiming that "the police have trampled . . . the fundamental principles of this Republic."[28]

At the center of this German radicalism was the immigrant socialist press, represented in Philadelphia by the *Tageblatt*, founded in 1877. In fact, several newspapers promoted ethnic versions of the labor movement. The *Irish World*, although published in New York, was widely read in Philadelphia. It praised working-class activism among the Irish while the *Trades* served as a voice for English and native-born trade unionists. As organized labor regrouped from the decimation caused by the depression, these three papers, like the ethnic factions of labor they supported, were more complementary than competitive. They reprinted or printed translations of articles run by the other newspapers and even encouraged workers to support all three. And, despite the different cultures and ideologies comprising working-class activism, all three groups cooperated in labor activities. On July 4, 1879, for instance, organized labor held a giant demonstration and picnic at Saenger Park. Speakers included Damon Kilgore, the Irish labor reformer, Congressman Hendrick Wright, a longtime friend of unions, the Socialist Adolf Douai, who spoke in both English and German, and Jacob Franz, an editor of the *Tageblatt.* Franz's speech, in particular, demonstrated the intricate tapestry of labor movement culture; he asserted: "The emancipation of the working people must be accomplished by themselves. . . . Thus, 'One for all, and all for one!' so help yourselves and only *then* God will help you."[29]

In many ways, then, working-class experience acted as a force for integration. German and Irish workers learned of American political culture from the Declaration of Independence (which was revised for an 1879 labor gathering), from the antislavery rhetoric which spoke of republican institutions endangered by "monarchical tendencies" and "wage-slavery," and from evangelists like Uriah Stephens and Thomas Phillips who told ethnic audiences of the unique blend of Christian and republican traditions which would carry labor to power. In turn, American workers promoted a mutual adaptation by translating Marx's writings on trade unionism, by applauding the heavily German Socialist Labor party, and by discussing the Lassallean program of state subsidies for cooperatives.[30] As the labor movement rebuilt its power, there seemed to be ample room for a variety of cultures.

The swelling of organized labor's power in the mid-1880s, however, heightened the persistent ideological and cultural differences between ethnic factions of the labor movement. As the great uprising associated with the Knights of Labor pushed Philadelphia's labor membership to 100,000 in 1886, debates over tactics, political activity, and organization took on a new urgency. This occurred just as an infusion of radicalized immigrants pushed the German community to the left. Craft unionists, Knights of Labor, Socialists, and anarchists all presented solutions to the social problems facing working men and women.[31] Moreover, these debates were interwoven with ethnic and religious splits, making the stakes seem even higher. In the aftermath of the bomb and riot at Haymarket Square in May 1886, the American public magnified its attention to organized labor. In turn, labor's various factions scrambled to maintain their following and assert their legitimacy.

In Philadelphia, as throughout the country, Germans were the target of much public furor. With spokesmen like Johann Most and radical military clubs like the Lehr- und Wehr-Verein, revolutionary sentiments appeared to thrive among German-Americans. The alleged Haymarket conspirators themselves were principally Germans. Similarly, the German-American working class dominated socialist and anarchist organizations as well as Paineite free-thought associations, all of which were at odds with the republican constitutionalism and millennial Christianity informing much of English and Irish immigrant and native-born labor activism.[32] The *Tageblatt* rapidly became the focus of these tensions when it hired a Chicago anarchist, Wilhelm Gorsuch, as an editor and employed printers from the anarchist Gutenberg Bund, after locking out printers from the regular typographical unions. Amid the rising strain, the storm around the *Tageblatt*'s actions shattered political cooperation. Different positions in this complicated affair were staked out by competing radical socialist and trade-union factions, which helped to further isolate the German-American Left from such possible working-class allies as the Irish-Americans.[33]

Ironically, by reinforcing the radical culture of German-American workers, the *Tageblatt* became more of an impediment to working-class solidarity than the German-language press had been in 1872. In August 1886, after several futile appeals to the *Tageblatt* to hire union printers, the Philadelphia Typographical Union sought a boycott of the paper by the Central Labor Union, a city federation of English and German-speaking unions. German strength in the CLU, however, overrode the appeal, causing English-speaking unions to withdraw. Rapidly, ethnic and political disputes began to spill over to other trades. Following their departure from the CLU, English-speaking unions threatened to cease buying union-label cigars because Cigarmakers' Union leader John Kirchner held anarchist sympathies. By December, the largely German brewery workers had difficulty obtaining non-German support for their strike, and German and non-German cigarmakers scabbed on each other. At a Knights of Labor parade, moreover, the appearance of a "red-flag brigade" aroused the ire of many non-German unionists and pro-labor politicians.[34]

Especially in the political realm, the *Tageblatt* affair became a divisive force. When various labor groups in the city established a United Labor party in September, German insistence on running socialist candidates rather than pro-labor reformers like lawyer Maxwell Stevenson caused many non-Germans to reject participation in the ULP. Printers' leader David Pascoe, editor of the *Tocsin*, which represented English-speaking unions, denounced the "unholy alliance" of the anarchist "scabs," nine-tenths of whom were not even U.S. citizens.[35] In December, the ULP meetings exploded over the seating of the *Tageblatt*'s Wilhelm Gorsuch, a former editor of the *Alarm*. Gorsuch's credentials came from an atheist organization, the Friendship Liberal League, not a labor union, and he disrupted the ULP with an attempt to have the words "Fatherhood of God" stricken from the party's platform. While attempts to launch a political campaign floundered, debate within the ULP degenerated to personal attacks; the *Tocsin* called Gorsuch a "bloodthirsty bombthrower," while Kirchner denounced the erstwhile reformer Stevenson as a "bobtail" candidate who defended strikebreakers in his legal practice.[36]

Needless to say, the ULP campaign ended in dismal failure and labor unity disintegrated. The *Tageblatt* affair, however, continued to reflect the ethnic and political divisions within the working class well into 1887 as other issues arose to widen those chasms. In October 1887, Philadelphia workers again split over candidates, even though this time they had returned to mainstream politics. English-speaking unions lined up behind the Republican candidate for sheriff, William Leeds, who supported several labor measures in the state legislature. German labor unions, however, led by the *Tageblatt* and the brewery workers, threw their support to the Democrats, who opposed the Sunday blue laws and the high-license law, which Germans argued were a direct assault on their employment and recreational opportunities. Most English-speaking unions did not return to a citywide labor federation until the 1890s.[37]

What do these two episodes reveal about the roles of class experience and the ethnic press in the immigrant community and more specifically about the impediments to a distinctly working-class politics? Obviously, class experience did at times encourage immigrant workers to look beyond their own ethnic group for support and even leadership. In a recent article, David Montgomery has suggested that class consciousness blended with old-world nationalism and American patriotism in ways that defy easy categorization.[38] Nevertheless, new terms were entering the political and cultural vocabulary of working-class immigrants, but without wiping clean the old slate.

The ethnic press also resists an easy fit with reigning assimilationist or pluralist perspectives that typify much of ethnic history. The German-language press was not able to simply overwhelm its working-class clientele with the ethnic elite's perspectives. Instead, it played a far more vital role among the German-American working class when it recognized the political and cultural demands of immigrant wage earners. Of course, with large-scale German immigration persisting into the 1880s, continually recomposing the working class, the ethnic press and the labor press interacted in an erratic manner, demonstrating just how difficult it was to translate class experience into an idealized form of class consciousness.[39]

What the experience of Philadelphia's German community in the Gilded Age appears to suggest is that ethnic and class perspectives overlapped and often competed for the loyalties of immigrant workers. Ethnic elites could ill afford to ignore the realities of working-class life even when labor confronted employers within the same ethnic group. The experience in Philadelphia mirrored that of Milwaukee, where "in politics, as in other organized community life, the frequent emergence of deep internal divisions . . . suggests the limitations of ethnic community."[40] Similarly, organized labor was trapped in a system where cultural issues often outweighed class interests, forcing the labor movement to tread lightly on subjects of profound importance to many of its members. Especially in the German-American community, the very complexity of the religious, class, and cultural differences among its members may have helped to push it toward dissolution.[41] If these episodes demonstrate any larger principle, it is that politics was a particularly volatile arena for organized labor. Sam Gompers and his allies understood this well; other heterogeneous labor movements, like the racially divided one discussed in Peter Rachleff's study of Richmond, Virginia, learned this at great cost.[42] What men like Gompers missed, however, was the difficulty of sustaining trade unionism without a proper appreciation of the role of the state.[43] This dilemma confronted organized labor for the next fifty years.

NOTES

1. Among the most recent attempts to answer this question, or at least move the discussion to a higher plane, see Eric Foner, "Why Is There No Socialism in the United States?" and the more controversial debates in *International Labor and Working Class History* (ILWCH) starting with Sean Wilentz, "Against Exceptionalism: Class Consciousness and the American Labor Movement" (vol. 26 [1984]); followed by responses in the same volume from Nick Salvatore and Michael Hanagan, and by Steven Sapolsky (vol. 27 [1985]); and ending with a

reply by Sean Wilentz (vol. 28 [1985]). The most complete collection of debates is contained in *Failure of a Dream?*

2. Here, we have been influenced by the excellent work of Richard Oestreicher, *Solidarity and Fragmentation*, and James R. Barrett, "Unity and Fragmentation."

3. The varying roles of the ethnic press in the acculturation of working-class immigrants were considered at a conference in Frankfurt, Germany, Feb. 12–15, 1985. A preliminary report by J. H. M. Laslett appeared in *ILWCH* 28 (Fall 1985): 85–88.

4. For the ethnic composition of Philadelphia's working class, we have relied heavily on two excellent essays: Bruce Laurie and Mark Schmitz, "Manufacture and Productivity," and Bruce Laurie, Theodore Hershberg, and George Alter, "Immigrants and Industry."

5. See the two fine essays by Bruce C. Levine, "Immigrant Workers, 'Equal Rights,' and Anti-Slavery," and "Free Soil, Free Labor, Freimänner."

6. Levine, "Immigrant Workers, 'Equal Rights,' and Anti-Slavery," pp. 40–48; Bruce G. Laurie, *Working People of Philadelphia*, pp. 163–68; Carl Wittke, *Refugees of Revolution*; Maria Wagner, "Representation of America in German Newspapers," pp. 321–30.

7. Lesley Ann Kawaguchi, "Making of Philadelphia's German-America," pp. 384–93.

8. See especially the discussion in Martin Shefter, "Trade Unions and Political Machines." On Candidus and the Philadelphia German community, see *Demokrat*, June 20, 1872; Kawaguchi, "Making of Philadelphia's German-America," pp. 296–303.

9. For descriptions of the transformation of German-dominated crafts in other settings, see Steven Joseph Ross, "Workers on the Edge," chap. 4; Susan E. Hirsch, *Roots of the American Working Class*; Laurie, *Working People of Philadelphia*, chap. 1.

10. James C. Sylvis, *Life, Speeches, Labors, and Essays of William H. Sylvis*, p. 41; David Montgomery, *Beyond Equality*, p. 238.

11. Edgar Barclay Cale, *Organization of Labor in Philadelphia*, pp. 42–59; "Minutes of Section 26, Philadelphia," Oct. 23, Nov. 6, 1871, in International Workingmen's Association Papers (microfilm ed.), State Historical Society of Wisconsin, Madison, reel 2.

12. David Roediger, "Ira Steward and the Anti-Slavery Origins of American Eight-Hour Theory"; Montgomery, *Beyond Equality*, pp. 249–60.

13. "Minutes of Section 26," Nov. 6, 1871; Feb. 19, 1872; Thomas J. Suhrbur, "Ethnicity in the Formation of the Chicago Carpenters Union," pp. 87–90.

14. *Public Ledger* (Philadelphia), June 8–11, 1872; *Demokrat*, June 11, 1872; *Freie Presse* (Philadelphia), June 11, 1872.

15. *Freie Presse*, June 11, 1872; *Demokrat*, June 12, 1872; *Evening Bulletin* (Philadelphia), June 13 and 18, 1872; *Philadelphia Inquirer*, June 11, 1872.

16. See especially the accounts in the generally pro-labor *Public Ledger*, June 11–25, 1872.

17. Kawaguchi, "Making of Philadelphia's German-America," chap. 6.

18. *Demokrat,* June 13, 1872; *Demokrat,* June 13 and 14, 1872; *Public Ledger,* June 18, 1872.

19. *Evening Bulletin,* June 18 and 20, 1872.

20. *Public Ledger,* June 19–21, 1872: *Demokrat,* June 18–20, 1872.

21. For the appeal of the "great republic of the west" for another immigrant group, see Herbert Gutman, "Labor in the Land of Lincoln."

22. *Demokrat,* June 20, 1872.

23. *Freie Presse,* June 11, 1872; *Demokrat,* June 12–14, 20, 1872; *Public Ledger,* June 12, 1872.

24. On arrests, see in particular the petition sent to the mayor, printed in *Demokrat,* June 14, 1872.

25. For the attempt to unite southern and northern Germans generally, see Kawaguchi, "Making of Philadelphia's German-America." For the change in the *Freie Presse,* see the testimony of Charles Lenz, in *Report of the [U.S. Senate] Committee Upon the Relations Between Capital and Labor,* 4 vols. (Washington, 1885), 1:244.

26. Laurie, Hershberg, and Alter, "Immigrants and Industry," pp. 108–11. For an excellent discussion of the explosive mix of craft traditions and deskilling, see Michael Hanagan, *Logic of Solidarity.*

27. For a survey of these debates, see Stuart Bruce Kaufman, *Samuel Gompers.*

28. "Minutebook, Philadelphia Branch, Social Democratic Workingmen's Party," 1876–77, in Manuscripts Division, Library of Congress, Washington, D.C.

29. *Trades,* July 12, Oct. 25, 1879, and passim.

30. *Trades,* May 24, June 29, July 12, Nov. 8, 1879, Jan. 17, Feb. 7, Apr. 17, 1880.

31. See Judith Lazarus Goldberg, "Strikes, Organizing, and Change"; Ken Fones-Wolf, *Trade-Union Gospel,* chap. 3.

32. For Most, see Frederic Trautmann, *Voice of Terror;* for the Lehr- und Wehr-Verein, see Christine Heiss, "German Radicals in Industrial America"; for German radicalism generally, see Paul Avrich, *Haymarket Tragedy,* and Henry David, *History of the Haymarket Affair.*

33. *Tocsin* (Philadelphia), Aug. 28, Oct. 2, 1886; "Philadelphia Typographical Union, Minutes," Oct. 16, 1886, in Historical Society of Pennsylvania, Philadelphia. Excellent background information on the *Tageblatt* affair is available in *The Samuel Gompers Papers,* vol. 2: *Early Years of the American Federation of Labor,* pp. 25–26, 37. The affair can be followed in the pages of three New York newspapers: *Der Sozialist,* Mar. 13, 21, 28, Apr. 10, 24, 1886; the *New Yorker Volkszeitung,* Mar. 3, 6, 8, 13, 15, 30, 31, Apr. 1, 2, 9, 1886; and the *Deutsch-Amerikanische Buchdrucker-Zeitung,* Jan. 15, Feb. 1, 15, Mar. 1, 15, Apr. 1, 15, May 1, 15, June 1, Oct. 16, Nov. 1, 16, Dec. 16, 1886, Jan. 16, Feb. 1, 16, Mar. 1, 16, May 1, June 1, 16, 1887.

34. *Tocsin,* Sept. 4, 2, Oct. 16, Nov. 13, Dec. 4, 1886, Jan. 8, 29, 1887.

35. *Tocsin*, Oct. 16, 23, 30, Nov. 13, 1886.

36. *Tocsin*, Dec. 4, 11, 18, 1886. For similar political splits in other cities, see Bruce C. Nelson, " 'We Can't Get Them to Do Aggressive Work' "; Oestreicher, *Solidarity and Fragmentation*, chap. 6; Ross, "Workers on the Edge," chap. 10.

37. *Tocsin*, Sept. 24, Oct. 1, 15, 29, Nov. 5, 1887. This type of cultural division supports the analysis presented by the ethnocultural political historians. See, for instance, Paul Kleppner, *Cross of Culture*.

38. David Montgomery, "Nationalism, American Patriotism, and Class Consciousness."

39. See the interesting points on this issue suggested by Herbert Gutman and Ira Berlin, "Class Composition and the Development of the American Working Class," pp. 380–94.

40. Kathleen Conzen, *Immigrant Milwaukee*, p. 224.

41. Conzen, *Immigrant Milwaukee*, p. 228.

42. Peter Rachleff, *Black Labor in the South*. See also Barrett, "Unity and Fragmentation."

43. Christopher L. Tomlins, *The State and the Unions*, chap. 3.

III

A Press and a Culture

Throughout the late nineteenth century, German-American radicalism was at times almost synonymous with the American left. And nowhere were the Germans more clearly important than in the radical press. In the upsurge of immigrant working-class activism that culminated with the Chicago Haymarket riot, German-language socialist and anarchist newspapers stood out prominently. Furthermore, during the suppression of a multilingual radical movement in the aftermath of Haymarket, authorities targeted editors of the German papers for special attention and retaliation. The Chicago police, perhaps even more than working-class activists, equated the radical movement with the radical press.

The prominence of the German-American radical community often led to an insular mentality. The German-speaking left developed its own clubs, benefit associations, singing societies, and athletic organizations. Perhaps the best means for recapturing the totality of this radical subculture is through the annual calendars, published by many of the German-American radical papers. In addition to providing a sampling of the latest political arguments, the calendars offered everything from recent fiction to hints for decorating. But their most important function was to provide a sense of community to German-American radicals, a sense of shared purpose and shared culture. This annual publishing event was the means through which the left educated its rank and file by offering its adherents a fully developed alternative to mainstream American life.

The insularity of the German-American radical subculture had serious implications for women. In a much more concerted way than

III. A Press and a Culture

American-born socialists, German immigrant leftists clung to a domestic ideal that left women's issues out of the mainstream of radical concerns. The debates raging in the women's pages, which began to appear in the German-language socialist newspapers after the turn of the century, testified to the difficulties that German-American women had in building bridges to the American women's rights movement. In the German-American radical press, male editors ensured that the correct political line privileged class over gender. Ironically, then, a press which offered such a vibrant political alternative to the dominant American culture could not assimilate one of the potentially most progressive parts of that culture.

Bruce C. Nelson

Arbeiterpresse und Arbeiterbewegung: Chicago's Socialist and Anarchist Press, 1870–1900

In April 1880 *Der Vorbote,* an official organ of the Socialist Labor party in Chicago, asserted "Die Geschichte der Arbeiterbewegung in den Vereinigten Staaten ist zugleich die Geschichte der Arbeiterpresse" (The history of the workers' movement in the United States is at the same time the history of the workers' press). That insight is important, for what we know of Chicago's socialist and anarchist movements has come largely from the *Socialist* and the *Alarm,* two of the movement's English-language papers. But between 1870 and 1900 Chicago's socialists and anarchists issued fifty-two newspapers, published in eight different languages: fourteen of them German, eleven Czech, nine English, eight Scandinavian, six Polish, three Lithuanian, and one Italian. Fewer than half of those titles have been preserved, but their publishing histories were crucial to the movement's development, their formats chronicle its organization, their circulation histories reveal the growth of a sympathetic following, and their contents reflect the movement's alienation and radicalization.[1]

Socialism in Chicago dates from 1853 when H. Roesch and J. Karlen briefly issued *Der Proletarier,* the city's first German socialist paper; in 1860 Joseph Weydemeyer and Julius Standau offered the *Stimme des Volkes* to one thousand subscribers for almost eight months. By the end of the Civil War, the city was home to a section of the International Workingmen's Association (IWA, the First International) which included German, Czech, Polish, Norwegian, and Danish branches. The IWA helped form the Workingmen's party of Illinois in 1874; two years later the WPI joined with several other organizations to found the Workingmen's party of the United States. In December 1877 the WPUS changed its name to the Socialist Labor party, which over the next four years captured 20 percent of the 1879 mayoral vote and elected one state senator, three state representatives, and five aldermen. In 1880, Chicago's CASLP split into two factions. One remained loyal to the party and committed to electoral socialism; the radical faction embraced armed revolution and founded the Revolutionary Socialist party (RSP) in 1881. Those radicals joined the International Working People's Association (IWPA) in 1883, and Chicago became the center of the American anarchist movement.[2]

Many of those who had been socialists in the 1870s became anarchists in the 1880s; after Haymarket most became socialists again. The frequency with which the movement changed its name obscures four essential continuities: of organization, of a cadre unconcerned with labels, of members who followed those leaders, and of ideological evolution. Beneath those changing labels lay a process of radicalization and a socialist movement. Beyond what the press reveals of that movement, it illuminates as well something of the city's working class and the processes of class formation. Those processes exploded in the Haymarket Square riot; they are chronicled in the city's socialist and anarchist press; and the best way to grasp that movement is to examine its public face.

The Emergence of a Multilingual Radical Press

The size and growth of Chicago's socialist movement can be seen from its polyglot press. In 1870 the left offered a socialist critique in at least three languages: *Narodni noviny* [National Gazette], a weekly edited by Lev Palda and J. B. Belohradsky, served the city's Czechs; *Der Deutsche Arbeiter*, a weekly edited by Carl Klings and published by the German Workers' Protective and Support Society; and *Dagslyset* [Daylight], a monthly edited by Marcus Thrane, aimed at the Dano-Norwegian community. From 1870 to 1886 Chicago's socialists and anarchists published twenty-two newspapers: eleven in German, five in Danish or Norwegian, four in Czech, and two in English; five were dailies, eleven weeklies, and two monthlies.

The most durable of these papers were published in German by the Socialist Publishing Society (SPS). *Der Vorbote*, the oldest, was founded in 1874 as a weekly, and the society grew out of the Verein Vorboten. In June 1876 the SPS confidently issued a second paper, *Die Volks-Zeitung*, as a tri-weekly. It expanded local news, leaving *Der Vorbote* with a weekly summary and larger audience. In May 1878 *Die Fackel* appeared as a Sunday weekly; one year later, as the SLP continued to grow in members and the SPS in confidence, the tri-weekly *Volks-Zeitung* became the daily *Arbeiter-Zeitung*.[3] Between 1874 and 1886, at least ten editors were hired and fired by the society: Carl Klings, Josef Gruenhut, Jakob Winnen, Conrad Conzett, Paul Grott-kau, Gustav Lyser, Wilhelm Rosenberg, Edward Liebig, August Spies, and Michael Schwab. All were immigrants, all but Swiss-born Conzett and Bohemian-born Gruenhut were German, all but Liebig and Grott-kau came from working-class families; seven of the ten held elected union office, and half had been journalists before emigration. Based on his study of German workers, labor leaders, and the labor move-ment in Chicago, Hartmut Keil has concluded that "listing the editors of *Vorbote, Chicagoer Arbeiter-Zeitung*, and *Fackel* is almost equivalent to enumerating Chicago's outstanding German labor leaders of the period." These men, like those Antonio Gramsci later labeled "organic intellectuals," used the papers as pulpits and forums.[4] By the time of the Haymarket Affair, the SPS issued three papers, a daily and two weeklies, and published seven days a week.

The German monopoly over Chicago's socialist press continued through the 1877 Great Upheaval. That fall Louis Pio, the founder of the Danish socialist movement, called for a national organization of Scandinavian workers in America, and announced a new paper, *Den Nye Tid* [The New Age], to be published in Dano-Norwegian. Pio was joined by Marcus Thrane, another exiled 48er, the father of the Nor-wegian labor movement. Even in exile, Pio and Thrane were perhaps the two most famous Scandinavian socialists of the nineteenth cen-tury. Yet Pio's comrades ousted him, in May 1878, when they found him simultaneously working on a Methodist paper. A freethinker, Thrane proved more acceptable, and the paper "adopted a strongly anti-clerical and atheistic stance" as it became an official SLP organ. In fall 1880 he too was ousted by a group of insurgents led by Peter Petersen and Olaf Ray. In October 1881 the RSP named *Den Nye Tid* an official organ; two years later it became one of the IWPA's organs. Combining socialism and rationalism, it survived through April 1884, perhaps even longer.[5]

An English organ, the *Socialist*, appeared in September 1878, six months after *Den Nye Tid*'s birth. When Cincinnati's *National Socialist* went under, the Chicago section bought its subscription list, paid off its debts, hired Frank Hirth, a German-born cigarmaker, and moved the paper to Chicago. Renamed the *Socialist*, its announced goal was to organize workers "into one grand political labor party for the purpose of securing labor's rights." Despite a circulation of 4,500, Hirth got fired about a month before the paper died in August 1879 and Albert

Parsons briefly assumed the editorship. With its death came grumblings about the loss of "German money" and the defection of the Irish from the SLP; in its wake Chicago's English-speaking socialists were without a paper for five years.[6]

Five other papers—three Czech, one English, and one German—appeared after the schism with the SLP and were anarchist papers. The Czech-language *Budoucnost* [The Future] appeared in June 1883, first as an eight-page biweekly, then as a weekly, issued from a small printing shop in the heart of the Bohemian colony. A contemporary account described it as "a very small sheet . . . having only a limited number of subscribers," and suggested that its articles were largely "translations from the German daily, the *Arbeiter-Zeitung*." Composed of recent immigrants exiled by the Austrian antisocialist laws, its editorial collective all worked outside the paper. Josef Pondelicek was a painter (and president of Chicago's first Bohemian painters' union); Jakub Mikolanda, a carpenter and officer in the carpenters' union; and Norbert Zoula a silversmith; only Josef Boleslav Pecka—cofounder of Czech social democracy—had any experience as a journalist.[7]

In October 1884, the *Alarm: A Socialist Weekly* was founded to serve Chicago's English-speaking radicals. The *Alarm* rejected electoral politics as it embraced armed revolution. Albert and Lucy Parsons shared editorial responsibilities with Lizzie May Swank, a native-born dressmaker active in the Working Women's Union. Although it was "owned and controlled by the IWPA," Parsons exercised little editorial control: "I had no right to shut off anybody's complaint. The *Alarm* was a labor paper, and it was specifically published for the purpose of allowing every human being who wore the chains of monopoly to clank those chains in the columns of the *Alarm*. It was a free press organ. It was a free speech newspaper." The *Alarm* appeared as a weekly for three months, then found "our expenses being too heavy [and] the prospects . . . gloomy" and reluctantly became a fortnightly. It was never solvent: the Alarm Publishing Association frequently scheduled picnics, dances, and festivals to keep it afloat.[8]

Chicago's last three anarchist papers had much shorter histories, and we know little about any of them. *Svoboda* [Freedom], an "anarchist journal" appeared in November 1883 and is mentioned in Max Nettlau's anarchist bibliography. *Lampcka* [The Lantern], a Czech weekly, was published from August 1885 through April 1886. The same day the police suppressed *Budoucnost*, they raided and closed *Lampcka*'s basement office. After describing it as "a Bohemian Anarchistic paper," the *Chicago Tribune* reported "the proprietor and editor . . . bears the name of Hradecny" and that he had fled the city after the riot.[9] In December

1885, one of the IWPA's twenty-six Chicago groups complained that the *Arbeiter-Zeitung* was "not radical enough." Led by Adolph Fischer, a compositor, and George Engel, a painter turned shopkeeper (both executed on November 11, 1887), Gruppe Nordwestseite began its own four-page monthly, *Der Anarchist,* in January 1886. Proclaiming itself an "Organ der Autonomen Gruppen der I.A.A.[International Arbeiter Association, the German translation for IWPA]," it reportedly followed the violent editorial line of Johann Most's *Die Freiheit,* but in its short life was never recognized as an official IWPA organ. Only four or five issues appeared before its editorial collective was arrested and the paper suppressed in the wake of the riot. The *Anarchist* may explain two competing Bohemian anarchist papers: if *Lampcka* was an anarchist paper it was probably more radical than *Budoucnost.* [10]

In 1886 then, Chicago's anarchists issued six or seven papers, five of them official organs of the International Working People's Association, published in three languages. *Der Vorbote, Die Fackel, Die Chicagoer Arbeiter-Zeitung,* and *Der Anarchist* appeared in German; *Budoucnost* and *Lampcka* in Czech; and the *Alarm* in English.

Contents

These papers shared editorial material but specialized by language. *Den Nye Tid* claimed to be "the only Danish-Norwegian Workers' newspaper and organ for the Scandinavian socialists in the United States"; judging from its first issue *Budoucnost* concentrated on Bohemian activities. While the *Arbeiter-Zeitung* occasionally reported meetings of the American group, the *Alarm* never covered any of the other ethnic groups within the movement. The SPS's papers were printed with fraktur type, few commercial advertisements, and infrequent illustrations. The daily had four pages, the Saturday political weekly eight, and the Sunday cultural issue twelve. The first page offered national and international telegraphic dispatches, the second carried editorials, the third page serialized a novel and carried advertising, and the last page held local, movement, and trade-union news. Every issue published directories, announcements, and reports of Chicago's labor and social-revolutionary movements. The daily concentrated on the local movement, *Der Vorbote* offered a weekly review but aimed beyond the city limits, and after 1881 *Die Fackel* offered a "Kleine Frauen-Zeitung" to women.

The WPUS's Union Congress had proposed that the socialist press "represent the interests of labor, awaken and arouse the class feeling amongst the workingmen, promote their organization as well as the trade-union movement and spread economical [*sic*] knowledge among them." All of Chicago's anarchist papers subscribed to *Den Nye Tid*'s credo:

> Its purpose is to safeguard and promote the interests of the worker and to spread socialist teaching among our countrymen. It will work to gather all workers in one association to establish a social order which will grant the worker his rights. It will oppose corruption, rottenness, exploitation and capitalist domination. It will fight against monopoly and the predatory nature of the system and will aim at liberating work from the yoke of capitalism. It will contain editorials on social, political and economic matters. It will bring news about the workers and workers' movement in all continents. . . . It will not be written in a haughty or pompous language, but in a style understood by the common man.

The *Arbeiter-Zeitung* applauded the *Vorbote* as "really the only socialist paper in America which under all circumstances will preach true and consistent class-hatred." The socialists reveled in baiting the bourgeois press; an infrequent cartoon showed a dog, variously labeled "Freie Presse" or "Staats-Ztg" baying at a moon labeled "Arb. Ztg."; and their editors provoked at least three libel suits. Under the header "Stadtrath," the *Arbeiter-Zeitung* carefully recorded the proceedings—and the machinations—of the city council and the boodle gang. The *Alarm*'s articles, as Paul Le Blanc noted, "ranged from the impudent, to the imprudent, to the totally outrageous" as Parsons and Swank filled its pages with lively social commentary; reports on strikes, union meetings, and demonstrations; editorial opinion and educational articles on revolutionary theory; extensive correspondence from its readers; and reprints from other socialist journals.[11]

Perhaps *Die Fackel*—whose masthead featured the torch of liberty and its own name engulfed in the flames of revolution—best expressed the movement's "feverishly combative character." The Sunday edition took as its slogan "Giving the serious and the funny its due, and despising nothing but the base." It published socialist poetry, songs, and plays; each issue serialized a novel (including ones by Émile Zola, Eugène Sue, George Sand, and Louise Michel); a regular column reviewed the city's theater. Its "Skizzen aus dem Leben der Großstadt," another regular column, reported fads and fashions, rumors and street conversation. In the remarkable hands of Gustav Lyser, a poet and playwright, the *Fackel* reveled in "the spirit of rebellion 'against everything,' against bourgeois culture and morality, conservative trade unionism, and above all, against the state." Lyser, and those who succeeded him, could be irreverent, satirical, witty, and sarcastic.[12]

These papers molded and then chronicled the evolution of their editors' and readers' ideology. *Der Vorbote*, *Die Arbeiter-Zeitung*, and *Die Fackel* began as the political organs of workingmen's parties, became socialist papers, and then broke with parliamentary socialism to become anarchist organs. The *Vorbote's* changing subtitles record that process. In 1874 it proclaimed "Organ der Arbeiterpartei für Stadt und Land"; then in 1876 became "Organ und Eigenthum der Arbeiter-Partei der Vereinigten Staaten." In 1878 it described itself as an "Unabhängiges Organ für die wahren Interessen des Proletariats"; and from 1880 through 1919 it remained the "Wochenausgabe der *Chicagoer Arbeiter-Zeitung*." Those changes reflect an evolution from artisan republicanism (note "Stadt und Land") to socialism, as does the name change from the *Volks-Zeitung* to the *Arbeiter-Zeitung*. Chicago's anarchist papers are most famous for their revolutionary rhetoric, for preaching class war, and for their fascination with the cult of dynamite. The *Vorbote* had presented the Lehr- und Wehr-Verein, a paramilitary organization, as "the workingman's answer to the servile militia" of the bourgeoisie. Lucy Parsons's broadside, "An Address to Tramps" advised, "Learn the Use of Explosives!" The *Alarm* published articles on "Assassination" and "Street-fighting—How to Meet the Enemy." The *Arbeiter-Zeitung* advertised Johann Most's pamphlet *Revolutionäre Kriegswissenschaft*—a handbook on dynamite, nitroglycerin, guncotton, and poisons—and offered its readers free instruction in the handling of arms. The *Anarchist* reveled in the fearsome image of the wild-eyed bomb-thrower, indeed it cultivated that persona. This was "bomb-talking," as Floyd Dell perceptively called it and, "it was done partly to attract attention . . . a way of shocking the public into attention. So desperate a means of securing an audience [was] certainly a sign of weakness."[13]

Beyond both rhetoric and image, Chicago's socialist and anarchist press addressed five different but overlapping audiences. The first was an immigrant audience, new to Chicago and America. The first page of the SPS's papers remained devoted to news from home, arranged by the subdivisions of the homeland: news from Berlin, from Nassau, from Hesse. Such telegraphic dispatches served an obvious purpose for the uprooted, but they also included reports from Europe: Scandinavia, France, Switzerland, Spain, and Russia. The German papers published daily market reports for foodstuffs (bread, meat, potatoes, sugar, coffee) to advise recent arrivals; they also published railroad timetables for immigrants, streetcar schedules to aid visitors, and the locations of fire department call boxes. In so doing they differed little from their bourgeois competitors, the Republican *Illinois Staats-Zeitung* and the Democratic *Freie Presse*. Moreover, both socialist and bourgeois papers featured the omnipresent steamship ads and those from the railroad companies for cheap western land.

These papers aimed more specifically at a second audience of workers, featuring, for example, the saloons which figured so prominently in working-class culture. Most advertisements—for food, clothing, doctors, housing, home furnishings, and entertainment—stressed their affordability and serviceability, not their fashion or extravagance. Parsons and Swank devoted much of their paper to readers' letters; the German papers and *Budoucnost* reported on proletarian fraternal and gymnastic societies, including the German Turnvereine and the Czech sokols; both Germans and Czechs published streetcar schedules and market prices; and they announced births, marriages, and deaths. If the English and Scandinavian papers addressed far-flung radicals, the German and Czech ones served concentrated and local communities.

Third, Chicago's socialist and anarchist press served several of the city's trade unions and these papers remain our best source on their activities. The German furniture and metal workers and the German typographical union had been the *Vorbote*'s founding supporters and all used it as their official organ. In March 1879, as the SLP was about to earn its greatest electoral success, the *Socialist* complained that only a handful of the city's trade unions were organized "on a socialistic basis." In 1884 the *Arbeiter-Zeitung* became the official organ of the new IWPA-dominated Central Labor Union (CLU), which could claim the membership of the city's eleven largest unions. Despite that affiliation, the socialist press announced the meetings of all three of the city's labor organizations: the conservative Trades and Labor Assembly, the reformist Knights of Labor, and the anarchist CLU. In the months before Haymarket, the membership rolls of all three rivals would grow meteorically.[14]

Fourth, these papers spoke to and for the party's membership. The German socialist party, SPD, earned considerable news space and long articles—like the *Fackel*'s "Sozialistische Katechism," which was later translated in the *Alarm*—explained socialist economics and anarchist politics to the reader. Lists of socialist books at reduced prices ran regularly. The fourth page of each paper offered a bulletin board which announced party meetings, reporting place and time, and identifying the lecturer and subject. Beneath those announcements lay a short account, a précis of the lecture and discussion, the election of officers, and the announcement of new members, a chance for the movement to publicize its growth and development. Some advertisers specifically addressed party members as they offered club regalia and discounts.

The German papers recorded the marriages, births, and deaths of party members and their families.

Finally, Chicago's socialist and anarchist press also cultivated an audience once described by Albert Parsons as the movement's "sympathetic following." In August 1877 the *Vorbote* asserted "Die Arbeiter-Bewegung [ist] eine Kultur-Bewegung," and these papers chronicle the cultivation of a movement culture—encompassing singing societies, theater groups, dances, festivals, picnics, parades, and the annual celebration of the Paris Commune—which recruited new members and invigorated the activists. The *Arbeiter-Zeitung* announced one event this way: "The Southside Group celebrates . . . its foundation festival. The program includes speeches and song. The comrades . . . are a jolly crowd and there we may expect a very enjoyable evening." A week later the same paper reviewed "a pleasant meeting combined with dancing. The main points were serious and humorous lectures and plays. The Socialistic Sängerbund did its full share. It seems that there exists no more fun and enjoyment anywhere than among the socialists as they only separated in the best of spirits early in the morning."[15] Movement culture served Chicago's socialists and anarchists from secular baptisms through rationalist funerals. These newspapers sought to explain that culture and to make it attractive to a sympathetic following.

The radical press tried to address five different but overlapping audiences: of immigrants, workers, trade unionists, party members, and sympathizers. These papers had staked out a field alien to the English-language press, below that of the bourgeois press, and far to the left of the commercial press. Gilded Age socialists and anarchists assumed that the fundamental tasks for its press were those of education, agitation, and organization. They embraced class differences as the only alternative to assimilation and they saw conflict as inevitable. And they were beginning to work out the dialectic of class and ethnicity. The radical press mobilized and educated the movement's active membership as it recruited and politicized a sympathetic following.

Publication and Circulation

Each of these papers was issued by a publishing society: all were cooperative ventures, which meant that only subscribers could buy stock (and few expected any dividends), that the staffs had to respond to the readership, and that editors were responsible to a board of directors. Comprising editors, reporters, compositors, and carriers, those boards tried to blur the traditional distinctions between management and labor. Composed of party members, societies hired and fired editors, and exercised some editorial direction, but their main role remained fund-raising. We know the most about the Socialist Publishing Society (SPS) which was the oldest and became the prototype for the others. It defined its mission as the "education and intellectual improvement of its members through the fostering of moral culture, history, political economy, statistics, philosophy and other subjects, by means of regular meetings, debates, lectures and addresses, pamphlets, newspapers, periodicals and publications." [16]

At the end of 1883 *Der Vorbote* reported that 15,729 books and pamphlets had been distributed by the Chicago groups. Two years later the *Alarm* published a more comprehensive report. During the preceding ten months, 387,537 books, pamphlets, and circulars had been distributed by Chicago's publishing societies: "The number of books and brochures sold was 6,527. (They were mostly valuable books, viz.: Marx, Lassalle, Bebel, Hyndman, Bakunine, Reeclus [*sic*], Gronlund, etc.) From the brochures of Comrade John Most there were circulated 5,000; Address to Tramps, by Mrs. Parsons, 10,000; 'How to Put Down the Commune,' 5,000; Communistic Manifesto, 25,000; Pittsburgh Proclamation, in English, German, French and Bohemian, 200,000; gratis copies of the *Alarm* were circulated 96,000." [17] But such productivity stretched the movement's resources. In 1876 *Der Vorbote* reported a weekly income of $108, expenses of $106.75, and a profit of $1.25; when the *Socialist* died three years later, it had a weekly income of $45 and expenses of $87. Each week threatened to be a socialist paper's last. The SPS kept publishing because it had conceded a union shop to (German) Typographia No. 9 which in turn subsidized the socialist press by working below scale. The bourgeois German papers resented that practice, as did the English printers' union which recognized that "the *Arbeiter-Zeitung* is a socialistic sheet and the members of the [International Typographical Union] are not permitted to work in its office." [18]

The SPS did not own a printing press until after Haymarket; instead its compositors set the type, then delivered the forms to a job printer for the press run. On the other hand, it occupied a three-story building, with a restaurant on the first floor, editorial and composing departments for the German papers and the *Alarm* on the second, meeting rooms and the IWPA's central library on the third. In contrast, both the Scandinavians and Bohemians owned their presses, although hardly comparable offices. *Lampcka* and *Budoucnost* issued from basements, and *Den Nye Tid* came out of another "hole"—"an unimpressive wooden building." According to one of its printers, "Daylight came from windows in the roof and at night there was an oil lamp. . . . All the book printing was done on a monster job press that was operated by foot power. We had great trouble getting anyone to feed and tread that press."[19]

Compared to its editors, staff, and compositors, Chicago's socialist and anarchist readership has remained largely invisible. What little information we can recover supports three conclusions. First, the German papers clearly dominated circulation, accounting for 80 percent of the total; while the Scandinavian, Czech, and English papers split the remainder. Second, the bulk of that circulation was by subscription and delivered by local news carriers. The German papers and *Budoucnost* had an elaborate distribution network that included carriers, news dealers, and the postal system; in contrast, the *Alarm* depended on single-issue purchases handled by news dealers. Third, and to reverse Richard Ely's insight, their "respectable circulation" carried with it "advertising patronage."[20]

The circulation histories of Chicago's radical papers measure the movement's growth. (See table 1.) The SLP's four papers had enjoyed a total circulation of 14,600 in 1880; the IWPA's seven papers enjoyed a total of 30,780 in 1886, an increase of 111 percent. Those 30,000 readers represented less than 4 percent of the city's population, but about 12 percent of its wage earners. Not only did circulation grow faster than the city's population but this discussion may underestimate readership, for it presumes that circulation equaled readership, that a paper was read by only one person. The *Alarm* asked, "Please pass this paper to a friend," and anarchist saloons became important distributors. According to the police, the city's "saloonkeepers always looked to it, the first thing in the morning, that plenty of anarchist literature and a dozen or so copies of the *Arbeiter-Zeitung* were duly on the tables of their places, and in some saloons beer-bloated bums, who could manage to read fairly [well], were engaged to read aloud such articles as were particularly calculated to stir up the passions of the benighted patrons."[21]

Subscription was a conscious decision, for anarchist papers did not entice their readers. Nor was the anarchist press the only ethnic press in Chicago: on the contrary, each paper had to compete with bourgeois foreign-language papers, some long and firmly established. Thus the *Arbeiter-Zeitung* competed with four other German dailies; the *Vorbote* and the *Fackel* competed with at least ten other German weeklies. The *Nye Tid* was up against five commercial Scandinavian papers, both dailies and weeklies; *Budoucnost* and *Lampcka* shared the Czech market with at least two other weeklies.[22]

Table 1
The Roster and Circulations of Chicago's Socialist and Anarchist Press, 1870–1886

Paper	First Issue	Last Issue	Language	Frequency	1872	1874	1876	1878	1880	1882	1884	1886
Narodni noviny	1868	1871	Cz									
Deutsche Arbeiter	1869	1870	G	d								
Dagslyset	1869	1878	N	m	400			260				
Arbeiterfreund	1874	1874	G	w								
Vorbote	1874	1924	G	w		700	3,050	3,000	5,000	6,500	7,115	8,000
Ch. Sozialist	1876	1879	G	d								
Arbeiter-Zeitung	1876	1919	G	d					3,000	4,850	5,326	5,780
Volks-Zeitung	1877	1877	G	d								
Arbeideren	1877	1877	N	w								
Ch. Volks-Zeitung	1877	1879	G	d								
Neue Zeit	1877	1879	G	w				1,500				
Fackel	1877	1919	G	w				600	5,000	7,150	10,000	12,200
Den Nye Tid	1878	1884	D-N	w					1,600	2,000	2,800	
Den Nye Verden	1878	1878	D									
Socialist	1878	1879	E	w				3,000				

Paper	First Issue	Last Issue	Language	Frequency	1872	1874	1876	1878	1880	1882	1884	1886
Tilskueren	1878	1882	D						800			
Svoboda	1883	1883	Cz									
Budoucnost	1883	1886	Cz	w							500	750
Ill. Volks-zeitung	1884	1884	G	w							2,000	
Alarm	1884	1886	E	w							2,000	3,000
Lampcka	1885	1886	Cz	w								750
Anarchist	1886	1886	G	m								300
Totals					400	700	3,050	8,360	15,400	20,500	29,741	30,780
Number change						+300	2,350	5,310	7,040	5,100	9,241	1,039
Percent change						+75	+336	+174	+84	+33	+45	+3

Notes: Column 3 "Language": G = German, Cz = Czech, E = English, D = Danish, N = Norwegian. Column 4 "Frequency": w = weekly, d = daily, m = monthly, 2w = biweekly.

Sources: N. W. Ayer and Sons, *American Newspaper Annuals, 1886–1900* (Philadelphia, 1886–1900); George P. Rowell and Co., *American Newspaper Directory, 1886–1900* (New York, 1886–1900); Michael Schaack, *Anarchy and Anarchists*; Frantisek Stedronsky, *Zahranicní krajanské noviny*; *Immigrant Labor Press in North America*.

Bruce C. Nelson

Throughout the 1870s and 1880s Chicago's radicals competed with a workingman's or labor press. In the 1870s the chief competition came from the *Workingman's Advocate*, which appeared in 1864 and died in 1877. In late 1879 and early 1880 several papers tried to present the Greenback party to Chicagoans; none survived more than a year. Then from 1881 to 1883, the *Progressive Age* proposed "to wage relentless war on the grasping and soulless corporations and monopolies which threaten the very existence of the Republic." The Trades Assembly endorsed that paper in September 1881, then bought it; in 1882 the Knights of Labor's District Assembly 24 extended its endorsement and it became, for a while, the Knights' official city organ. When a new editor championed temperance, the Trades Assembly withdrew its support and started the short-lived *Western Workman*.[23] A fourth competitor came from the SLP's remnants who hoped "to annihilate the *Arbeiter-Zeitung* . . . to kill that paper so dead that . . . there will be no more Anarchists." The *Illinois Volkszeitung*, a weekly coedited by Julius Vahlteich and Hermann Walther, appeared in May 1884 but issued from New York; only the inner pages came from Chicago. Within a year the Chicago section repudiated that paper when it fell into the hands of a clique which had "betrayed the party."[24]

Measured by either longevity or circulation the radicals won that competition. The growth of a socialist and later anarchist readership was neither the result of entrapment nor the product of default. These papers could speak to Chicago's immigrant workers; they tried to speak for them as well.

The Great Upheaval and the Haymarket Affair

In 1884 the forerunner of the American Federation of Labor had designated May 1, 1886, for the inauguration of the eight-hour working day. The proposal died for lack of interest. A year later, the unskilled and unorganized workers revitalized that movement, and the skilled and organized found themselves drawn into something they had not started and seemingly disdained. On the eve of what Selig Perlman labeled the Great Upheaval of 1885–86, Chicago's labor movement embraced only a minority of the working class: about 10 percent of the city's wage earners had been enrolled and none of the city's trades was fully organized. It was the unskilled and unorganized, rather than the Knights of Labor, Trades Assembly, or CLU, who became the driving force for the eight-hour day. Indeed, the Trades Assembly did not establish its Eight Hour Committee until October 1885; as late as December only eleven of its twenty-five member unions had endorsed the movement. At the local and national levels the leadership of the Knights of Labor was similarly unenthusiastic. In January 1886 the *Alarm* complained that "the Trades and Labor Assembly has done little or nothing. . . . Thus far the only large mass-meetings in behalf of the 'Eight Hour Movement,' have been held by those who have been accused of being opposed to the movement . . . the 'ignorant foreigners' who follow the red flag."[25]

The anarchists initially dismissed the eight-hour movement, regarding it as a compromise. But led by some of its most active unionists the CLU dragged the IWPA into that struggle; as the winter of 1885–86 set in, both organizations became enthusiastic. They scheduled weekly, then almost daily mass meetings in every part of the city, addressing audiences in as many as seven languages. Their papers carefully recorded the frenzy of unionization. By spring the *Vorbote's* last page was filled with the announcements and reports of union meetings. Under the heading "Stadt Chicago" the April 21 issue, for example, reported meetings of the Möbel-Arbeiter [Furniture Workers] Union No. 1; a mass meeting outside Pullman where the Metall-Arbeiter Union gained fifty new members and the Möbel Arbeiter Union No. 3 initiated seventy-five; the Linseed Oil Arbeiters; the masons; the tanners; the butchers (with forty-five new members); the carpenters (fifty-four new members in two new locals); the saddlers ("50 neue Mitglieder"); and the Metall-Arbeiter Union, which gained ninety-six new members for a total "über 900." The anarchists carried a sense of urgency to the movement, and they also brought a cadre of organizers.[26]

The anarchist press continued to be provocative and inflammatory. From December 1885 to March 1886 the *Arbeiter-Zeitung* offered free weapons instruction at an anarchist saloon; the *Alarm* simultaneously advertised an armed section of the American Group; the Lehr- und Wehr-Verein and the Bohemian Sharpshooters, another socialist paramilitary group, were seen drilling on the prairies; the CLU's leading unions declared their militancy. Military rhetoric permeated every discussion of the labor movement and class relations. On May Day, the *Arbeiter-Zeitung* called: "Bravely forward! The conflict has begun. An army of wage-laborers is idle. Capitalism conceals its tiger claws behind the ramparts of order. Workmen, let your watchword be: No Compromise! Cowards to the rear! Men to the front! The die is cast." The anarchist press held a strategic position during the Great Upheaval. The CLU's official organ remained labor's only voice by default: the *Knights of Labor* did not appear until March, and the Trades Assembly depended on the sufferance of the commercial press. But whatever the source, Chicago's businessmen responded to that rhetoric by expanding the police force, massing Pinkerton detectives and police specials, and mobilizing the state militia. The Commercial Club reviewed both cavalry and infantry riot drills, and Philip Armour, the meatpacker, subscribed $2,000 for a new Gatling gun for the militia.[27]

On May 3, 1886, the police attacked a group of strikers outside the McCormick Works. August Spies raced back to the *Arbeiter-Zeitung's* offices to dash off a broadside for a protest meeting; the composing-room foreman added the word "Revenge." The next night another detachment of police, the "flower of the Central Detail" marched into the Haymarket Square prepared to break up a small group of workingmen. A bomb exploded in their ranks, chaos ensued. Seventy policemen and an unknown number of workers were killed or wounded.

Proper Chicagoans knew whom to blame. The day after the Haymarket Riot, the police marched into the SPS's offices and arrested everyone they found. They returned that afternoon, arrested a few more, and confiscated manuscripts, galleys, books, and records. A second set of raids hit fifty anarchist halls and the Czech newspapers. At Florus Hall the police found "a subscription list . . . to the Arbeiter-Zeitung"; at *Budoucnost's* office they got "a complete list of subscribers." In June a grand jury indicted thirty-one Chicagoans for conspiracy in the Haymarket Riot. Only eight men actually stood trial, and six—George Engel and Adolph Fischer from the *Anarchist*, Albert Parsons from the *Alarm*, Michael Schwab, August Spies, and Oskar Neebe from the SPS—were directly connected to the city's anarchist press. (Mikolanda, from *Budoucnost*, was later convicted for a separate offense.) The Haymarket trial convicted, and then executed or imprisoned, the movement's most prominent leaders. A decade-long red scare, conducted by both the public and private sectors, intimidated the active membership and sympathetic following.[28]

After Haymarket

Despite the executions and intimidation, the radicals and their newspapers did not disappear. The Socialist Publishing Society's three papers reappeared first. With type set and ready to go to press on the Thursday after the riot, no shop in the city had been willing to print the papers. Oskar Neebe then secured new offices, the society finally bought its own printing press, and *Die Arbeiter-Zeitung* resumed publication on May 8, 1886. Facing the mayor's promise to suppress any inflammatory material, Spies and Schwab continued to write "the principle [*sic*] editorial matter" from their jail cells. After their executions, a new set of editors successively filled their positions. Once hailed by

Marx as "the philosopher of the proletariat," Joseph Dietzgen resigned his position on New York's *Der Sozialist* and edited *Die Arbeiter-Zeitung* for almost two years until his death in April 1888. Albert Currlin, a major figure in St. Louis's 1877 general strike, stayed a bit longer. They shared editorial responsibility with Gustav Belz, president of the metal workers' union and secretary of the CLU. Jens Christensen and Simon Hickler took over after Belz's untimely death in October 1888, and managed the three papers through the 1890s.[29]

Prace [Labor] reincarnated *Budoucnost* in October 1886. Again edited by Josef Pecka, it issued from the same office. Both papers started as dailies, then became weeklies; but the former was an anarchist paper, an official IWPA organ; edited and printed by anarchists, the latter was a labor paper funded by local Bohemian unions. The carpenters in Local 54 provided capital and a publication committee, promising "to make it the publication of all labor groups, to be supported by all labor groups, so that it would continue to function on a permanent basis." The local considered its outright purchase, but with only 250 members and a treasury of $400 the deal collapsed. "A great many difficulties arose," then "All locals were requested to contribute to the support of this publication, and all members instructed to purchase and read it, to pay up an advance subscription." The CLU twice extended its financial support, to no avail; the carpenters pulled out. *Prace* died in July 1887, leaving "bad feelings and hot blood amongst the [union's] members, in some for years, in some forever."[30]

In spring 1887, Joseph Buchanan moved his *Labor Enquirer* from Denver to Chicago. Buchanan held membership cards in the International Workingmen's Association and the Knights of Labor; with a foot in two camps (like Parsons), he was misunderstood by both. The *Chicago Labor Enquirer* appeared as a biweekly; facing two rivals, it remained insolvent, the post office refused to deliver it, and news carriers were warned not to touch it. Buchanan cut back to a weekly, hoping for expansion, but the subscription list "was never more than one twentieth of what it should have been." He cut his staff and set his own type. The *Alarm* conceded that Buchanan was "a revolutionary socialist," but complained that "the *Enquirer* could never be called a socialistic paper. It advocated radical reform in a vague sort of way that left the reader in considerable doubt." From New York the Socialist Labor party warned that Buchanan had rejected "the control of organized labor." In August 1888 he dismissed his staff and sent his paper's obituary and subscription list to Henry George. The next day Buchanan resigned from the SLP—but he had already been expelled.[31]

The *Alarm* reappeared in November 1887, eighteen months after the

Bruce C. Nelson

riot, six days before the executions. A four-page weekly like its name-
sake, it survived for twenty-two months, but was published in Chicago
only for the first five. A Knight, and a member of the SLP and later the
IWPA, Dyer Lum, the new editor, had come from an anarchist paper
in Kansas and had been a contributor to the first *Alarm*. While Lucy
Parsons and Sarah Ames invited Lum to edit the new paper, August
Spies feared competition with Buchanan's paper and warned the CLU
not to extend its support. With Lizzie Holmes returning as assistant
editor, the new paper looked like the old; but Lum was not Parsons.
He highlighted free thought, disdained the United Labor party, all but
ignored the labor movement, and addressed the *Alarm* to a shrinking
readership. After the paper moved to New York, a single column on
the third page carried "Our Chicago Letter." The second *Alarm* had
changed.[32]

Three Scandinavian papers were published in the 1890s, on soil left
fallow for a decade after *Den Nye Tid*'s death. For eighteen months
in 1889–90, Louis Pio issued *Samfundet* [Society] as an "Illustrated
Monthly for Scandinavian Literature, Family and Community Life." In
it he published articles on cooperatives, Marx, parliamentary socialism, and the local community. *Revyen* [The Review] appeared in March
1894 as a Danish weekly and ran through September 1921. Edited by
Christian Botker, a journalist who arrived in Chicago in 1891, it neither
sought nor earned the SLP's endorsement, but reportedly enjoyed
the largest circulation and longest life of any Danish socialist paper.
Edited by John Glambeck, a clerk, *Arbejderen* [The Worker] appeared
in July 1896, survived only four years, but was an official SLP organ.
Like *Revyen*, *Arbejderen* maintained its autonomy through 1921, but at
the cost of militancy. Both sold their subscription lists to commercial
immigrant papers.[33]

By May 1889, the radicals had restored their press to pre-Haymarket
levels. The SPS still published three papers: *Prace* replaced *Budoucnost*,
the *Labor Enquirer* and Dyer Lum's *Alarm* stood in for Parsons's original *Alarm*, and *Den Nye Tid*'s editor had returned with *Samfundet*. That
roster continued to grow. Between 1886 and 1900 Chicago's socialists
and anarchists issued thirty-six newspapers, published in seven languages: seven each in English and Czech, six each in German and
Polish, three each in Danish and Lithuanian, and one in Italian. (See
table 2.)

Three new German papers appeared after Haymarket. The Central
Labor Union announced a new official organ in February 1888. The
Arbeiter Stimme "will be a weekly," reported the *Alarm*, "and 25,000
copies are to be guaranteed for five weeks at least." The *Arbeiter Stimme*

became the CLU's German competitor to the Trades Assembly's new English *Record;* we know nothing, however, about its editors, editorials, circulation, or even its history (if any) beyond those five issues. Five years later, the SLP's German section reactivated the *Illinoiser Volks-Zeitung.* Subtitled "Den Interessen den Arbeitenden Volkes gewidmet" and published by the Deutscheverein Druckerei with a Typographia No. 9 union label, it appeared in March 1893, and probably ran several months. In spring 1896, Max Baginski offered the *Sturmglocke* as an anarchist weekly; it collapsed after four issues. These three papers remain unknown beyond their first issues.[34]

Chicago's Czech socialists and anarchists tried repeatedly to establish a solid journal in the 1890s. *Pravo Lidu* [Rights of the People], a daily "Dedicated to the Interest of the Working People," ran from May 1893 through August 1894 and was succeeded by *Duch Volnosti* [Spirit of Freedom], a monthly organ of the IWA. *Hlas Svobody* [Voice of Freedom], another daily, ran from January through May 1896, followed immediately by *Pochoden* [The Torch], a weekly, from June 1896 through May 1899, and *Revoluce,* an ephemeral social-revolutionary paper issued in 1897. In March 1900 the Czech section of the Socialist party in America began *Spravedlnost* [Justice], first as a weekly, later a daily; it survived through 1941. Josef Pecka, the former editor of *Budoucnost* and *Prace,* stayed on to work on *Pravo Lidu* and *Hlas Svobody* and represented the old guard; Frantisek Hlavacek, who debuted in Chicago with *Pochoden* and later edited *Spravedlnost,* represented newer, younger immigrants.[35]

The SLP's English section issued two new papers in the 1890s. An eight-page weekly, *Chicago Labor,* was printed in St. Louis, and only the last page carried local news. In sixteen months, from August 1893 to December 1894, it went through at least three local editors, including John Glambeck, the section's Danish organizer, and J. Hubert de Witt, a "young, brilliant and energetic young man." Local reports were buried on the last page, jammed between local ads; before reaching them, a Chicago reader had to wade through the SLP's national platform, reports from the New York sections, and national ads. After sixteen months Chicagoans wanted their own paper, and the *Socialist Alliance* appeared as the monthly organ of the Socialist Trade and Labor Alliance in July 1896.[36]

Perhaps the most fascinating phenomenon of the 1890s was the development of a socialist press within Chicago's Polish and Lithuanian colonies, communities traditionally regarded as either priest-ridden or Democratic. Between 1889 and 1900, five radical Polish papers—four weeklies, one biweekly—appeared in Chicago; only one has been

Table 2
The Roster and Circulations of Chicago's Socialist and Anarchist Press, 1886–1900

Paper	First Issue	Last Issue	Language	Frequency	1886	1888	1890	1892	1894	1896	1898	1900
Vorbote	1874	1924	G	w	8,000	5,000	3,150	3,575	4,000	7,300	6,150	5,000
Arbeiter-Zeitung	1876	1919	G	d	5,780	5,000	4,600	5,800	7,145	15,120	12,560	10,000
Fackel	1877	1919	G	w	12,200	7,500	16,000	20,000	24,160	24,600	19,800	15,000
Budoucnost	1883	1886	Cz	w	750							
Alarm	1884	1886	E	w	3,000							
Lampcka	1885	1886	Cz	w	750							
Anarchist	1886	1886	G	m	300							
Prace	1887	1887	Cz	w	2,000							
Labor Enquirer	1887	1888	E	w		2,000						
Alarm	1887	1889	E	w								
Arbeiter Stimme	1888	1888	G	w		5,000						
Glos Wolny	1889	1890	P	w								
Samfundet	1889	1890	D	m								
Nowe Zycie	1889	1896	P	w				5,000	7,000			
Freedom	1891	1892	E	m								
Reforma	1891	1892	P	w								
Chicago Labor	1893	1894	E	w								
Grido d. Oppressi	1893	1894	It	w								
Pravo Lidu	1893	1894	Cz	d					400			
Ill. Volks-Zeitung	1893	1896	G	w								
Gazeta Robotnicza	1894	1894	P	2w								
Revyen	1894	1921	N	w						2,000	2,000	
Duch Volnosty	1895	1895	Cz	m								1,080

Paper	First Issue	Last Issue	Language	Frequency	1886	1888	1890	1892	1894	1896	1898	1900
Sturmglocke	1896	1896	G	w								
Hlas Svobody	1896	1896	Cz	d						400		
Socialist Alliance	1896	1898	E	m						10,000		
Pochoden	1896	1899	Cz	w							400	
Arbejderen	1896	1900	D	w							2,800	2,800
Amerikos Lietuvis	1897	1897	Lith	w								
Revoluce	1897	1897	Cz	w								
Social Democrat	1898	1898	E	w								
Anarchistas	1899	1899	Lith	m								
Workers Call	1899	1902	E	w								
Sila I Postep	1899	1901	P	w								
Kurejas	1900	1901	Lith	w								
Robotnik	1900	1906	P	w								
Spravednost	1900	1941	Cz	w								5,000
Totals					32,780	24,500	23,750	34,375	42,705	59,420	43,710	33,880
Number change					−3,039	−8,280	−750	10,625	8,330	16,715	−15,710	−9,830
Percent change					−10	−25	−3	+45	+24	+39	−26	−22

Notes: Column 3 "Language": G = German, Cz = Czech, E = English, P = Polish, D = Danish, It = Italian, N = Norwegian, Lith = Lithuanian. Column 4 "Frequency": w = weekly, d = daily, m = monthly, 2w = biweekly.

Sources: N. W. Ayer and Sons, *American Newspaper Annuals*, 1886–1900 (Philadelphia, 1886–1900); George P. Rowell and Co., *American Newspaper Directory*, 1886–1900 (New York, 1886–1900); Henryk Nagiel, *Dziennikarstwo polskie w Ameriyce*; Frantisek Stedronsky, *Zahranicni krajianské noviny*; Frank Lavinskas, *Amerikos Lietuviu Lakrasciai*; *Immigrant Labor Press in North America*.

preserved. *Glos Wolny* [the Free Voice] came to Chicago in 1889 as a socialist paper but sold its subscription list, fourteen months later, to the Polish Roman Catholic Union (PRCU). *Nowe Zycie* [New Life] came next and ran almost seven years, from 1889 to 1896. *Reforma* started in Chicago in 1891 as a socialist paper, moved to Buffalo and affiliated with the PRCU within a year, and then returned to Chicago. *Gazeta Robotnicza* [Workers' Gazette], "an atheistic and anarchistic journal" edited by Jozef Rybakowski, a baker, issued from January through May 1894. It "promoted anarchism," complained a bourgeois Polish paper, and "became a source of lies and ridicule against religion, society, and private property." Finally, *Siła I Postep* [Strength and Progress] began as a free-thought paper but later served as the organ of the SLP's Polish section from 1899 to 1901.[37] At the turn of the century Jouzas Laukys, a printer, offered three successive Lithuanian papers. The first, *Amerikos Lietuvis* [American Lithuanian], a "radical socialist" paper, lasted but three issues in 1897; *Anarchistas* was intended as a monthly, but enjoyed only a few issues in 1899; and the third, *Kurejas* [the Creator] "attempted to publish anarchist, free-thinking and nationalist ideas" in nineteen issues in 1900.[38]

The roster of Chicago's socialist and anarchist press from Haymarket to 1900 comprised thirty-six papers, published in seven languages, including three dailies, twenty-five weeklies, one biweekly, and six monthlies. The number of papers may be misleading, for few endured; but that growth, and its penetration into new communities, was remarkable. Circulation (based largely on German figures) fluctuated wildly in the 1890s, reflecting not only the business cycle but also the cycle of repression. Total circulation grew from about 32,780 in 1886 to a high of 59,420 in 1896, then fell to 38,880 in 1900—somewhere between 2 and 4 percent of the city's population. Scourged by both political repression and economic depression, the life expectancy of the radical press varied by language. The German papers proved the most durable, the Scandinavians came second, followed by the Polish and Czech papers. In comparison the English papers all died young. None survived as long, but the gaps in their publishing history were never glaring. A new paper, with a new name and editors, always appeared. The effort of founding and maintaining a multilingual press was apparently justified.

After the Knights of Labor purged the anarchists, some of Chicago's trade unions let repentant socialists back in, at the cost of their propaganda but not their militance. Stripped of their politics, ex-radicals proved good unionists. The relationship between the socialist press and organized labor changed too. As anarchists became a liability, as socialism became expendable, the intimacy of that relationship was lost in the 1890s. The class-consciousness of the 1880s gave way to craft sectionalism. The Möbel-Arbeiter Union got its own paper in 1883 (*Die Möbel-Arbeiter Journal*, published in New York), as did the German and Czech bakers (1889, the *Chicagoer Bäcker-Zeitung; Cesky pekar*), the saddlers (1891, *Sattler und Wagenbauer*), the furniture workers (1896, *International Wood Worker*), and the carriage workers (1899, *Carriage and Wagon Workers' Journal*). If several unions stayed close to the Socialist Publishing Society, most moved on, not to business unionism but back to the SLP, then to Debsian social democracy, still later to the Socialist party and the Industrial Workers of the World.[39]

A decade of repression changed the content and trajectory of the radical press. The inflammatory rhetoric, the ads for the Lehr- und Wehr-Verein, the articles on dynamite, even the initials IWPA, disappeared immediately. In Haymarket's wake the press dropped its "anarchist" pretensions, renounced revolution, and reembraced socialist electoral politics. Even after Judge Tuley's 1889 decision that "anarchists have the same rights as other citizens," discretion reduced the names and detail in meeting reports. The socialist press still covered the labor movement, but with a bit less urgency, and, after Dietzgen's death, much less theory. When the Pullman strike broke out in May 1894, *Der Vorbote* and *Die Arbeiter-Zeitung* offered extensive coverage and voiced their outrage. But as the strike dragged on, both papers reduced their coverage. Beyond an almost perfunctory solidarity, Chicago's former anarchists became distant and uninvolved, and their initial sympathy gave way to a cynical defeatism and then disgust. By 1909 *Die Arbeiter-Zeitung* conceded that "the pain and fury" of the Haymarket tragedy had "been corrupted to sweet nostalgia." A year before, *Die Fackel*'s editor complained:

> Where are they gone, the many who only a few years ago helped to build and to extend the new working-class movement? Many have turned completely bourgeois, and only a small number at least keep in touch with the organized workers by reading a radical paper of some kind. . . .
>
> While it used to be that those active in the movement for at least ten years, some years later, one could count oneself fortunate if he saw the same faces for five years. But nowadays, they participate no longer than two years.[40]

If we measure by date of birth, by progeny, by circulation, or by longevity, it would be difficult to underestimate the saliency of the German radical press to the socialist and anarchist movements. The German socialist papers appeared first, issued more titles, enjoyed

Bruce C. Nelson

higher circulations, and survived longest. While *Der Vorbote's* fifty-year run (1874–1924) was remarkable, mere survival should not be the only way of judging the radical press. *Die Fackel* died in 1919, *Die Arbeiter-Zeitung* and the *Vorbote* hung on through another red scare. As late as 1924, with a circulation of about eight thousand, the *Arbeiter-Zeitung* was still owned by the Zeitung Publishing Company, the Central Committee of the Socialist party, Brewery Workers', Beer Bottlers', and the Bakers' and Confectionary unions.

Writing thirty years ago, Carl Wittke argued that the foreign-language press in America was "the voice, the mirror, and the most active catalyzer of the life of any immigrant community." Chicago's foreign-language press illuminates those communities far better than the *Tribune* or *Inter Ocean.* But Wittke's argument remains blind to class, generalizing from bourgeois papers while largely ignoring the proletarian press. It is clear that Chicago's polyglot socialist press became a voice, mirror, and catalyst in the city's working-class communities. Thus *Der Vorbote's* assertion that "the history of the labor movement is simultaneously the history of the labor press" takes on new meaning. *Die Arbeiter-Zeitung,* for example, tells us more about Chicago's German workers than either the Republican *Illinois Staats-Zeitung* or the Democratic *Neue Freie Presse.* While their contents are lost to us now, the presence of *Glos Wolny, Kurejas,* and *Grido degli Oppressi* were important to the development of an urban socialist movement a century ago. Because Chicago's population was multiethnic, its historians will have to be multilingual if we are to move from labor, radical, or social history toward a history of society.[41]

NOTES

I want to thank Frances Mateyko, Paul Street, Richard Altenbaugh, and the editors for their critiques of earlier drafts.

1. *Vorbote,* Apr. 3, 1880, p. 1. *The Immigrant Labor Press in North America* should become the standard guide and finding tool.

2. See Henry David, *History of the Haymarket Affair;* Paul Avrich, *Haymarket Tragedy;* and Bruce Nelson, *Beyond the Martyrs.*

3. "Zur Geschichte der Chicagoer Arbeiter-Zeitung, des Vorboten, und der Fackel," *Chicagoer Arbeiter-Zeitung* [*ChAZ*], June 21, 1888, p. 1; Jacob Winnen, "Geschichte der Arbeiterbewegung von Chicago," *Fackel,* Mar. 4, 1917, p. 1; and Renate Kiesewetter, "Institution der deutsch-amerikanischen Arbeiterpresse," pp. 12–15.

4. Hartmut Keil, "German Immigrant Working Class of Chicago," p. 167.

5. Louis Pio, *Til de skandinaviske Arbejdere;* Johannes Wist, "Norsk-Ameri-

104

kanernes Presse," pp. 82–83, 87–88, 92–93; Jens Engberg, *Til Arbejdet! Liv Eller død!* and Oddvar Bjorklund, *Marcus Thrane*.

6. *Vorbote*, Oct. 6, 1877, p. 5; *Socialist*, Sept. 14, 1878, p. 1; *Proceedings of the SLP Convention, 1879–1880*, 7, Socialist Labor Party of America Records [SLP Records], Wisconsin State Historical Society [WSHS], microfilm edition, 1970, reel 35.

7. *Budoucnost*, June 16, 1883, p. 1; "A True Bohemian" to editor, *Chicago Mail*, May 10, 1886, p. 1; Francis Hlaváček, "Zlomky českého počátečního," pp. 79–81; Josef Polišenský, "Český podíl na předhistorii Prvního máje," in *Začiatky českej a slovenskej emigrácie do USA*.

8. *Alarm*, Dec. 27, 1884, p. 2; Albert Parsons, *Anarchism*, p. 173; Herbert Gutman, "Alarm: Chicago and New York," pp. 380–86.

9. *Svornost*, May 7 and 11, 1886, both p. 4; *Chicago Tribune*, May 7, 1886, p. 2. In *Dějiny Čechů v Americkych* Jan Habenicht identified *Lampcka* as an "anarchistic" paper (p. 607), although Tomáš Čapek (*Padesát Let Českého Tisky v Americe*, p. 131) identifies it as a "humoristicko-satiricky" weekly. The contradiction cannot be resolved: there are no issues extant.

10. *Vorbote*, Dec. 23, 1885, p. 8. The Julius Grinnell Collection has two issues of the *Anarchist*; see John Kebabian, *Haymarket Affair*.

11. *Formation of the Workingmen's Party*, p. 31; Louis Pio, *Den Lille Amerikaner*, p. 12; Paul Le Blanc, "Revolutionary Socialism," p. 199.

12. Paul Buhle, "German Socialists and the Roots of American Working-Class Radicalism," p. 230.

13. Floyd Dell, "Socialism and Anarchism in Chicago," p. 391; cf. George Schilling to Lucy Parsons, Dec. 1, 1893, George Schilling Collection, Illinois State Historical Library, Springfield.

14. *Socialist*, Mar. 15, 1879, p. 4; Hartmut Keil, "Knights of Labor."

15. *Vorbote*, Aug. 4 and 25, 1877, both p. 2; *ChAZ*, Apr. 26, 1884, p. 4; Apr. 13, 1884, p. 4; Nelson, *Beyond the Martyrs*, pp. 127–52.

16. Cf. "By-Laws of 'The Chicago Socialist Press Association,'" *Socialist*, Feb. 1, 1879, p. 8; and "Protokoll-Buch von der Illinoiser Volkszeitung Publishing Association, 1884–1885," Thomas J. Morgan Collection, Illinois Historical Survey, University of Illinois (microfilm edition: Urbana, 1969), reel 7; Kiesewetter, "Institution der deutsch-amerikanischen Arbeiterpresse," pp. 28–49; *Vorbote*, Apr. 1, 1876, p. 1.

17. *Vorbote*, Dec. 22, 1883, p. 6; *Alarm*, Nov. 28, 1885, p. 1; *Formation of the Workingmen's Party*, p. 18.

18. Kiesewetter, "Institution der deutsch-amerikanischen Arbeiterpresse," pp. 74–82; *Vorbote*, July 14, 1877, p. 2; *Fackel*, June 8, 1879, p. 8; *ChAZ*, June 27, 1882, p. 4; Thomas Robinson, "Chicago Typographical Union #16."

19. See a report from a Danish printer who worked with Pio in *Ugebladet*, June 22 and 29, 1922, trans. in Marion Marzolf, *Danish-Language Press*, pp. 42–43.

20. [Adolph Douai?], "Bericht über den Fortgang der sozialistischen Bewegung: Amerika"; Richard Ely, *Labor Movement in America*, p. 278.

Bruce C. Nelson

21. From 1880 to 1886 the city's population grew by 64 percent; Michael Schaack, *Anarchy and Anarchists*, p. 216.

22. Elisabeth Pitzer, "Bürgerliche Presse und Arbeiterpresse im Wandel"; Habenicht, *Dějiny Čechů v Americkych*, pp. 604–9; Frederick Buchstein, "Anarchist Press in American Journalism," pp. 43–45, 66.

23. Neither the *Telegraph* nor the *Standard of Labor* have survived. For *Progressive Age*, and a brilliant exegesis of its leading columnist, see Richard Schneirov, "Knights of Labor in the Chicago Labor Movement," pp. 328–36, 318–27.

24. "Notes on Meetings of the SLP," Mar.-June 1884, Morgan Collection, reel 6; H. Walther to NEC, Jan. 9, 1885 (reel 5), L. Bonstein to NEC, Jan. 19, 1885 (reel 6), SLP Records.

25. Selig Perlman, "Upheaval and Reorganization"; *Alarm*, Jan. 23, 1886, p. 2; Keil, "Knights of Labor," pp. 301–23.

26. *Vorbote*, Apr. 21, 1886, p. 8; cf. *Chicago Tribune*, Apr. 19, 1886, p. 2; Bruce Nelson, " 'We Can't Get Them to Do Aggressive Work.' "

27. *ChAZ*, May 1, 1886, quoted in *Concise History of the Great Trial*, pp. 20–21; *Chicago Tribune*, May 1, 1886, p. 2.

28. *Inter Ocean*, May 9, 1886, p. 2; *Chicago Tribune*, Sept. 1, 1886, p. 8; Nelson, *Beyond the Martyrs*, pp. 190–200.

29. *Alarm*, June 23, 1888, p. 4; Eugene Dietzgen, "Joseph Dietzgen"; on Belz see *Vorbote*, Sept. 5, 1888, p. 7; and his obituary, *ChAZ*, Oct. 10, 1888, p. 1.

30. Quotations from "History of Local No. 54," trans. H. Vydra (typescript, ca. 1922), pp. 9–11, Archives of the Chicago District Council, United Brotherhood of Carpenters and Joiners of America; František Štědronský, *Zahraniční krajanské noviny*, p. 104; Rudolf Bubenicek, *Dějiny Čechů v Chicagu*, p. 361.

31. Joseph Buchanan, *Story of a Labor Agitator*, pp. 331, 350–51, 452; *Vorbote*, Feb. 23, 1887, p. 7; *Alarm*, Sept. 1, 1888, p. 3. The *Enquirer's* rivals were the *Knights of Labor* and the *Daily Star Telegram* "published by the Knights of Labor Publishing Co."; a single clipping of the latter has survived in the Albert Parsons Papers, WSHS.

32. *Vorbote*, May 14, 1888, p. 4; May 30, 1888, p. 1; see Frank Brooks, "Industrialization and Radical Ideology."

33. *Samfundet*, May 1, 1899; *Arbejderen*, Mar. 11, 1897, p. 2; July 6, 1899, p. 2; *Revyen*, May 15, 1897, p. 1; May 5, 1900, p. 2; Danielsen, "Early Danish Immigrant Socialist Press," pp. 64–72.

34. *Alarm*, Feb. 25, 1888, p. 1; *Vorbote*, Mar. 14, 1888, p. 8; Karl J. R. Arndt and May E. Olson, *Deutsch-amerikanische Zeitungen und Zeitschriften*, pp. 58, 78. On the *Record*, see *Vorbote*, July 11, 1888, p. 8; there are five issues of *Illinoiser Volks-Zeitung* (Apr.-May 1893) at WSHS.

35. Štědronský, *Zahraniční krajanské noviny*, p. 106; Čapek, *Padesát Let Českého Tisky v Americe*, p. 132; Hlavácek, "Zlomky českého počátečního," pp. 82–90.

36. The Labor News Company of St. Louis, "a socialist newspaper union," offered "an eight page paper, [with] local matter . . . confined to the last page."

By 1895 it was published under different names in thirty-three cities. *Chicago Labor*, Aug. 12, 1893, p. 8; *Socialist Alliance*, June 1897, p. 1.

37. Henryk Nagiel, *Dziennikarstwo Polskie w Ameryce*, pp. 14, 108–9, 112, 118–20, 127; Waclaw Kruszka, "Gazeciarstwo polskie w Ameryce," 5:57–58, 60, 65–66, 73; Stanislaw Osada, *Prasa i publicystyka polska w Ameryce*, pp. 24–25, 26, 28; quotations from *Dziennik Chicagoski*, Apr. 21, 1894, p. 1.

38. Frank Lavinskas, *Amerikos Lietuviu Lakrasciai*, pp. 20, 34; *Immigrant Labor Press in North America*, 2:156, 166.

39. *ChAZ*, Nov. 1, 1886, p. 4; *Vorbote*, Nov. 10, 1886, p. 8; see *ChAZ*, July 16, 1888, p. 4.

40. Tuley quoted in David, *History of the Haymarket Affair*, p. 482; *Vorbote*, May-Oct. 1894; *ChAZ*, May-Oct. 1894, passim; *ChAZ*, Nov. 12, 1909, p. 2; *Fackel*, May 24, 1908, p. 4.

41. Carl Wittke, *German Language Press in America*, p. v; *Vorbote*, Apr. 3, 1880, p. 1.

Carol Poore

The *Pionier* Calendar of New York City: Chronicler of German-American Socialism

German radical immigrants to the United States were constantly seeking to expand the public reached by the socialist and labor press. One of the best examples of these efforts is the *Pionier*, an "illustrated people's calendar" published annually by German-American socialists connected with the *New Yorker Volkszeitung* (*NYVZ*) in New York City. The length of time over which this publication appeared and its high quality make it a fascinating and significant record of the importance these immigrant socialists attached to creating alternative reading matter for the working-class audience they had in mind. This discussion of the *Pionier* will treat the following points: (1) a brief historical overview of the genre of the calendar in Germany and its reworking by Social Democrats, (2) the publishing history of the *Pionier* within the context of the German-American socialist cultural milieu, and (3) an analysis of the *Pionier* itself.

After the invention of the printing press in the fifteenth century, calendars expanded from being mere tables of the days of the year, church holidays, and astrological and meteorological dates to include more and more practical information, didactic writings, stories, and various other forms of prose and poetry. They became popular reading matter, and it is easy to imagine that among groups of the population who could just barely read, such calendars were probably one of their only contacts with the printed word.[1] During the eighteenth century, in the course of the Enlightenment, various writers and pedagogues in Germany made efforts to raise the niveau of such calendars in order to use them for educating the lower classes. In the nineteenth century military, pedagogical, medical, or theological calendars began

108

to appear, creating a flood of calendar literature directed at specific occupational groups. Alongside this development, a number of well-known writers produced short stories which they called "calendar stories." These were not necessarily even meant to be published in calendars, but by choosing this genre designation writers indicated that they were creating a short prose form which would, or should, have a broad popular appeal. Perhaps the most important example from the twentieth century is Bertolt Brecht's *Kalendergeschichten* (1949), a collection of his stories, poems, and anecdotes which he compiled upon his return to Europe from exile. In these small, modest pieces, Brecht sought to revive a popular tradition of resistance to illegitimate authority, in opposition to the racist, chauvinist appeals to the *Volk* under the Nazis. It is worth quoting Michael Hamburger's introduction to the English translation of *Tales from the Calendar* (1961) in this regard:

> In giving the book its title . . . Brecht consciously recalled the "peasant calendars" of an earlier age, when collections of satirical tales, fables, aphorisms and little descriptions of historical or everyday episodes were a traditional form of popular instruction and entertainment in rural areas. Though the form degenerated sharply after 1848, it maintained a shadowy existence, and Brecht's deliberate revival of the name and his choice of the contents are in accord with his clearly expressed view that the function of literature, whether in drama, verse or prose, is to stimulate, through entertainment, the wits, the social consciousness and the moral sensibilities of ordinary men and women.[2]

This form of calendar and of reading matter is familiar to all of us today. With respect to alternative groups, we need only to think of feminist calendars, ecology calendars, alternative history calendars—or in the Federal Republic of Germany: "red" calendars, calendars for progressive teachers, calendars for the civil-rights efforts of people with disabilities, and so forth.

From its beginnings, German Social Democracy valued highly this kind of popular reading matter.[3] Along with various workers' calendars published in socialist circles, the Social Democratic party itself began to publish a calendar entitled *Der arme Conrad* ("Poor Conrad"—referring to the revolutionary peasants' league of this name in the Peasant Wars of 1524–26) immediately after its unification congress in Gotha in 1875. By 1878 the circulation of this calendar was about 60,000. Other party calendars also appeared, their combative, assertive edge blunted by censorship under the antisocialist laws of 1878–90. But one party calendar, the *Neue-Welt-Kalender*, was published continuously from 1883 to 1933. The Communist party of Germany (KPD) also published calendars beginning in the early 1920s, about which very little information

Carol Poore

is available. We might surmise, though, that both the social democratic and the Communist calendars (as well as the *Pionier* in the United States) became somewhat less influential as time went by, due to the proliferation of other forms of mass entertainment and information— the growth of the press, magazines, movies, radio, sports, and other leisure pursuits which workers took part in.

An article published in Germany in the "Allgemeiner Arbeiter-Kalender für das Jahr 1886" stated the "cultural task" of the calendar as follows: "There are in fact books which are found in the poorest huts and which are therefore best suited to fulfill the mission of edu-cating and enlightening the people: they are the calendars. A calendar is probably to be found in the most straitened household, and in some families it is the only source of intellectual stimulation for the whole year. Therefore, it is here that the lever should be applied, in order to have a meaningful effect on the education of the lower classes."[4] This emphasis on education and enlightenment was nothing new in itself, but Social Democrats sought to transform the content of this education in accordance with their own goals. They kept the tradi-tional structure and layout of other calendars, but the reading matter was often selected with a view toward its socialist political or cultural content. This would include calendar stories which depicted the life of the proletariat, satirical sketches attacking the parasitical, lazy rich, historical and biographical pieces, and reports on the labor movement abroad. Many of the authors were party functionaries—some, though not all, self-taught workers. During the period of the antisocialist laws, however, it was possible to continue this sort of satirical, polemical, informative writing only in the social democratic press published in exile (for example, in Switzerland), and the calendars published during this time took on a more entertaining and much less overtly political character.[5]

Coming from such traditions, it seems quite natural that German socialist immigrants to the United States would establish calendars with similar goals, aimed at a working-class reading audience. Besides the *Pionier*, I have located two others: the *Kalender des Philadelphia Tage-blatt* (for the years 1899–1904; for 1903 and 1904 it is simply a reprint of the *Pionier* but published in Philadelphia), and the *New Jersey Arbeiter-Kalender* (for 1899, edited by Albert Gabriel in Newark "under the aus-pices of various unions"). No doubt these calendars were published over a longer period of time than I have found, and no doubt more calendars connected to the labor and socialist movements were pub-lished in other cities, but these were precisely the kind of ephemera rarely deemed worthy of collecting and preserving.

110

Fortunately, however, the *Pionier-Kalender* has been preserved. It was published annually by the *NYVZ* from 1882 to 1933, averaging about one hundred pages per issue.[6] Furthermore, I have found two volumes of an *Illustrierter deutschamerikanischer Volkskalender* from the years 1938 and 1939 which are obviously continuations of the *Pionier*, judging from their layout and contributors.[7] These two volumes were published by the "Arbeiter Kranken- und Sterbe-Kasse" (Workers' Sick and Death Benefit Society of North America, a large mutual aid society made up primarily of Germans with headquarters in Brooklyn). They are designated as the first and second volumes of the *Volks-kalender;* therefore, it seems likely that due to the financial difficulties and reorganization of the *NYVZ* beginning in 1933, no *Volkskalender* was published in New York from 1934 to 1937. Probably the calendar did not last for long past 1939, since the Workers' Sick and Death Benefit Society dwindled in membership and became more and more exclusively concerned with providing financial benefits to its aging members rather than with other cultural tasks.

It is impossible to determine the circulation of the *Pionier*, although we can certainly see that it met with a good reception from the fact that it was published regularly over such a long period of time, that the Philadelphia *Tageblatt* copied it, and that for a number of years, the copies preserved note that they are the second or even third printing of the calendar. Circulation figures for the daily *NYVZ* during this period certainly show popular support: in 1878, for example, there were 4,000 subscribers, but 5,500 copies of first issue sold; by 1880 there were 10,200 (that the *Pionier* was already launched in 1882 testifies to the importance the *NYVZ* attached to putting out such a calendar); and the numbers grew, until in 1932 there were 23,000 subscribers.[8] The calendar cost twenty-five cents for most of its life; by 1939 it cost forty-five cents—which might indicate that the circulation figures for the *Pionier* would be similar to those for the *NYVZ*.[9]

Perhaps the most impressive and touching thing about this publication to a reader who turns its yellowing pages today is the very high quality of its layout, printing, illustrations, and contents, indicating the time and great care which its editors and writers put into it. Who wrote for the *Pionier*? Its contributors included many of the German-American socialist journalists active in the political and union movements in New York—the reader familiar with the history of German-American socialism will recognize the names of Adolf Douai, Alexander Jonas, Hermann Schlüter, Jacob Franz, Julius Grunzig, Sergius Schewitsch, Ernst Schmidt (from Chicago), Julie Zadek-Romm, and many others. They were generally intellectuals who cast their lot with socialism—although there were a few self-taught workers who also contributed. As was the case with the rest of the German-American socialist press, many pieces were taken over from the German press or calendars, but certainly a noteworthy amount of the material in the *Pionier* was written specifically for it and dealt with working-class life in the United States. Very little material was translated from English for inclusion, but a few notable examples are chapters from Jack London's *Iron Heel* and Frank Norris's *The Octopus* and reports by Job Harriman on labor struggles in the West. In other words, the *Pionier* focused significantly on American life and experiences, but generally from a German-American socialist perspective.

The general makeup of each issue was as follows: first, a picture on the title page, which might be a portrait of a revolutionary leader like Marx or Lassalle or a reproduction of a painting (perhaps from revolutionary history such as Adolph Menzel's paintings of 1848, but perhaps also a landscape or genre painting). Next would come the actual calendar section, with an illustration accompanying each month of the year, and lists of important dates including events from American and European progressive history. The longest part of the calendar was devoted to reading material, usually introduced by a poem for the year. The volume closed with advertisements and greetings from many socialist and labor fraternal organizations in New York City, and lists of books which could be ordered from the *NYVZ*.

In discussing the reading material, it is important to stress from the outset that by no means all of it was overtly political. Those pieces expressing a clearly socialist standpoint were definitely in the minority, but this accords with the editors' apparent goals—to integrate a socialist perspective into other reading experiences and needs, and into daily life. They wanted to appeal to a broad audience, not just to those who were already familiar with socialism, and who were politically committed. Therefore, the calendars offered a real potpourri of topics, literary genres, and fiction and nonfiction. It would be impossible here to give an exhaustive description and analysis of the extremely varied contents of the *Pionier* over fifty years. Instead, the following discussion will focus on the effort to develop alternative, entertaining reading matter which was meant to stimulate independent, critical thought and a will to resist the increasing commodification of all areas of life under capitalism.

The calendar contained a wide variety of anecdotes, jokes, poetry, and stories. The jokes might be directed against capitalists and the rich, but more often than not they could have been (and probably were) taken over from some nonsocialist German sources (jokes about

teachers and pupils, shrewish wives, drunken husbands, etc.). The
poetry selections sometimes reprinted the inspired expressions of the
1848 revolution or included works by later socialist writers which reflected on historical events or called for solidarity. A good number
were also sentimental lyrics which sang of love and landscape. The
stories were also quite mixed. Some were clearly selected mainly for
their entertainment value and could have been found just as well in
the nonsocialist press (these usually dealt with some kind of love affair). Others had a more pronounced socially critical thrust, but it is
important to note that these two tendencies existed along a continuum
rather than being two sharply distinct themes. Even some of the more
sentimental love stories and poems stated at times that love was more
important than money, that there was hardly a place for true love any
more in this increasingly materialistic world, or that free love was infinitely preferable to unhappy marriage based on private property and
status-seeking. On the other hand, the stories and sketches which
depicted the life of the proletariat or drew on themes from the labor
movement often spiced up their naturalistic descriptions with liberal
doses of sentimentality.[10] For example, *NYVZ* editor Sergius Schewitsch contributed a sketch entitled "The Hun" to the 1890 volume. It
is the story of a Russian immigrant who becomes a scab during a strike
in Johnstown, Pennsylvania, out of ignorance and lack of knowledge
of English. Treated badly by the strikers, he falls in love with a young
German woman who believes that surely he would support his fellow workers if he only understood the situation. Finally, a great flood
rushes through the valley one day, and he risks his life to save her.
But when he returns to try to find the body of her dead father, the
townspeople shoot him dead, believing he is robbing the corpses. In
the end, "Marie was waiting in vain. There was one less 'hun' in the
world" (p. 19). Or, in "Molly" (1906), Meta Lilienthal told the "everyday story" of a working-class woman who has an illegitimate child
and has to leave it with an old woman while working as a nursemaid.
The child receives poor care and finally dies. In 1933, Paul Mattick
contributed a story called "The Bees" about a miner in an IWW strike
led by Bill Haywood. In trying to prevent picket lines from being set
up, the police kill the miner, who leaves behind a wife and children as
numerous as "bees." Obviously, the writers of such stories sought to
depict conflicts which were neglected in other literature. They wanted
to stir the emotions and the consciences of their readers at the thought
that such injustice and misery could exist in the land of opportunity.

The nonfiction pieces in the calendar can be divided roughly into
three subject areas: popular science (articles on nature, astronomy,

travel, engineering, etc.); political, historical, and economic analyses; and literary and art history. An early article (from 1886) on modern railway travel established the tone struck in many of these pieces, when it acknowledged the speed and convenience of the train, but noted that along with this, people were losing a sense for the deliberate enjoyment of natural beauty and only wanted to say that they "had been there." A later article by Meta Lilienthal on "The Art of Enjoyment" (1910) noted that it would be a terrible accusation against our civilization if it were in fact true that working people trapped in cities in a monotonous working life were not really able to enjoy nature or beauty for their own sakes, with knowledge and appreciation. Along these lines, it was in fact the goal of much of the reading matter to encourage the reader to resist passive consumption by cultivating knowledge and aesthetic appreciation, and by pointing out the inequities in access to enjoyment under the capitalist system.[11] A good example is a series of articles on science and nature written by the self-taught Wilhelm Gundlach (1828–1913). Gundlach came to the United States in 1868 and was a freethinker, member of the First International, contributor to the *NYVZ*, and teacher in the German free schools. As his eulogy in the *Pionier* noted in 1914, however, his wife held the family together since he had no head for business! He viewed his main task in life as popularizing science for children and workers, and set out to do this in the articles he wrote for the *Pionier*. In "The Forces and Beauties of Nature" (1905), he notes that workers really need to be able to get out of the cities and enjoy nature, but that they have to pay to do this, while in the meantime, the rich are building their homes in lovely places like Mount Desert Island in Maine. After describing the flora, fauna, and geological features of some places that workers might visit if they had the money, Gundlach muses over the question of how many of the earth's treasures would be destroyed in the interests of capital. Similarly, in a 1906 article entitled "The Wonders of Nature in the Vicinity of New York," he assured his working-class readers that most well-off people would not be able to have such deep enjoyment of the wonders of nature as they would if they immersed themselves in study and really opened themselves to the many profound impressions to be experienced in nature. Then follows an informative article on the geology of New York harbor, where the emphasis lies on really looking at one's surroundings and knowing something substantial about them. Gundlach succinctly expressed the premise underlying all of these articles in a piece he wrote on Darwin in 1909, where he asserted that capital kept people ignorant, but that knowledge meant power (echoes of Wilhelm Liebknecht).

Another group of articles focused on history (usually of socialism) and on workers' struggles in the United States and Europe. For several years, a kind of editorial signed by the "Calendar Man" painted grim pictures of working-class life in the United States, explained the theory of surplus value in simple terms, and admonished its readers that the only possible response was to work for the realization of socialism by joining the Socialist Labor party or later, the Socialist party. Also, an annual "Year in Review" section provided a brief analysis of events of importance to workers in the United States and Europe. As early as 1924, the *Pionier* commented on the rise of Nazism in Germany. In 1931 it noted that General Ludendorff was calling for the annihilation of German Jewry, for the enslavement of Slavic peoples on German soil, and for the executions of the "stab-in-the-back traitors" (p. 21). In this same year, it explained the success of the Nazi party as due in part to its appeal to youth, but above all to the representatives of big industry and high finance who were supporting Hitler as the last hope of the bourgeoisie. Realizing that fascist dictatorship was a threat to the entire German working class, the "Year in Review" section expressed the hope that the two German workers' parties would unite against fascism rather than fight against each other (p. 102). The 1939 volume reported on the triumph of Nazism, on the Kristallnacht, and on the new wave of German Jewish exiles coming to the United States. It also contained an article by one Dr. Bernhard F. Mueller, "On the Problem of Race: Aryans and Jews," debunking Nazi racism (p. 56–58).

All of these articles, along with the dates selected as worthy of remembrance in the calendar section, were expressions of alternate views and perceptions of what was important in history and of efforts by oppressed groups of people to resist authority and assert their own subjectivity. However, the other side of this, which was characteristic of much of German-American socialism, was that in many of the pieces where the writers set out to give an explicitly political analysis of conflict, they tended to develop an accusatory or exasperated tone directed against what they saw as the unrevolutionary American working class. The editorials and news summaries would often end by bemoaning the fact that American workers were too dense to realize that they were oppressed, or too willing to enter into compromises with "petty-bourgeois" parties, or that yet another year had passed without anything of note to report about the workers' movement in the United States. However, such condescension appears only infrequently in the *Pionier*, and it is not a feature of the publication in general—a point to which we will return.

A third topic which occupied a significant amount of space was literary and art history—for example, a series of articles by Clara Ruge on social art and drama in the United States.[12] Her illustrated pieces on social art in America (1910 and 1917) discuss sculptures, paintings, and drawings, many by immigrant artists who often took their subject matter from working-class life in New York. The articles surveying modern social drama in America (1922 and 1926) focus on O'Neill and the Provincetown Players and also on antiwar plays. In her 1910 article, Ruge explained how she hoped to connect cultural and political goals: "The more we awaken an interest in artistic efforts among the people, above all among progressive workers, the more urgent their demands will be for intellectual pleasures, for the highest joys of life. The result is that the workers will grasp the social struggles of the present from a higher cultural standpoint, and they will engage in economic and political struggles with more perseverance and greater knowledge" (p. 81). This belief that aesthetic education (a salute to Schiller!) would necessarily lead to deeper, more knowledgeable political commitment and action can be taken as the driving hope underlying such socialist cultural efforts as the *Pionier* in general.

The belief in progress through enlightenment is also evident in the way in which the calendar used illustrations. These were many and various in each volume, including drawings, cartoons and caricatures, reproductions of paintings, photographs of sculptures, etc. Sometimes they would be accompanied by a short analysis pointing out important artistic techniques or social content, again from the perspective that the readers should learn to look at these artworks (and at the world) with a knowledgeable and critical eye. Like the reading material discussed here, although some of the art depicted struggles of the oppressed or important historical figures, much of it was clearly intended for the simple enjoyment of the readers, such as the numerous paintings of beautiful seminude or nude women, of mothers and children, of cute dogs and other animals, and of pleasant landscapes. It is easy to imagine that readers would have found this calendar a source of pinups, of reproductions of paintings, and of little political posters to tear out and hang on their walls. In fact, an anonymous author reflected on this in the women's section of the calendar in 1922, in an article entitled "On Hanging Pictures. A Part of Proletarian Culture." S/he made the point that workers (meaning women, who generally did the decorating) should think about what they hung on their walls and not have "petty-bourgeois" or "bourgeois" pictures, specifically ruling out pictures of soldiers and of church weddings! The author particularly recommended works by Käthe Kollwitz as appropriate (her works were frequently reproduced in the *Pionier*). This example shows the efforts that these people were making to act consciously, even in the smallest aspects of daily life.

If it was to be mainly women who thought about and were responsible for decorating their homes, in part with illustrations like those reproduced in the *Pionier*, what can we say in more general terms about women and this publication? To what extent was it concerned with issues of specific importance to women, and to what extent did women contribute to it? At first, as was characteristic of German-American socialism in general, the *Pionier* devoted little space to questions of women's emancipation, and almost all of its contributors were men. Occasionally, however, there would be exceptions to this. In the first volume from 1882, for example, an immigrant named Doris Epstein wrote a piece entitled "Academic Experiences" on the difficulties she had experienced as a woman trying to study medicine in Leipzig and about her hopes to continue her studies in the United States. In 1883, the socialist journalist Alexander Jonas, who had been active in free thought and women's rights circles in New York during the 1870s, contributed an imaginative lecture from "Before the Ice Age" entitled "The Emancipation of Men." This recounted a story about a society at the North Pole where the roles of men and women were reversed and described a convocation of "men's rights advocates" who were ridiculed by the women present. During the 1880s and 1890s, a few stories appeared by writers like Minna Kautsky (reprinted from the German social democratic press) and Julie Zadek-Romm (who was active in German-American socialist circles in New York and who later edited the women's pages of the *NYVZ* until her death in 1916).

Over time, during the early twentieth century, the number of contributions by women increased, until a section of the calendar entitled "For the Woman of Labor" began to appear in 1922 (simply called "For Women" in 1938 and 1939 under the sign of the Popular Front). This section was usually about ten to twenty pages long and contained household hints, discussions of such topics as child-rearing, health, and sex education, as well as stories, illustrations, and political and cultural articles. In these statements we can see how the contributors understood their cultural task. One woman who wrote several pieces during the 1920s was Lily Lore, probably the wife of *NYVZ* editor Ludwig Lore. In her articles called "What the Movement Can Mean to Us" (1922) and "I Do My Duty!" (1923), she chastised housewives who said that they were too busy with family duties to come to meetings, or who were afraid to develop their own opinions, and urged them to become active in the workers' movement.

Other articles later on urged women to resist war with all the means at their disposal by becoming active in the struggle against capitalism. One article from 1922 took a question as its title—"Working Woman, What Do You Read?" It can be taken as a programmatic statement for the goals of these women's pages. It criticized working women who thoughtlessly read or even subscribed to a bourgeois newspaper, who believed that the news was the same in any paper, and who read mainly for the short stories (here we could deduce that the short stories the *Pionier* contained would have made women more likely to read it). It pointed out that the bourgeois press would support factory owners against striking husbands of working-class women readers, and that its women's pages were written for women with money to squander on high fashion and gourmet recipes. Only one conclusion should be possible for the working-class woman, to "learn, read, and think," to read the *NYVZ* and the New York *Vorwärts* (and by extension, the *Pionier*).[13] In other words, as the anonymous writer stated, the reader should consciously try to "connect" what she read in the press "with (her) own daily life" (p. 70). Again, we find the contradiction in some of these political and cultural statements that the writers (especially Lily Lore) sometimes adopt a rather accusatory and condescending tone toward women who were not active in the workers' movement, and it is easy to imagine that this would have put off some readers because of its arrogance. However, the actual content of the women's pages in the context of the entire calendar did have a definite thrust toward empowerment in many areas of daily life, toward encouraging women to think and act for themselves, and toward synthesizing political, cultural, and emotional needs in their lives.

Under the pressure of events and developments in the United States and Germany, a publication like the *Pionier* could not have lasted much longer than it did. The days in which Marxist socialism had been most firmly rooted in the German-American ethnic group had long since passed, and the older immigration of Germans had long been increasingly integrated into English-speaking America. By the late 1920s, there is a feeling in the pages of the *Pionier* that it was not expressing so much of a mission to effect social change in the United States as it had earlier. An article from the 1931 volume which described a group trip back to "the old homeland" planned by the *NYVZ* for the following year expressed the writer's lingering feelings of being out of place in New York in the following way: "Yes, I speak their language, and I make their gestures, so that I don't put people off or stand out in the crowd. You do some things because they really are better than what you did before. You do other things to keep from becoming a stranger to your child. For I don't want my little girl to feel foreign in her homeland. She shouldn't want to emigrate and then become homeless inside like we of the older generation are now and will probably be until we die" (p. 50).

It is quite telling in this context that the 1938 and 1939 volumes were put out by the Workers' Sick and Death Benefit Society, an organization devoted especially to taking care of its aging radical members. Yet even at this late date, such an organization, and by extension, these last volumes of a publication like the *Pionier*, were anchored in an alternative, radical German-American sociocultural milieu which disappeared only after the war. Looking through the advertisements and congratulatory notices in the back of the calendar in 1933, and even in 1939, we see how active this socialist- or labor-oriented fraternal milieu still was—with mention of workers' singing societies, labor lyceums, various benefit societies, union activities, recreational and old age homes, etc.

One of the best personal statements about this milieu in which the *Pionier* was read is the memoirs of Meta Lilienthal, *Dear Remembered World* (1947).[14] She was born in New York about 1876; her parents were highly educated German Jewish immigrants, active in women's rights and socialist circles. Between 1906 and 1919, writing sometimes under the pseudonym "Hebe," she produced half a dozen pieces for the *Pionier*, mostly on various aspects of women's history. She also published a translation of August Bebel's *Woman and Socialism* (1910) and other writings on women's rights. One chapter in her memoirs is devoted to the man she remembered fondly as her "spiritual parent," Alexander Jonas (founder of the *NYVZ*). She recalled that he would play with her like a child himself, but that also, on their walks through the city, "he aroused my consciousness of social wrong." It was Jonas's influence, she states, that led her "to champion social causes and to take an active part in public life" (p. 38). During her childhood, her parents' home was visited by a stream of "social reformers," including Henry George and Wilhelm Liebknecht, and she was always included in these gatherings. She describes the atmosphere there as follows: "As I participated in my parents' intellectual life, so also did I in their merrymaking. Sometimes these serious minded people, these idealists and world reformers, would play games and perform charades and sing together, to familiar tunes, humorous verses that one or another of the group had composed. On these occasions there was much laughter. The men, particularly, shed their dignity and reverted to their student days" (p. 178).[15] She recalled particularly vividly a New Year's

Carol Poore

Eve spent alone with her father in about 1890, when he read Heinrich Heine's poems to her, talked of "countless things good and beautiful," and made a toast "to our fellow men" (pp. 180–81).

Publications like the *Pionier* sought in their own way to speak to all sides of life in this milieu, as we see in the following statement by its unknown editors upon the fiftieth anniversary of the calendar in 1931:

> This year the *Pionier* is appearing for the fiftieth time. Every year for half a century it came as a loyal chronicler into the homes of German working men and women. It came to entertain, gladden and teach them, and last but not least, to give them renewed courage for the hard struggle of the progressive workers' movement on the stony soil of this country. The growing popularity every year of this genuine people's calendar shows that it did justice to its tasks. From the beginning, the calendar always had as its motto: for the worker the best is just good enough! The *Pionier* never offered the shallow, trivial reading of other calendars which spoils people's taste and makes them forget how to think. Like its mother, the *NYVZ* and its weekly edition, the *New Yorker Vorwärts*, the *Pionier* always sought to educate the workers, to inspire them to fight for their class, and to enable them to understand the beautiful and the noble.
>
> If it accomplished these tasks in a modest way, it owes this to the active support and contributions of its large family, the men and women comrades. (p. 97)

Writing her memoirs after 1945, Meta Lilienthal gave an assessment of her "dear remembered world" which could just as well have applied to the *Pionier*, and the German-American radical press in general: "As, heartsick and disillusioned, I contemplate the material and spiritual wreckage of our present day world, I find it difficult to picture the kind of world my parents thought they were helping to build. But I do not feel that their ideal was a mistaken one. The social objectives for which they were striving—economic security, physical well-being and personal happiness for the great mass of mankind—still seem to me the goals most worthy of human achievement" (p. 176).

NOTES

1. For general information on the history of calendars and calendar stories in Germany, see: Gero von Wilpert, *Sachwörterbuch der Literatur*, p. 319; Ludwig Rohner, *Kalendergeschichte und Kalender*; Rudolf Schenda, *Lesestoffe der kleinen Leute* and *Volk ohne Buch*. On the history of German social democratic calendars, see Cäcilie Friedrich, ed., *Kalendergeschichten*. Most of my discussion of these calendars is based on Friedrich.

2. Michael Hamburger in Bertolt Brecht, *Tales from the Calendar*, trans. Yvonne Kapp and Michael Hamburger, p. 9.

3. Friedrich, *Kalendergeschichten*, pp. x-xi. See also the entry on calendars in *Lexikon sozialistischer deutscher Literatur*.

4. Friedrich, *Kalendergeschichten*, pp. ix-x.

5. *Lexikon sozialistischer deutscher Literatur*, pp. 268–70.

6. All volumes but 1920 of the *Pionier* are available between the Wisconsin State Historical Society and the New York Public Library.

7. The 1938 volume is available in the New York Public Library. Both the 1938 and 1939 volumes are in the Heinrich Bartel Collection of the Milwaukee County Historical Society.

8. Publishing information on the *NYVZ* is taken from the second edition of Karl J. R. Arndt and May E. Olson, *German-American Newspapers and Periodicals*.

9. An item from the socialist curiosity cabinet: Friedrich Sorge regularly sent the *Pionier* to the household of Marx for Helene Demuth, as we know from Engels's letters to Sorge of Sept. 29, 1889 and Oct. 18, 1892. Noted in Friedrich, *Kalendergeschichten*, pp. 262–63.

10. The actual effect of naturalistic depictions of misery and poverty has been hotly debated in socialist circles ever since the naturalism debate within German Social Democracy of the 1890s. See *Naturalismus-Debatte*.

11. For a more in-depth discussion of the problematic aspects of such attempts at "aesthetic education," see Peter Brückner and Gabriele Ricke, "Über die ästhetische Erziehung des Menschen"; and also Carol Poore, *German-American Socialist Literature, 1865–1900*.

12. Clara Ruge also wrote short plays which were published in the *NYVZ's* "modern library." To be found in the New York Public Library are her *On the Road: Drama in One Act; Raub: Soziales Drama;* and *Die Wiederkehr, ein Drama aus der Kriegszeit*. They are quite forgettable.

13. I was able to find one volume of the *Staats-Zeitung Kalender* from 1912 in the New York Public Library. The *Staats-Zeitung* (which still exists) was the main "bourgeois" competitor with the *NYVZ*, and the two newspapers were constantly feuding. To judge by their competing calendars, the *Pionier* was infinitely superior, as the *Staats-Zeitung* calendar contains nothing but dates and tables, with no effort at providing reading matter or an attractive layout.

14. The following works by Meta Lilienthal can be found in the New York Public Library: *Dear Remembered World; From Fireside to Factory;* and *Women of the Future*. Meta Lilienthal is also known by her married name, Meta Stern.

15. A wonderful recent evocation of this atmosphere is the scene in Margarethe von Trotta's film, "Rosa Luxemburg," of the Social Democrats' ball.

Ruth Seifert

Women's Pages in the German-American Radical Press, 1900–1914: The Debate on Socialism, Emancipation, and the Suffrage

In 1900, the *New Yorker Volkszeitung* (*NYVZ*) introduced a special "women's corner," particularly addressed to the wives of German workers and working women. Soon the women's corner expanded to become a women's page published weekly in the Sunday supplement of the *NYVZ*. The reason for establishing that page had less to do with concern for women than with the Socialist party's realization that it was hardly possible to build a viable cultural and organizational network among workers without the support and active engagement of women. The women's corner was to give ideological coaching to women, to make them familiar with socialist theory in general and the socialist position on the "woman question" in particular.

The belief that more attention to the woman question was necessary gained ground in the social democratic movement after the turn of the century. In Germany, the circulation of the *Gleichheit*, a social democratic monthly on women's issues read primarily by female functionaries, rose steadily from 4,000 in 1900 to 112,000 in 1913.[1] In New York by 1914, all but one of the foreign-language socialist newspapers had a women's page. Only the Finnish socialists of New York voiced the opinion that for them a women's page was anachronistic.[2] The *NYVZ* started a page edited by Johanna Greie-Cramer, who made it her explicit aim to familiarize women with socialist class theory. Greie-Cramer, too, was convinced that the socialist movement could not do without the consent and active engagement of working-class women. Moreover, some socialists, men as well as women, saw that gender conflicts disturbed the unity of the working class and that ideological efforts were necessary to tackle that problem.[3]

From the viewpoint of the Social Democratic party of Germany (SPD) these ideological efforts were aimed not so much at integrating feminism into socialism but at convincing women of the overriding importance of the class struggle.[4] The Socialist Labor party as well as the German-American socialists ascribed a low priority to female concerns.[5] In spite of sympathies for the feminist cause, Johanna Greie-Cramer, just like Clara Zetkin in Germany, always put the class struggle before the gender struggle and resisted the enticements of the bourgeois women's movement. "The modern proletarian woman," she instructed her readers, "has no reason to get enthusiastic about the emancipatory endeavors of the world of the bourgeois woman. However, under certain circumstances, and if her own class interest is not affected, she will stand up for these demands, too, because it is a question of justice and equity."[6] Her view of that problem was quite in accord with the party's official stance on the woman question: "the central theme of the women's struggle must not be interpreted as being directed against men, but rather it should include men, for the same forces which repress and tyrannize men keep women in bondage."[7]

As the women's page developed, though, it became clear that there was no uniform or generally agreed upon point of view on the woman question within the German-American socialist movement. This was partially due to the ideological situation to which German-Americans were exposed. In Germany, the Social Democrats were virtually the only large movement that had the power to make their demands for gender equality heard. The mainstream of the bourgeois women's movement in Germany was conservative, with only a small radical wing. The situation was different in the United States.[8] Socialist women in New York became acquainted with progressivism, feminist radicalism, anarchism, and, most important, the suffrage movement. These movements advanced specific demands other than those the Socialist party deemed the most essential. Even though the editorial staff of the women's page regularly was recruited from class-conscious socialists, these women were also exposed to—and often fascinated by—the ideas and the personalities of the suffrage movement. While Greie-Cramer adhered to the opinion that the woman question was a secondary problem that would be resolved by the victory of the working class and that any cooperation with the bourgeois women's movement was a cardinal mistake, other editors and correspondents of the women's page did not share that viewpoint totally. Thus, the

NYVZ's women's page was never merely an instrument of instruction, but became a forum for discussion and negotiations about discourses of gender relations, women's issues, and life-styles.

In that respect, the women's pages in German-American papers differed greatly from comparable publications of the SPD, where neither controversies nor dissenting positions were frequently heard. In Germany, attempts to keep so-called bourgeois feminism at a proper distance were successful.[9] There, topics of gender that could not be integrated into the discussion of the class struggle were banned from official discourse as of only "private" interest.[10] In 1910, Meta Stern, daughter of the German-American freethinker Auguste Lilienthal and Greie-Cramer's successor as editor of the "women's corner" of the *NYVZ*, published an article on New York socialist women in the *Gleichheit*. In carefully chosen, nonprovocative words, she pointed out that the American situation was different from the German: "Here the position of socialist women towards the bourgeois women's movement is still an open question, there are no sharp demarcations. Socialist women support the women's movement as long as they do not have to give up socialist principles."[11]

The women's page of the *NYVZ* published articles on a variety of topics which were considered to be of interest to women. In general, there was one editorial written by a member of the staff, and articles were frequently taken from the *Gleichheit* and other social democratic publications in Germany. The women's page also published contributions taken from the *Neue Generation*, the organ of the Bund für Mutterschutz (Association for Mothers' Protection), the moral reform movement founded by the liberal Helene Stöcker. Translations from other foreign-language women's pages were fairly common. As the American suffrage movement became increasingly important, the women's page also included articles taken from the *Progressive Woman*, a socialist women's publication loosely affiliated with the Socialist party, and the *Woman's Journal*, the official organ of the national suffrage movement. Articles by Charlotte Perkins Gilman, a leading feminist intellectual of her generation and author of *Women and Economics*, were printed with editorial approval by 1910.

The women's page also invited and published letters by readers. In the months just after the page was started, a flood of letters enthusiastically welcoming the women's page reached the editors. Women pointed out that the women's page was the first thing they read when they received the *NYVZ*, and that they were particularly eager to read the letters to the editors to learn about the lives of other women.[12] These letters are a unique source for the historian, giving insights into the concerns of rank-and-file German-American working-class women that are not otherwise readily available. They show that among at least some of these women the need to discuss the gender situation was overwhelming. Women correspondents also tried to make sense of the social and cultural problems they faced and often were not content with the characterizations of social issues offered to them by the socialist movement. Many were not prepared to view the world merely through the perspective of class theory; that they should fight for socialism first and for female concerns later did not make sense to them.

In the course of time, a gender-based analysis of social and everyday problems became increasingly important for the editorial staff of the women's page as well as for rank-and-file American socialist women. These discourses on the gender struggle that were new to the socialist movement were never antisocialist.[13] The destructiveness of class society was an immediate experience of most women involved in political life. At the same time, however, they saw the necessity of changing or at least reforming gender relations. This meant introducing other topics into the women's page than those the party, or even the editorial staff, preferred. The letters reveal that these working- and lower-middle-class women expressed their experiences as much in terms of gender as in terms of class. Women carried on discussions in letters to the *NYVZ*, trying to create a female perspective on such concerns as abortion, unhappy marriages, or prostitution that were tied up in a hegemonic male discourse. A vivid discussion among female readers on free love and marriage—rather an anarchist than a socialist topic—was carried on in 1901, and, not being political in the classical sense, was at first not wholeheartedly welcomed by the *NYVZ* or by Greie-Cramer. Both the female and the male readers' response to that topic was so strong, however, that for a short time the discussion was even carried into the "Löwenrachen," the "general" page for letters to the editor, which had been almost exclusively the domain of male readers. In general, the topics discussed in the "Löwenrachen" were not related to those on the women's page, but typically were questions of agitation, union organization, and general politics. For the *NYVZ*, questions of gender relations were a female topic and a female problem, not considered to be of great interest for male readers.

The "Löwenrachen" was different from the women's page in another way: male contributors to the "Löwenrachen" had no problem signing their letters with their entire name, while the women who sent letters to the women's page either signed with their initials or merely called themselves "a working woman," "a socialist woman" or "a German woman." Often they doubted their own capabilities and apologized for their "dumb writing" or "deficient thinking," invoking the notorious female lack of self-assurance and self-esteem.

Attempts on the part of Greie-Cramer to lead the audience back to the "actual" problem, zealously emphasizing the economic basis of female hardship, caused unrest among German-American social- ist women. As early as September 1900, there were complaints that women's letters to the column "For Women" were ignored and that the editor of the *NYVZ* should feel obliged "to lend a helping hand" to women, "since the existence of the women's corner is very helpful to our cause." [14] Yet, in 1903, the *NYVZ* printed fewer and fewer letters ad- dressed to the women's page and by 1904 the letters had—with just a few exceptions—disappeared. The articles presented in "For Women" in 1904 were almost exclusively written by men and had such titles as "Baby's Gymnastics," "On Fairy Tales," "Children and Poetry," or "What to Do against Coarse Skin." Articles on the wives of prominent socialist men were popular now, portraying the hard-working, wise, and practical homemaker creating a cosy home for husband and chil- dren and endowing him with motherly care.[15] There were no hints in the newspaper as to discussions or conflicts in the editorial staff on this policy. After the editors reduced the scope of the women's page, reports on the activities of the women's branches in New York reveal that there were obstinate attempts on the part of socialist women's branches to reactivate it. They had regular meetings with the editorial staff of the *NYVZ* to negotiate the conditions for resuming the page. By fall 1906 their efforts were successful. The women's page was re- sumed under the direction of Meta Stern (in the years to come she wrote under the pseudonym of "Hebe"), who, in her first editorial, made clear what her intentions were: "From today on, this part of our newspaper belongs to us women in a more defined sense than before. It is to represent the interest of working-class women, in particular, socialist working-class women." [16]

Between the turn of the century and the beginning of World War I, the conflicts fought on the women's page were characterized by a spe- cific kind of ambivalence about an explicit dedication to female emanci- pation, an implicit clinging to patriarchal prerogatives, and the attempt to reconcile these positions with socialist thought.[17] Women editors and readers tried forcefully to write feminist demands into socialist theory and to make the movement accept their claims. As the Ameri- can women's movement grew stronger and fascinated both the editors of the women's page and its readers, the necessity to deal with feminist demands in the socialist press became more acute. Thus, the women's page was to some extent successful in introducing gender-related topics into the German-American socialists' discourse in America.

This was clearly an effect of exposure to the American gender situation. Before the end of the nineteenth century, special women's pages were not known in the German-American labor press, but discourses on woman and definitions of femininity abounded.[18] These articles primarily expressed the irritation of German-born men about the situation with which they were confronted in the United States. Comparisons made between the situation in the new home and the old country played an important role in the discussions of gender relations carried on in the German-American socialist press. As the immigrants were confronted with a gender situation different from that in the German Reich, their reaction to the American situation was ambivalent and underwent changes in the course of time. Whereas in the United States "the 1880s and 1890s saw the emergence of a novel social and political phenomenon—the New Woman,"[19] this kind of social and political awakening of women did not take place in Germany before the 1920s, when a "social earthquake" in the wake of World War I brought about a drastic change in gender relations.[20]

Before World War I, female self-assertion or even militance was neither common nor acceptable to German-American socialists in their everyday culture.[21] Even though Bebel's book *Woman and Socialism* was published in the United States in 1883, its impact on the treatment of the woman question in the socialist movement seems to have been negligible.[22] In spite of theoretical lip service paid to women's emancipation, German-American socialists still cherished their traditional domestic life. According to a recent study, the Italian and Jewish ethnic cultures in America were the most patriarchal of the European immigrant groups,[23] but the German-American situation appears to have been quite similar. Time and again, there are hints in the German-American newspapers about the "cheekiness" and "impertinence" of American women and the "meekness" of American men. When talking about gender relations in their new home, words like "emancipation," "liberation," and "female consciousness" were not used in the socialist press. American gender relations were negatively contrasted to the neatness of the German ethnic setting, where patriarchal values still guaranteed an idyllic orderliness in marriage and family life—at least from a male point of view. In that respect, German-American socialists were much in accord with their bourgeois counterparts who "endorsed the myth that theirs was the only land where marriage was holy."[24]

When trying to keep women in their place and encourage men to defend their hegemonic position, socialist newspapers worked with images of "true womanhood" and expressed contempt for so-called male subservience. When reporting that a female cyclist defended herself against verbal harassment by hitting a man in the face, the *Chicagoer Arbeiterzeitung* commented that the man took the "humiliation" as they called it "with the usual American submissiveness toward everything [*sic*] that wears an apron or a petticoat." Moreover, he had to suffer derision from passersby, and, "to top it all," as the *Chicagoer Arbeiterzeitung* commented, even a policeman who was consulted "decided that the young lady was right."[25]

In an article entitled "The New Woman," the *Chicagoer Arbeiterzeitung* defined their idea of what she is supposed to be, drawing a line between the liberated "bourgeois American" and the socialist "new woman": "The monster, which brainless journalists have proclaimed as the 'new woman,' in reality has nothing to do with that type of woman." Whereas in their opinion bourgeois women were a "mixture of falseness, coquetry and foolishness," the middle-class and the proletarian woman were thought to be different. These women had learned trades "to be able to make a living on [their] own." Thus, the *Chicagoer Arbeiterzeitung* claimed, "it is no longer necessary for her to play the doll, she stands independently at the side of the man and can possibly free herself from his despotism, because she can make it alone."[26]

The *NYVZ* adopted a similar position in 1896, pointing out that "the 'New Woman's Movement' started with the introduction of bloomers and has not advanced much further during the past century . . . whereas working women have gained many a nice success" and are thus also distinguished from the "idle woman world" of the bourgeoisie.[27] Obviously, only *wage work* distinguished the "new woman" from "the old doll" in the view of the German-American labor press. In reality this meant a tremendous double burden for women, since their responsibility for housework was by no means lessened by these developments. Apart from that, they were to subscribe to the official discourse by maintaining all "womanly characteristics."[28] These views on women changed drastically when women themselves got a chance to voice their opinions on the women's page of the *NYVZ*. Many contributors to the women's page were well aware of the gains the "new woman" had made in the United States. To be sure, socialist women were eager to point out that it was only possible to be a "new woman" with a certain level of education and amount of income. Nevertheless they comment approvingly on a type of woman "for which the English language has already found a new name . . . : 'Bachelor Girl.' The

Bachelor Girl does not consider her life a failure. . . . Her work satisfies her. . . . Even without a husband, she has a home. Had the women's movement achieved nothing but this change in the position of the unmarried woman, just this would already have been tremendous progress."[29]

While most women welcomed the development of gender relations in the United States that granted more independence to them, many German-American men were less enthusiastic about the differences they perceived. In a letter to the women's page, Robert Uhlig from Trinidad, Colorado, expressed his irritation about a certain weakening of traditional gender arrangements in the United States that obviously gave more independence and leeway to women than he was prepared to accept. He contrasted the sensible German wife with the unruly and unreasonable American woman:

> American women yell a lot, while German women are quiet and do their work; it is clear that our German comrades know what they want and cannot learn anything from our suffragists. . . . In the United States, women didn't even fight for the suffrage. Rather, the men gave it to them, because they hoped that then more women would settle in the states in question. . . . And this suffrage movement has had such great effect that today there is hardly any opposition to it. American men and women are the most stupid, for it is here that prostitution has spread more than anywhere else. Nowhere have I seen so many unmarried women, even though there is a surplus of men.[30]

Uhlig's views did not go unchallenged. The editors of the women's page commented on his letter tersely and ironically, contending that "our correspondent's lack of information is remarkable. The granting of the suffrage in Colorado was preceded by a tremendous agitation campaign. The Suffrage Association there was one of the strongest."[31] The editorial staff was increasingly tired of having to deal with certain male arguments. These women had immersed themselves in socialist theory and they were familiar with both anarchist thought and the feminist ideas of the American women's movement. In addition, they could draw on their own experiences as women in a male-dominated movement.[32]

German-American feminists' knowledge and ability to reflect profitably on their own situation stood in stark contrast to their lack of power. At a time when they had discussed and analyzed woman's situation among themselves, they had to deal with self-confident men whose intellectual prowess may have been weaker but who could enforce their will on the level of the debate. When answering a male reader who had insisted on the naturalness of conventional gender arrangements, the editors of the women's page called his ideas "weird opinions," pointing out that they were "terribly tired, after having refuted the same ancient arguments a thousand times, to have to refute them 1001 times, particularly for someone who claims to be a socialist." Resignedly, they recommended that he "diligently read the women's page and study Bebel's book *Woman and Socialism*."[33]

Until 1908 the suffrage movement was mentioned time and again on the women's page. Female suffrage was a long-standing demand of the Social Democrats and part of their platform in Germany. In October 1901 the Social Democratic Women's Association of New York had passed a resolution demanding the suffrage for women.[34] In 1903 the central committee of the Social Democratic Women's Association decided "to start an energetic agitation for women's suffrage."[35] But although the demand for women's suffrage was never questioned, it was not considered to be of outstanding importance. This was reflected in attitudes toward suffrage among the rank and file as well as in the various socialist organizations. Female functionaries and agitators alike complained of working women's indifference toward suffrage and politics in general, but also of the remarkable lack of willingness on the part of the men to allow women to participate in political life.[36] Further, the party did not even attach much importance to any agitation among women.

This situation changed dramatically around 1908, when the American suffrage movement gained impetus and when it was successful in attracting the interest of working women to a larger extent than did the socialist movement itself. As a consequence, the years before World War I saw suffrage emerge as a major political issue in the socialist movement. What has been noted for American socialist women was true for German-Americans, too: "Only when the suffrage movement threatened to entice females away from the party, and pit the wives of socialists against their husbands," did a greater interest in agitating among women develop.[37] The women's page pleaded, "We have to reach the masses of working women whom we tend to lose to the suffrage movement. The women's movement must be taken seriously."[38]

From 1908 on, the suffrage question became the most important single issue discussed on the women's page. The suffrage movements of all foreign countries and American states were covered extensively and approvingly. Suffrage, however, carried in its wake other, no less important, problems for the socialist movement. On the one hand, it was closely connected with general theoretical judgment of the bourgeois women's movement and the tactical question of how socialists should behave toward it. On the other hand, it was tied up with the long-neglected question of suffrage agitation among working women.

German-American socialists were stirred by these developments. First, there was the danger of losing working women to the suffrage movement. Moreover, as more states granted suffrage, it became clear that universal suffrage was about to come and that working women would be potential voters. By 1913, suffrage was no longer a side-show for socialists. Instead, party activists felt that one of the "most urgent tasks of socialist agitation" was to drive home to proletarian women the outstanding importance of female suffrage for the socialist cause. "Now it was held that proletarian women must not be taken by surprise by the new rights and duties which the conquest of female suffrage bestows upon them. . . . They must be educated to realize the full importance of this weapon, which suffrage puts in their hands."[39] Only when suffrage seemed close at hand did the party ascribe so much importance to women.

One way of trying to make working women stick to the cause was the attempt to enforce party discipline. In 1910, after lengthy discussions had been carried on in the women's page, an "open letter to a young socialist" was published. A young German woman had inquired if membership in the Suffrage Association was compatible with membership in the Socialist party. This young socialist explained that she had arrived at the conviction that the woman question was the most compelling issue of the present time. The women's page answered with an open letter because, as they claimed, "this is not a personal matter: Lately many socialist women have grappled with this problem and thus a public discussion is desirable." The answer was that participation in the suffrage movement was superfluous for a socialist woman, because the Socialist party was itself the largest pro-suffrage party. The young woman was asked to reserve all her energy for socialist agitation, because her special interest in the woman question obliged her to dedicate herself to the socialist movement and to work for women's suffrage as a socialist.[40]

Socialist women, however, did not seem to be very impressed by attempts to discredit the suffrage movement and to lure them away from it. Party discipline on the woman question failed to hold German-American women.[41] Within the editorial staff of the women's page, both theoretical positions—one propagating the "correct," i.e., orthodox socialist view of the woman question, the other pleading for cooperation with bourgeois women—coexisted. Whereas agreement grew within the socialist movement that increased agitational efforts were necessary so that the socialist movement would not be damaged considerably by the exodus of working-class women, the editorial staff of the women's page remained split over questions of strategy and tactics in dealing with the women's movement.

The faction of feminist socialists gained ground, however. An article published in 1909 brushed away "the old saw according to which the woman question could be solved together with the social question"[42] and asserted that until a short time ago, the Socialist party had not even displayed any serious interest in women's suffrage and women's political emancipation. Another article lavished praise on the women of the *American Suffragette* (which spoke for the radical wing of the suffragists) and cheered the American tour of suffragists Emmeline Pankhurst and Dora Montefiori, describing them as "two gorgeous women."[43] Teresa Malkiel, garment worker, socialist organizer, and columnist of the women's page, commented that "socialist women, too, are full of admiration for Pankhurst. However, they do not forget that she completely neglects the economic slavery of both men and women."[44]

Opinions expressing overt sympathy or solidarity with the women's movement were anything but the exception on the women's page; one unsigned article (probably written by Meta Stern) claimed that the position held by the SPD in Germany should not be adopted because "in the United States there is actually only *one* women's movement. . . . In the United States things are different from England, different from Germany, probably different from any other European country. First of all, here no strict demarcations can be drawn between a bourgeois and a proletarian women's movement. In its beginnings, the American women's movement was completely bourgeois: But during the last couple of years it has had great success among working women and this is the very reason why it has grown so strong. Many working women support the women's movement."[45]

Even Auguste Lilienthal, by that time over seventy, interjected a furious letter into the discussion, calling socialists who opposed co-operation with bourgeois women "old, fossilized and orthodox." She ridiculed the idea of "pure and undiluted socialism"—while at the same time emphasizing her devotion to the socialist idea.[46] This letter provoked letters by other women who emphatically agreed with her. One of them, Frances Schmeling, wrote: "I am a socialist and I will remain one. But I will fight for women's suffrage till my last drop of blood. I think we should not build a Chinese Wall around us, but fight along with all women all over the world for our political liberties, because only united will we win."[47]

The overwhelming majority of socialist women on the editorial staff as well as among the rank and file shared this opposition to strict separation from bourgeois women. They thought that it was their duty "to work for the achievement of female suffrage and to work hand in hand with the women of other classes for at least part of the day."[48] This faction characteristically was represented by women who spoke English and who had connections with English-speaking socialists and feminists. But for the socialist hard-liners any cooperation with bourgeois women was a major ideological mistake. This faction was headed by Greie-Cramer, Charlotte Schneppe, and Dr. Anna Ingermann. Julie Romm, who became editor of the women's page in 1911, also seems to have been closer to this group than to the feminist sympathizers even though her position was not as defined as that of the others.[49] Ludwig Lore, a central figure in this camp, was a German socialist who had immigrated in 1905 and later became editor of the *NYVZ*.[50] Between 1905 and the beginning of World War I, Lore made himself a specialist on the woman question among German-American socialists. He agitated untiringly in the German-American women's branches of the New York area, where he made speeches on various issues.

The faction centered on Greie-Cramer and Lore vehemently opposed the idea of an autonomous feminist cause and publicly disapproved of the position of the National Women's Committee.[51] In their opinion "these women do not want to and cannot understand that we have to make a precise and clean class division. . . . Among the comrades who are in the foreground now, because they speak English and because the movement must and is supposed to be 'English' the strangest opinions are rampant. In any case, they do not sufficiently emphasize the class struggle."[52] This view found fewer and fewer followers among the rank and file; columnists and readers alike increasingly found it absurd and saw advantages in working together with bourgeois suffragists. "Comrade Lore always has letters at hand which he cites," a "socialist woman" wrote to the page. "He claims that it was a woman who wrote him insisting that we should only work with the Party. Well, but if the Party does not do anything? Should we then just sit down and wait? . . . Here, we do not yet have a proletarian women's movement. . . . We should not be so fanatical but instead follow up good developments wherever they occur. Sisters, seize any opportunity to agitate, also among bourgeois women."[53]

During a conference called by the Women's Committee of Local New York, Lore himself saw no problem in agreeing with a bourgeois man.[54] Four men—Morris Hillquit, Algernon Lee, Ludwig Lore, and Robert Bruere, debated the merits of socialist suffrage clubs. Hillquit and Lee were in favor of them, but Lore sided with upper-class urban reformer and union supporter Robert Bruere—after having put much effort into convincing socialist women that any kind of cooperation with bourgeois women was harmful to the movement.[55] It is interesting to note that this kind of public behavior by a socialist man did not require any explanation.

Bourgeois women, meanwhile, worked toward an accommodation with socialist women and made use of the socialist press. When the National-American Woman Suffrage Association (NAWSA) sent a message to the convention of the Socialist Women's Society, it was published on the women's page.[56] In a letter signed by Dr. Anna Howard Shaw, president of NAWSA, Ella Hawley Crossett, president of the New York State Suffrage Association, and Ida Husted Harper, chairwoman of the National Press Committee of NAWSA, the suffragists congratulated socialist women on the platform of the Socialist party and asked for their cooperation in the great movement that was underway.[57]

The cooperation between socialist and suffragist women reached a peak in 1909 during the shirtwaist-makers' strike in New York. Suffragists concerned with the condition of working women joined the Women's Trade Union League and helped organize the strike. The shops went on strike in September 1909 and strikers were supported with money and publicity by bourgeois women. During a meeting called by Alva Smith Belmont, Mary Averell Harriman, and Anne Morgan at the Colony Club, strikers presented their case. Mrs. Belmont and Anna Howard Shaw spoke at a huge rally in New York's Hippodrome, for which Mrs. Belmont paid the bill.[58] Ironically, however, the women's page did not mention the involvement of bourgeois women in the strike. Almost a year passed before the women's page referred to the shirtwaist-makers' strike again, remarking that during a conference in the Labor Temple, socialist women had voted overwhelmingly against cooperation with bourgeois women. "However," the women's page continued, "a couple of days after the stormy conference socialist women organized a huge rally for the striking shirtwaist-makers together with bourgeois women of all shades. Two months later, socialist women invited all of the bourgeois suffrage associations of New York to their great suffrage demonstration in Carnegie Hall. . . . A couple of months later, bourgeois suffragists held a rally in Union Square and invited all socialist women. They accepted the invitation and participated with their banner and a socialist woman presented a socialist speech from the platform of a bourgeois women's association."[59]

German-American socialists got increasingly worried about losing working women to the feminist cause. In the winter of 1910 the German Agitation Committee for Women was reorganized and started holding rallies aimed at agitating and organizing working women. Also in 1910 the women's page started a campaign addressed to the readers. It ran under the heading, "How can we reach working-class women?" and invited suggestions and new ideas for agitation among German-American working-class women. One explicit aim was to reach married women, who were considered to be completely submerged in home and family. "Occupied with the eternal sorrows and strife," the women's page proclaimed, "the homemaker's intellect withers away completely."[60] A couple of months before, this very discussion had taken place in the "Löwenrachen." Now an agitation campaign was started in the socialist press; pamphlets addressed to women were published in all socialist papers. The first one, which appeared on the women's page of the *NYVZ* in January 1911, was written by Teresa Malkiel and entitled "To the Working Woman."[61] This article appealed to the working woman exclusively as a class subject and did not have any feminist implications.

Readers also participated actively in the discussion of how to reach working women. German-American women tried to give advice on how to deal with female political apathy in letters to the women's page. Suggestions included the increased distribution of leaflets, visiting housewives at home, talking to them as woman to woman, and demanding that at least every fortnight meetings should be called exclusively for women and girls.[62] Some letters pointed out that the special situation of women in a class-based and sexist society made smooth and easy alliances impossible. In the opinion of one correspondent, the greatest hindrance for women to take part in political life was the socialist husband. She observed that even though socialist men were prepared to go to extremes to defend their own rights, they saw women primarily as housewives and as mothers of small children. She concluded, "My opinion is: Women have to defend their rights on their own and have to fight. They, too, have to go to the extreme to find out the truth."[63] Another reader agreed that men did not really want women as fighting comrades in the movement, not least, she claimed, because then it would become more difficult for men "to enrich their knowledge in the tavern with a couple of drinks."[64] The fact that often socialist men were almost hostile to the women's cause was also revealed by a report of a socialist woman on a German local's meeting when a petition on suffrage was discussed. Rejecting a plea addressed to the men to help in distributing the petition, one comrade got up asking "whether or not we are in a local of the Socialist party here or in a philanthropic association supporting the weak and helpless."[65] The women's page cited this kind of behavior as another bad example of the conduct of male comrades and pleaded for a more unified class consciousness.

Given these conditions, the discussion on how to reach the working woman proved difficult. It was continued on the women's page for about two years until 1913. Finally it was openly acknowledged that it had become necessary for the party to offer something to socialist women activists, for the women's movement had become more and more attractive. The socialist movement had to address the question of its relationship to the suffrage movement more seriously and thoroughly. One obstacle in women's agitation, the women's page claimed, was "our indefinite, insecure, and inconsistent attitude toward other, nonsocialist women's organizations." "The lack of unity, the inconsistency and indifference within the party itself regarding women's agitation" was deplored.[66] Socialist women increasingly solved the problem on their own, without recourse to the party's stance. They held offices in the Socialist party while at the same time being active in the suffrage movement side by side with bourgeois women. They also supported the Women's Trade Union League. Still, the women's page admitted, these women were as good comrades as any.

These developments also influenced relations between German and American socialists and created conflict between German-American and English-speaking sections on questions of suffrage and women's agitation. In this conflict, starting around 1911, the women's page retreated from its one-time independent and defiant position back to a more orthodox one. To be sure, the women's page still published articles advocating feminist positions. One example is the lengthy contribution by Esther Sinovieva-Deutsch in 1913 entitled "Women's Clubs and Professional Associations," which militantly and intelligently advocated an autonomous women's struggle.[67] Also, they reported on the activities and standpoint of both the German sections and the English-speaking ones. However, the editorial staff now seemed to avoid open discussion and seemed to favor the orthodox stance.

Tensions peaked when no consensus could be reached on the participation of German speakers during "Woman's Day" in February 1912. The official explanation for not accepting German-American speakers was that they would not be understood by everyone. As a consequence, German-American women held their own rally. The women's page claimed that there was absolutely no reason to have so many English-speaking contributors, and that the Socialist Women's

Committee had made a tremendous mistake and weakened the movement by excluding German-American speakers. Nevertheless, until World War I, Woman's Day was never again a joint project. The English-speaking branches held their Woman's Day; a bloc composed of German, Bohemian, and Hungarian women rallied separately. The women's page editors deemed this development "unfortunate" but finally allowed that even though the branches did not march together, they intended to strike together.[68]

Dissent on theoretical positions had its effect on all levels of socialist organization. English and German women's agitation committees split their activities, and German-American women now generally cooperated with Bohemian and Hungarian branches. The German Women's Agitation Committee was eager to point out that they did not have any connections to the Women's Agitation Committee of Local New York, and that they concentrated on German women exclusively.[69] Whereas the National Women's Committee was now in turn accused by the *NYVZ* of displaying insufficient tolerance toward other language branches, there were countercharges that German-American women's branches were not open enough toward other positions.[70] Thus, the gap on the woman question between German-American and other American socialists widened. German-American women who had tried to unify socialist and feminist positions tended to drift into English-speaking groups. In early 1913 Meta Stern, at one time chief editor of the woman's page, became secretary of the English-speaking Women's Committee of Local New York.[71] Teresa Malkiel, too, seems to have contributed more now to the *Call* than to the *NYVZ*, and when the women's page took over one of Malkiel's articles from the *Call* in 1914, it did so commenting that the editors did not "quite agree with Malkiel's conclusions"[72] that women were better socialists than men. Malkiel had contended that in the socialist movement for women, history repeated itself: "As long as agitation was exclusively up to the men, we constantly had to fight a deficit. . . . But not now, since women have taken over. . . . They first and foremost think of the work that has to be done. . . . Recently they have been called the live wires of the movement and this is what they are."[73]

The women's page of the *NYVZ* did not systematically pursue the discussion of theoretical differences over the woman question. To be sure, time and again articles were printed advocating a socialist-feminist position. However, the accompanying comments always included a rejection of that position. Even though the problem could not be ignored altogether, it became clear that within the editorial staff a more orthodox line had won out again. So, the debate on how to reach working women was carried on without explicit reference to the problems emphasized by feminist-oriented women. As Greie-Cramer had done before,[74] the staff now pursued a policy sympathetic to the behavior of male socialists. To be sure, there were men whose conduct toward women was questionable, the argument went, but one should not forget that men were in a quandary, too. One columnist pointed out that sometimes socialist men would like to act differently but could not do so due to external coercion. Coercion was defined as the production process on the one hand and gender traditions, which supposedly weighed heavily on men, on the other. The question of power relations between men and women was simply not posed in this argument. Instead, men were portrayed as the helpless victims of a tradition that accidentally ascribed a privileged position to them. Women's double work burden was not discussed. The possibility for change was projected into the future; as time went on, it was hoped, things would gradually change and equality would come.[75]

Action was again called for when woman suffrage for the state of New York was imminent. By 1913 nine states had incorporated suffrage into their constitutions. For the NYVZ this was reason enough to dedicate an entire extra page to the question of how the socialist movement should react. It would be "depressing and humiliating" if suffrage were granted in New York and socialist women behaved indifferently.[76] Suffrage was primarily welcomed because it was deemed to be a decisive instrument in the class struggle. Therefore, the NYVZ could without ideological problems support a rally of all socialist women in Greater New York presided over by Teresa Malkiel. It was held at the Labor Temple in March 1913, primarily for preparing foreign-born women for their naturalization. There was consensus that as many foreign working-class women as possible should be reached to ensure their participation in the next elections. In view of the overall importance of this issue for the socialist movement, men were also called on to participate. The naturalization campaign was supported by all branches and filled the women's pages of the NYVZ. In 1914, Malkiel, in addition to her other tasks, started to work as an unpaid agitator for women's suffrage[77] and soon an agitation committee was formed consisting of Rose Schneidermann, Anna Ingermann, Meta Stern, Pauline Newman, and others to raise money for another socialist suffrage campaign.[78]

By now, however, World War I had started and even though suffrage was still an important topic on the women's page, events in Europe increasingly preoccupied German-American socialists. For many German-Americans, men as well as women, who still had relatives and friends in the German Reich, political developments in their new home became secondary to the war in the old country. "The European war has thrown a burning flame into our ranks," the women's page stated, "and has temporarily paralyzed our interest in the suffrage question."[79] As distinct from the "Löwenrachen," the women's page refrained from any overt political comments. Whereas the "Löwenrachen" vehemently opposed support for war credits on the part of the Majority Socialists in Germany, the women's page primarily dealt with the plight of the civilian population and the human consequences of the war. It also reflected on the emotional importance of European developments for German-Americans. "The best we have to offer, especially our materialist philosophy, developed on German soil," the women's page wrote, "now, all of a sudden, all connections are temporarily cut. . . . We are groping about in the dark, seizing any bit of unproven news."[80]

The women's page adopted a pacifist-feminist standpoint. In discussing radical German feminists and leftists Anita Augspurg and Lida Heymann as well as American pacifists Ellen Key and Carrie Chapman-Catt, it pointed out that bourgeois women, too, worked for international solidarity and passionately condemned the war.[81] An article by Meta Stern called "Fight the War" summed up this position, claiming that the women of this world were no enemies to each other and that all women had a historical mission to complete, which would bring about a world without wars.[82] German-American socialists continued to conduct suffrage agitation and rallies, but when suffrage finally was granted in the state of New York, for German-American socialists it was overshadowed by the World War, which for them posed a major political and emotional problem.

NOTES

1. Annik Mahaim, Alix Holt, and Jacqueline Heinen, *Frauen und Arbeiterbewegung*, p. 66.

2. In 1914 Teresa Malkiel in a letter to socialist women's groups of New York pointed out the necessity to reserve a page for women in their newspapers. The Finnish women responded that they did not consider a women's page necessary, since they had been working together with men in locals for some period of time. *NYVZ*, May 9, 1915.

3. See, e.g., *NYVZ*, Mar. 15, 1903, when it was also stated that "in the working class's great struggle for emancipation, one can by no means do without the active participation of women."

4. Richard Evans points out that Social Democracy changed from a workers' movement to a family movement, making it necessary to extend social demo-

cratic thought from men to all members of the family (*Sozialdemokratie und Frauenemanzipation*, p. 235).

5. Catherine Clinton, *Other Civil War*, p. 189.

6. *NYVZ*, Jan. 21, Mar. 16, 1902.

7. *NYVZ*, Mar. 16, 1902.

8. For the various feminist positions of the time see June Sochen, *Movers and Shakers*, pp. 31–95.

9. Jean Quataert, "German Socialist Women's Movement," pp. 286f.

10. As late as 1920, Henriette Fürth confirmed in the *Gleichheit* that sexual behavior was "the most private affair of any person," thus banning sexuality from the realm of politics (30, July 17, 1920).

11. Meta Stern is also known as Meta Lilienthal. *Gleichheit*, 7, 1910, p. 111.

12. For example, *NYVZ*, May 3, 1905.

13. The term "discourse" is here meant in the Foucauldian sense, a "policy of speech" that selects what is or is not talked about in a given culture. Foucault assumes that power produces discourses and that there is no knowledge that is not constituted within power relations. See Jeffrey Weeks, "Foucault for Historians," p. 111.

14. *NYVZ*, Sept. 16, 1900.

15. See the portrait of Sybille Hess, wife of Moses Hess, in *NYVZ*, Feb. 28, 1904.

16. *NYVZ*, Oct. 7, 1906.

17. On a reduced scale, these contradictions also occupied the German Socialists. Here, a position won out that has been called the "inner conservatism of socialist emancipation theory," meaning the acceptance of bourgeois family ideology and the associated ideal of woman. The idealization of petit bourgeois family life was also characteristic for leading socialist women in Germany. See Birgit Koehn, Helga Milz, et al., "Verlässliche Frauenspersonen und Luxusdamen," pp. 160–202. Jean Quataert also points out the "delicacy" with which female leaders in Germany approached family life and the apparent fear to tackle that topic (*Reluctant Feminists*), p. 158.

18. Ruth Seifert, "Portrayal of Women in the German-American Labor Movement."

19. Carroll Smith-Rosenberg, *Disorderly Conduct*, p. 176.

20. Atina Grossmann, *New Woman*. See also Manes Sperber, *Vergebliche Warnung*, p. 213.

21. This was quite similar to the situation of social democratic women in Germany. Jean Quataert points out that antifeminism in the rank and file and by party functionaries was often deplored by socialist women, since "traditional ideals partially frustrated socialist women's efforts to create a new consciousness of the equal worth of males and females." This was, however, not seriously tackled "until the post-World War I period and later." Only then "did socialist women clearly recognize and lament this gap." Quataert, "German Socialist Women's Movement," pp. 419, 417.

22. When discussing Bebel's merits in respect to the so-called woman ques-

tion, it should be noted that more recent interpretations suggest that Bebel's "Woman" was primarily an attempt to establish male hegemony in an unstable proletarian context, where the discourses on women of the bourgeois culture had become dysfunctional. See Roswitha Burgard and Gaby Carsten, *Die Märchenonkel der Frauenfrage*, and Ruth Seifert, "Bebel Revisited."

23. Mary P. Ryan, *Womanhood in America*, p. 169.

24. Priscilla Robertson, *Experience of Women*, p. 200.

25. *Chicagoer Arbeiterzeitung*, Sept. 9, 1895.

26. *Chicagoer Arbeiterzeitung*, Sept. 9, 1895.

27. *Chicagoer Arbeiterzeitung*, Mar. 8, 1896.

28. In Germany, the Social Democrat Edmund Fischer as late as 1905 had advocated a "wife-mother-housekeeper" model in a socialist framework that was not fundamentally challenged by socialist women, who, on the whole, "concentrated on the goal of furthering the revolution and promoting class consciousness; they devoted less attention to questions of love, marriage and family relation." See Quartaert, *Reluctant Feminists*, pp. 100f.

29. *NYVZ*, Nov. 22, 1908.

30. *NYVZ*, May 2, 1909.

31. *NYVZ*, May 2, 1909.

32. See, for a similar example among Jewish women, Maxine S. Seller, "Defining Socialist Womanhood," p. 418.

33. *NYVZ*, Jan. 10, 1909.

34. *NYVZ*, Oct. 20, 1901.

35. *NYVZ*, Feb. 1, 1903.

36. For socialist men's attitudes see Ruth Seifert, "Portrayal of Women in the German-American Labor Movement."

37. Ryan, *Womanhood in America*, p. 196.

38. *NYVZ*, Nov. 20, 1910.

39. *NYVZ*, Feb. 16, 1913.

40. *NYVZ*, Oct. 30, 1910.

41. In Germany, the situation was different. In 1908, legal restrictions on female organization were revoked. The possibility of joining the party, however, was not without its liabilities, because now women's activities were restricted by party directives. In Germany, even though women grumbled, on the whole, they stuck to the party line. See Quartaert, *Reluctant Feminists*, p. 148.

42. *NYVZ*, Apr. 18, 1909.

43. *NYVZ*, Aug. 15, 1909.

44. *NYVZ*, Sept. 26, 1909, and Oct. 31, 1909. Teresa Malkiel had contributed to the women's page of the *NYVZ* for a couple of years before she entered the editorial staff in 1910.

45. *NYVZ*, Nov. 28, 1909.

46. *NYVZ*, Dec. 5, 1909.

47. *NYVZ*, Dec. 12, 1909.

48. *NYVZ*, Mar. 14, 1909.

49. In October 1911 she took a stand against Lore claiming that no such sharp demarcation should be drawn between women's economic and political struggles. See *NYVZ*, Oct. 29, 1911.

50. In the spring of 1911, Ludwig Lore and his wife Lilly became editors of the *Little Socialist Magazine*. See *NYVZ*, Apr. 16, 1911.

51. Greie-Cramer and Ludwig Lore in *NYVZ*, Apr. 18, 25, 1909. See, for example, Aug. 1, 1909, when the women's page comments on a speech which Lore gave in Branch 5 entitled "Women and Prohibition": "Comrade Lore does not consider this topic interesting, but talked about it nevertheless. From the socialist point of view, there is no men's or women's position, only a class position."

52. *NYVZ*, Apr. 18, 1909.

53. *NYVZ*, Apr. 11, 1909.

54. *NYVZ*, May 7, 1911.

55. *NYVZ*, Mah 7, 1911. A couple of months later it turned out that the debates on socialist suffrage clubs were superfluous since working women were not attracted by them. *NYVZ*, Aug. 20, 1911. Regarding Robert Bruere see Melvyn Dubofsky, *When Workers Organize*, p. 25.

56. The Socialist Women's Society was a cross-ethnic association with primarily educational objectives. It was independent of the Socialist party; however, many members were party members as well. *NYVZ*, June 6, 1909; *NYVZ*, Oct. 24, 1909.

57. Christine A. Lunardini, *From Equal Suffrage to Equal Rights*, p. 23.

58. Eleanor Flexner, *Century of Struggle*, p. 242.

59. *NYVZ*, Oct. 2, 1910. Dubofsky has pointed out that Theodore Roosevelt, too, took the opportunity to sound "the trumpet for yet another moral crusade" by demanding better living conditions for these "future mothers" (*When Workers Organize*, p. 83).

60. *NYVZ*, Dec. 4, 1910.

61. *NYVZ*, Jan. 11, 1911.

62. This was a demand raised in a letter by Elizabeth Paul of Evergreen, Long Island, who called herself "an older woman." *NYVZ*, Feb. 4, 1912.

63. *NYVZ*, Jan. 1, 1911.

64. *NYVZ*, May 7, 1911.

65. *NYVZ*, Nov. 5, 1911.

66. *NYVZ*, Apr. 29, 1911.

67. Sinovieva-Deutsch published a series of articles in the *NYVZ*, Feb. 23, Mar. 16, Apr. 6, 1913.

68. *NYVZ*, Mar. 3, 1912, Feb. 22, 1914.

69. *NYVZ*, Jan. 1912.

70. *NYVZ*, Nov. 26, 1911, and Mar. 24, 1912.

71. *NYVZ*, Apr. 20, 1913.

72. *NYVZ*, June 21, 1914.

73. *NYVZ*, June 21, 1914.

74. See Greie-Cramer in the *NYVZ* on Apr. 6, 1902.

75. *NYVZ*, Apr. 13, 1913.
76. *NYVZ*, Feb. 16, 1913.
77. *NYVZ*, Jan. 17, 1915.
78. *NYVZ*, Dec. 19, 1914.
79. *NYVZ*, Mar. 21, 1915.
80. *NYVZ*, Aug. 13, 1914.
81. *NYVZ*, Feb. 21, 1915.
82. *NYVZ*, Aug. 13, 1914.

IV

Radical Visions

German-American radicalism was a varied and complex set of people, newspapers, and political and cultural institutions. The editors had diverse backgrounds, coming from all over Germany and going to most corners of the United States. They were Catholic, Lutheran, and freethinker, and came in waves after 1848 and 1871, jostling the earlier immigrants with new ideas as they were jolted by what they saw in their new home. In the second half of the nineteenth century, German-American radicalism developed from its roots in the tradition that the 48ers brought with them and confronted a working-class trade unionism that grew apace after the Civil War. These editors and their newspapers spoke with different voices that were shaped by their immigrant roots and by their American circumstances, by the date of their migration and the place they chose to settle, by the state of American industrial capitalism and the strength of the American political and civic institutions pitted against them.

It is in the lives of of these editors that the most striking difference between German-American radicalism and German socialism is evident. Freed from the constraints of party discipline, the absolutist state, and the strong presence of established religions, German-American radicals developed in ways that would have been unthinkable in Bismarck's Reich. To be sure, there was the Socialist Labor party, which copied the old-world Marxist political forms, demanding strict discipline and hewing to a line that was based in abstract theory. But it remained an isolated phenomenon, only to have important influence when it tried to cooperate with the broader-based left. One could not imagine a figure such as Robert Reitzel, a man whose broad sympathies and wide intellectual range moved him across the radical spectrum, flourishing in Bismarckian Germany. Ludwig Lore, balancing a feeling for a theoretical Marxist line with a more sensitive reading of American political culture, tried, and ultimately failed, to develop a communism that would meet the demands of the aging generation of radical German-Americans in the 1920s and 1930s. Josef Jodlbauer, the Austrian parliamentary deputy who came in the 1910s and left in the 1920s, ran up against the flip side of American pluralism. Though a myriad of radical groups and papers existed, and the radical critique was strong and pointed, the ability of American political culture to absorb shocks and to defeat radicalism by a mixture of repression and inattention ended his quest in disillusion and reverse migration. But what comes through most strongly in the divergent radical visions presented here is the call for a more just society, a call that still strikes chords that echo throughout American history.

Richard Oestreicher

Robert Reitzel, *Der Arme Teufel*

What does such an Arme Teufel have to do? O, worthy readers, so
much, so endlessly much! He must clutch to his heart all of the
grandeur and beauty which all of Nature and all of the works of
mankind have to offer . . . he must relive all of world history. . . . The
Arme Teufel endures it laughingly when someone rates him at the
highest level, as every roguish fool tries to take him in with praise . . .
but his heart grows angry when he must see how unashamed
ignorance struts in the robes of wisdom, how parasitic evil sucks the
vitality from the veins of innocence which bears it, how mankind
cheers for lies which appear unadorned, and how the truth has been
masked so long that mankind can no longer distinguish between truth
and lies. But if an Arme Teufel's heart sometimes grows angry, what
does he have to fear? His Fatherland is the world; his religion is do
what seems right and hesitate before no one, not even the God-
bogeyman tailored especially for big children; his party will never
demand a share of booty; his income cannot be cut.

> Robert Reitzel, "Unser Programm," *Der arme Teufel*, Dec. 6, 1884.

Poet, literary critic, essayist, journalist, and radical propagandist,
Robert Reitzel was perhaps the most lively and imaginative, certainly
the most irreverent, literary voice of nineteenth-century American
Germania. As his eight-page Detroit weekly, *Der arme Teufel*, expanded
its readership from a regional base to an international audience, Reitzel
became the most eloquent exponent of a brand of German radicalism bridging the generational gap between the liberal Enlightenment
rationalism and literary romanticism of disappointed 48ers and the
revolutionary proletarianism of the late-nineteenth-century immigrant

left. To contemporary radicals who rediscover him he is an appealing figure, anticipating the political concerns, moral tone, and style of the New Left far more than most of the socialist intellectuals who followed him.[1] His career also illustrates poignantly a contemporary dilemma—the bittersweet anguish of those who unswervingly maintain a radical faith in a nonradical era.

By the late nineteenth century, in both American Germania and Germany, Marxist socialism had become so hegemonic that it was virtually synonymous with the German left. To be sure, socialists vigorously debated strategy and tactics. Yet German-American counterparts of Kautsky, Bernstein, or Luxemburg all saw themselves as part of the Marxist tradition. Indeed, the flourishing of that tradition in their homeland served as powerful emotional compensation for their relative lack of success in America. But a generation earlier, the intellectual spectrum of the German-American (and German) left had been broader. The 48ers and their successors from the 1850s to the 1880s had included Paineite radical democrats, Freidenker, anarchists, utopians, Lassalleans, as well as Marxists. While followers of all these tendencies endorsed the emerging labor movement, many of them were not workers but intellectuals, professionals, shopkeepers, occasionally even owners of substantial businesses. For such shopkeepers or professionals the emotional wellsprings of their radicalism had more to do with anticlericalism, rationalism, or radical egalitarianism than class struggle at the point of production.[2] Although Reitzel actively sympathized with workers' struggles, and he gave the funeral oration over the graves of the Haymarket martyrs in 1887, his *Der arme Teufel* depended on radical shopkeepers and nonconformist intellectuals more than on radical artisans or trade union activists. His story suggests that scholars who want to understand the German-American radicalism of his generation will have to look to the Turnvereine and Free Thought clubs of German-American communities as much as to their union halls.

Reitzel was born in the village of Schopfheim in Baden in January 1849. His mother and her brother had been closely linked to the revolutionaries Friedrich Hecker and Georg Herwegh; his mother named him after Robert Blum, a Leipzig revolutionary orator who had just been killed in Vienna. However, his father, a local schoolmaster afraid for his position, wanted nothing to do with his wife's radical associates. Indeed, on the night Reitzel was born, his uncle, with the police on his heels, had sought refuge in the Reitzel household, and his father had tried to turn him away from the door.[3]

Not surprisingly, his family life was unhappy. His mother and father quarreled. His father, whom Reitzel described as authoritarian and puritanical, beat him regularly. His mother tried to shield him, to instill in him her radical faith, and to support his literary interests, but she died of consumption when he was sixteen. Expelled from the gymnasium in nearby Mannheim, he nonetheless gained admission to the University of Heidelberg. Officially he majored in theology and philosophy because divinity students from poor families received a stipend, but he studied little theology, devoting himself far more to "love, wine, revolution, and freedom."[4] In 1870, with the university degree still far from completion, his exasperated father issued an ultimatum: join the army or go to America. Reitzel's older brother had fled to America the year before. The choice was clear—America!

With a bit of nostalgia for his homeland, but also the enthusiasm of an adventurous vagabond, he boarded a ship bound for America. He had little in common with the upstanding German burghers among his fellow passengers, but amused himself by composing ribald rhymes with another young student, the future pastor of an "enlightened" St. Louis congregation and eventually one of his loyal subscribers. One sample is included in his biographical essay, "Abenteur eines Grünen":

> I love because love I must,
> I love on orders from above,
> And when I cannot love anyone,
> Dammit! then I start on getting drunk.[5]

As he landed in New York harbor, "even in a free country," he discovered "to my horror . . . a customs inspection existed. The suitcase had to be opened." Unfortunately, his ancient trunk no longer had any clasps, and he had laboriously tied it shut. Once he had ripped it open for the customs clerk to rifle through, he could no longer close it. His fellow passengers rushed about him to catch the ferry to Castle Garden. No one would help the bedraggled student dragging the trunk with its contents spilling out. "I already had a foretaste of what awaited me in America" (p. 44).

"To return to my theological career, even if I had passed my state certification exam, did not appeal to me." He made the rounds of the German newspaper offices, publishers, and book dealers with no success. As his meager funds disappeared, "my pride and ambition sank ever closer to zero." A German brickmaker who had advertised for help would not take him, but referred him to the proprietor of a small German restaurant. Frau Pfaff looked suspiciously at his glasses, but decided to take a chance. He could start as an apprentice waiter. He made three dollars in the five days he lasted (pp. 45–48).

Expelled from his boardinghouse, still unemployed, he slept on stoops or in the backs of bakery and butcher wagons parked on the streets. Finally, along with other unemployed young German and Irish immigrants he joined a railroad track crew bound for upstate New York. Wielding a pickaxe, "there I learned respect for work . . . the higher the sun rose, the more tired and unwilling my arms became . . . by evening my hands were covered with blisters. . . . How little do we reflect, when we are pulled by a locomotive, traveling smoothly and comfortably through the world, how many thousands of hands had to work like slaves for us to ride over this new door to heaven" (p. 57).

Reitzel and four other young Germans decided that laying tracks was not the life for them. Together they set off on the tramp, through New York and Pennsylvania, working odd jobs along the way. Unemployed once again in central Pennsylvania, Reitzel and his comrades debated their next destination. He remembered one of his sarcastic student songs about a minister from Freiburg, Carl Pistorius, "Pistor," who escaped Death by shipping him off "to Baltimore" (p. 68). Why not Baltimore?

By Baltimore, Reitzel found himself alone, penniless, hungry, and forlorn. As he passed a church, the words on a small sign caught his attention: "Rev. Pister, the pastor of this congregation lives at . . ." With a dose of "gallows humor once again in my breast," he banged on Rev. Pister's door. The good minister turned out to be a kindly man who took the bedraggled ex-divinity student under his wing, fed him, cleaned him up, and decided to groom him for the ministry (pp. 79–80).

A few weeks later he gave his first sermon to Rev. Pister's congregation. It was, as he recalled years later, a harrowing experience: "The first sermon!—The first duel, the first fight, the first explanation of love, the first hangover—all child's play compared to the first sermon. I had certainly already taken history exams, directed many toasts, and sung many songs, but to stand on a pulpit, in a black robe with long overhanging sleeves, the center of attention of all the wise-looking, dumbly gaping, mischievous, and pious eyes, and there to preach the Word of God—I do not wish on my worst enemy the dreams I endured the nights preceding this sermon" (p. 99).

A bit more coaching and advice from Rev. Pister ("above all . . . keep it short!") and he passed his certification examination before three ministers representing the German Reformed Church synod. He was assigned to a congregation in nearby Washington with an annual salary of six hundred dollars—more money than he had ever earned before or would thereafter. Beyond enjoying his newfound fortune,

Reitzel had notions of using his clerical authority to propagate humanistic ethics. His sermons, anticipating his later literary interests, drew far more on German literature, on the beauty of nature, and on the ideal of freedom than on theology, of which he knew little and cared less (pp. 99, 117–21, 126).

At first many of his parishioners proved to be surprisingly tolerant and flexible. Perhaps there was a sprinkling of 48ers amongst them who found the new pastor's philosophy to their liking. When descriptions of some of his preachings reached church authorities, the congregation agreed to leave the Reformed Church and become an independent congregation rather than expel their unorthodox minister as the synod demanded. But Reitzel was drifting farther and farther from any compromises with respectability. He had begun to spend much of his spare time with the Washington Freie Gemeinde, the local club of organized freethinkers. He appeared on his pulpit Sunday mornings obviously suffering from the aftereffects of Saturday-night revels. A delegation of parishioners suggested "The people are complaining . . . it is after all a church. . . . we truly have nothing to take exception with . . . but our wives are very dissatisfied that you appear on the pulpit without your cassock. . . . You must know, Herr Pastor, that a minister is still always a minister. . . . if you could just show just a little more discretion" (p. 144).

Discretion was never Reitzel's strong suit. "There is nothing worse for progressive aspirations," he would write twenty years later, "than halfway measures, there is nothing more disgraceful for a true freethinker than compromise." In 1874 he quit his ministerial career rather than adjust to his parishioners' requests.[6]

Over the next ten years he supported himself as a lecturer and writer for the German-American free-thought movement, traveling widely and developing a reputation as a brilliant speaker and writer. In 1884 local admirers in Detroit invited him to settle there, offering financial support for a weekly journal. The first issue of *Der arme Teufel* appeared on December 6, 1884.

He quickly established himself as one of the intellectual leaders of Detroit's radical Germania, the featured speaker at such German community events as the annual Paine festival sponsored by the local Turnverein or the annual commemoration of the Paris Commune. Radical Germans in Detroit had a highly organized subculture within the local German community including German unions and a German city labor federation (the Central Labor Union), an active local of the largely German Socialist Labor party, a German labor press, and a variety of cultural institutions including singing societies, the Turn-

Richard Oestreicher

verein, and private schools run by freethinkers. German union leaders, socialists, and radical intellectuals had a ready audience among the city's large, mainly working-class, German population. German immigrants and their children, who often still lived in ethnic neighborhoods, made up 27 percent of Detroit's population in 1890. In 1880, 86 percent of the German-born were employed in working-class occupations; in 1900, 83 percent. The German neighborhoods of Detroit's East Side were the city's most enthusiastic base of support for craft unions, boycott and shorter hours movements, radical plays and left-wing lectures, and the local Independent Labor party, which elected several of Detroit's state legislators in the mid-1880s.[7]

Although certainly an enthusiastic supporter of radical political movements, at first Reitzel devoted most of his columns to literary criticism and free-thought diatribes. He mocked the bourgeois celebrants of German literary Kultur who lionized Goethe and Schiller as German national heroes without actually reading a line that they had written. If the self-appointed conservative spokesmen of German-American ethnic identity actually read Goethe and Schiller, Reitzel observed, such worthies would probably advocate book-burning. He carried on an editorial joust with Herr Muller, the editor of the local German Catholic *Die Stimme der Wahrheit*. Muller, outraged over Reitzel's sacrilegious sarcasm, attacked the "freethinker garbage" of the "god blasphemer Reitzel" almost every week. In a regular column entitled "Stimmemuller," Reitzel gleefully repeated Muller's weekly charges or woefully chided Muller for forgetting him when no anti-Reitzel material had appeared. "Is it possible that I have insulted friend Muller?"[8]

When some of the local socialist stalwarts criticized Reitzel for not paying enough attention to political economy, he lambasted his comrades for lack of imagination. In a critique of the first issue of *Der Socialist*, the new central organ of the SLP, he argued that socialists were only preaching to the converted. Socialist newspapers were boring, with virtually every article nothing more than a repetition of the party program in various forms. He attended most of the frequent speeches of prominent socialist lecturers, but he found their orations, for the most part, long-winded. The anarchists, who at least spoke with more feeling, were more to Reitzel's taste. When Michael Schwab, soon to be one of the Haymarket defendants, spoke in Detroit in the spring of 1886, Reitzel noted that he spoke "simply, but with warmth." And he "stuck to the point" and did not use the talk as another opportunity to argue about "the unpleasant house-fight between anarchists and socialists." Schwab also talked too long. "In the workers' movement people still have the idea that a speech is not a speech if it isn't at least two hours long."[9]

While he scorned Marxist orthodoxy and the cult of the proletariat, Reitzel's loyalties were nonetheless unequivocal. "The world belongs to all. That sounds nice in theory, only unfortunately it is quite different in practice." There was no way to change that except through struggle. The socialists lacked a sense of the long history of human inequality. Socialists who ridiculed plays and literature as "Spielerei" did not appreciate the role of liberal values in changing human culture. Yet he seemed torn, perhaps doubting his own assertions about the significance of cultural activity. The same editorial which began with a plea for a sense of history and cultural change ended with a celebration of the invention of dynamite which would "guarantee the final victory of the weak and unarmed, . . . just as the cannon had allowed the peasants and townspeople to attack the knight's castle . . . against illegitimate authority . . . every weapon is justified."[10]

The events of the spring of 1886 the rise of the Knights of Labor, the national eight-hour-day strike, the Haymarket bombing, and especially the subsequent arrest and sentencing of the eight Chicago anarchists accused of inciting the unknown bomb thrower—pushed Reitzel toward a more activist resolution of this tension between philosophical ideals and praxis. Reitzel recognized far more quickly than most of his contemporaries that the trial of eight anarchist leaders and the death sentences of seven of them were an effort by the "moneybags" to "crush or at the very least to turn back the labor movement for a decade." Perhaps he was speaking to his own inner voice, as much as to the audience of 1,700 Detroit supporters of the accused men, when he told them one month before the executions, "There is a time when writing is enough, there is a time when one must strike hearts with the spoken word, there is a time when weapons mean more than pen or word. We now stand in the midst of the second time, the third is at the door."[11]

From the start Reitzel almost instinctively grasped the historical significance of what came to be known as the Haymarket Affair. He was shocked and astounded when most of his journalistic compatriots reacted differently, not only in the mainstream press but also, with only a few exceptions,[12] most of the editors of the English-language labor and of German-language liberal and free-thought newspapers:

> If pitiful whining and servile, brutal rage was ever the order of the day in this republic, it is so right now after the streetbattling of the Old World

has first made an appearance in one of our big cities. . . . But that after the inevitable defeat of the first outposts of struggle such a choir of a hundred thousand fools would be shot up out of the old swamp, I would not have imagined. . . .

Every stump speaker who painfully awaits an electoral campaign in order to win himself a new robe of office, every statesman who has swindled himself an office, every porter for whom a grocery store beckons as reward for faithful service, every newspaper writer—has become like Luther, who pledged freedom to the last drop of his blood, when he meant the freedom of the powerful, but became the pitiless hangman's preacher when dealing with justice for farmers and proletarians.[13]

Reitzel traveled to Chicago to report on the trial for his readers. He had already met several of the defendants on their earlier speaking tours through Detroit and had been impressed then with their warmth and feeling. They had written him from Cook County jail, thanking him for standing by them when so many others, even on the left, sought safety in silence or joined the chorus of denunciation, hoping to preserve their own legitimacy from the taint of anarchism. At the trial, the contrast between the quiet dignity of the defendants and the ferocity of their judicial antagonists deepened his affection for the men and his respect for their integrity. These men were not criminals! They were Arme Teufels who refused to confess any sins to their hypocritical oppressors, refused to beg for clemency. They would die rather than renounce their ideals. "Do with me what you please, your honor," Oscar Neebe, the only one of the eight defendants not sentenced to death, told the judge. "Hang me with my comrades." Louis Lingg told Reitzel, "my young Landsmann," that "in our situation, there is nothing more contemptible than the principle of self-preservation."[14]

Over the next year, as Reitzel became more and more engrossed in the defense of the convicted men, his tone changed from sarcasm and defiance to fear, desperation, and, as he finally came to see clearly that five of the men were indeed doomed, bitter anger and sadness. First, after the trial, defiance: "Hang them, hang them if you dare! You have the power and the might and the glory, but—not forever. Amen." After the Illinois State Supreme Court upheld the verdict in September 1887, deepening fear: "The second throw in the horrible game of dice for the lives of the seven men has come up snake eyes and it means death. . . . The execution is scheduled for November 11 between 9 in the morning and 2 in the afternoon."[15]

"We must protest," with growing desperation he implored the audience of the Detroit protest meeting just twenty-six days before the executions, "from one end of this country to the other. . . . A free word at the right time is a free deed. . . . Now is the time for the voice of the people to tip the balance of the scales. Man! it is your brother, Woman! it is your son, who will be murdered there. Humanity! they want to dishonor and annihilate your greatest goodness on those gallows. If today you cannot hate, if today your hearts cannot be roused to indignation, then it will be to your infamy if you ever again dare to complain of any injustice committed against you."[16]

Time was running out. "The day of revenge draws near, the revenge of the moneyed rabble against the workers. . . . Sensitive hearts who could not believe in the total vulgarity of the ruling class awaited the tiniest glimmer of justice from the Supreme Court of the United States." However, the Supreme Court, on November 2, 1887, nine days before the scheduled executions, refused to overturn the verdict.

> The pessimists inside and outside of the Chicago Bastille were once again correct. . . . The shame of letting seven men who belong to us, who have dedicated their lives to the people, be butchered in our midst without our raising a hand—?! Can that be? Must it be?
>
> To be sure, the Parisians once stormed the Bastille with a pair of ordinary pickaxes. But that was long ago; and the Chicagoans are no Parisians, and if a Camille Desmoulins exists today, he howls for a booty-party in an election meeting, and in September the trees no longer have any green leaves.
>
> And yet I still have hope that this *dies irae* can still come to be a *dies illa*[17] to which the people look forward with joyful redemption, instead of with pain and fury, a day on which the reminder of the dead poet to the people . . . finally comes true:
> Lightning after the thunder!
> O that is only one day,
> Only one until we are free![18]

On November 6, 1887, Louis Lingg committed suicide in his cell. Finally on November 10, less than twenty-four hours before the scheduled execution, Governor Oglesby commuted the sentences of Michael Schwab and Samuel Fielden to life imprisonment. The mounting protests and appeals for clemency had saved two of the men. Spies, Parsons, Fischer, and Engel were hanged the next day.

Reitzel was invited to give one of the two funeral orations at the gravesite of the five martyrs. He began in anger: "Friends of freedom! My first word over these coffins shall be an accusation, not against the moneyed rabble . . . but instead against the workers of Chicago. For you have let five of the best, most noble, most persistent champions of your cause be murdered in your midst." Still he looked forward:

Here over these coffins is the place where a vow will be taken in every heart: We must realize what these people strived for, we want to give the rights of man, which we were long ago given on paper, practical value.

We are no Christians, who leave that to the rage of their lord God, we must take it ourselves with our own hands, and since we can anticipate no heaven, so we must do everything on earth that has to be done.

We must have organization so that the murder of law will not be permitted by those who have the power in their hands.

We must show to the world that the red flag is the symbol of love. . . .

These dead will truly and in truth live on. They were crucified on Good Friday. This Sunday is an Easter Sunday and must become a day of resurrection forever.

So certainly these trees will once again sprout green leaves, so certainly will these dead remain living within us, in the workers of Chicago, in the idealistic thoughts of humanity in the entire world.

Never has right been crushed with hangmen!

Never have gallows strangled the truth!

Never are there boundaries for thoughts!

We have no need to mourn for these dead. . . . as the cross was once the symbol of love, so the gallows will become in the nineteenth century the symbol of freedom. But we must mourn for our own humiliation, our own irresolution, our own cowardice.

Let us depart from these graves with the words of Herwegh in our hearts:

We have loved long enough,

We will finally hate![19]

Like many others who committed themselves to the defense, Reitzel was never the same after these events. Despite his graveside claims for the future, he found it hard to maintain the optimistic spirit of most of his earlier writings. Yet he kept the faith he had vowed to keep at the graveside of the martyrs. The following year, he was a central figure in the factional struggle within Detroit's Turnverein between conservatives who wanted to divest the Turners of their radical image and radicals who saw the rationalist culture of the Turners as the bedrock of the social struggle. In 1890, he was the key spokesman for Detroit's German left when they opposed the plan of German businessmen for a German Day parade, a kind of German St. Patrick's Day. Reitzel and other leftists opposed such nationalistic displays on principle, but equally important they challenged the right of German businessmen to represent the German community in Detroit. "German Days," Reitzel wrote, "will be appropriate when the humane ideals that were driven out of Germany in 1849 can be returned." German Day went on, but all of the German unions boycotted the event. The first year, perhaps because of the novelty of the event (and also because many employers gave their workers the day off) there was a large turnout. But by the following year, even the Detroit *Volksblatt,* the local German Democratic daily and one of the boosters of the event, admitted that "the parade was a colossal washout . . . a disgrace." Reitzel and his friends had shown their influence in the community.[20]

Although Reitzel had already been well known within German-American Freidenker circles, his role in the Haymarket Affair helped to broaden his reputation. His practice of publishing subscription receipts in his journal with the names and cities of out-of-town subscribers allows us to reconstruct the expansion of his readership. In the first year of publication, subscriptions trickled in quite slowly, at an average rate of only 13.2 per week, and nearly three-quarters (73 percent) of his out-of-town subscribers lived in Michigan or the surrounding states of Ohio, Indiana, Illinois, and Wisconsin (see table 1). Four nearby cities with large German populations—Saginaw, Cleveland, Chicago, and Milwaukee—accounted for nearly half (46 percent) of the listed subscribers. There were few East Coast subscribers (13 percent in New England, New York, New Jersey, and Pennsylvania combined)—only ten in New York City and five in Brooklyn, the nation's first and third largest cities, both with enormous German populations.[21]

In the following year his circulation started to expand beyond this narrow regional base of Michigan and surrounding states. The weekly rate of subscription receipts, an average of 21.9 per week, had nearly doubled from the previous year. East Coast readers now represented about one-sixth (16 percent) of the new out-of-town subscribers, and the percentage in the five state area of Michigan and surrounding states had fallen to closer to half (60 percent).

These trends in the geographic distribution of Reitzel's readership would continue until his death in 1898. In 1890, when the weekly rate of new subscriptions had risen to 32.7 per week, East Coast readers now represented one-fifth (20 percent) of new out-of-town subscribers, and the five-state Michigan area less than half (44 percent). The paper had at least scatterings of readers all around the country.

By 1895, as total circulation continued to expand to a peak of about 7000,[22] the weekly rate of subscription receipts had risen once again to 39.9 per week.[23] Reitzel's readership had become international. The original base of Michigan and the four adjoining states now provided only a little over a third (38 percent) of the subscribers. East Coast subscriptions had swelled to nearly another third (33 percent). Reitzel had subscribers in more than half a dozen countries, including Ecuador, Rumania, Germany, and Switzerland, as well as a large contingent in London.

Table 1
Out-of-Town Subscribers of *Der arme Teufel**

	1885[1]		1886[2]		1890[3]		1895[4]	
	N	%	N	%	N	%	N	%
Northeast								
Boston	12	2.2	9	1.2	42	3.1	25	2.0
Other New England	10	1.9	13	1.7	35	2.6	69	5.6
New York City	10	1.9	34	4.6	58	4.3	133	10.8
Brooklyn	5	0.9	7	0.9	9	0.7	24	1.9
Other New York	5	0.9	13	1.7	32	2.4	20	1.6
New Jersey	9	1.7	34	4.6	26	1.9	83	6.7
Philadelphia	9	1.7	2	0.3	17	1.3	35	2.9
Other Pennsylvania	7	1.3	8	1.1	55	4.1	14	1.1
Total Northeast	67	12.7	120	16.1	274	20.4	403	32.6
Michigan Region								
Saginaw/E. Saginaw	39	7.4	17	2.3	9	0.7	3	0.2
Other Michigan	60	11.4	59	7.9	80	6.0	10	0.8
Cleveland	99	18.8	94	12.6	130	9.7	6	0.5
Other Ohio	28	5.3	72	9.7	60	4.5	58	4.7
Indiana	8	1.5	30	4.0	62	4.6	42	3.4
Chicago	70	13.3	43	5.8	187	13.9	209	16.9
Other Illinois	35	6.6	40	5.4	38	2.8	36	2.9
Milwaukee	33	6.3	81	10.9	7	0.5	73	5.9
Other Wisconsin	14	2.7	12	1.6	14	1.0	28	2.3
Total Mich. region	386	73.2	448	60.1	587	43.7	465	37.6
Other Midwest								
Minn'lis/St. Paul	0	0.0	41	5.5	8	0.6	36	2.9
Other Minnesota	1	0.2	6	0.8	3	0.2	47	3.8
St. Louis	23	4.4	53	7.1	99	7.4	115	9.3
Other Missouri	0	0.0	10	1.3	40	3.0	16	1.3
Iowa	4	0.8	17	2.3	14	1.0	14	1.1
Total other Midwest	28	5.3	127	17.0	164	12.2	228	18.4
Other U.S.								
D.C.	29	5.5	20	2.7	42	3.1	2	0.2
California	6	1.1	8	1.1	103	7.7	22	1.8
All other	8	1.5	19	2.5	161	12.0	63	5.1
Total other U.S.	43	8.2	47	6.3	306	22.8	87	7.0
Foreign	3	0.6	3	0.4	11	0.8	54	4.4
Total	527		745		1342		1237	

Table 1 *continued*

	1885[1]		1886[2]		1890[3]		1895[4]	
	N	%	N	%	N	%	N	%
Weekly average subscriptions received	13.2		21.9		32.7		39.9	

1. Subscription receipts listed May 9, 1885, through Feb. 6, 1886.
2. Subscription receipts listed Feb. 13, 1886, through Oct. 2, 1886.
3. Subscription receipts listed Jan. 4, 1890, through Oct. 11, 1890.
4. Subscription receipts listed Mar. 23, 1895, through Oct. 19, 1895.

*Based on receipts for subscriptions published in the issues during the time intervals listed below. Since some subscribers paid up as much as several years in advance, the totals for each location may more accurately reflect the rate of new subscriptions rather than the cumulative total of subscribers in good standing at that location. In some cities subscriptions were apparently collected by officers of Arme Teufel clubs or Turnervereins and sent in several dozen at a time. Sometimes there were long intervals during which no subscriptions were received from a particular city, and then a batch of several dozen appeared all at once. Some of the anomalies in the table may be the result of this procedure.

It is difficult to judge the relative importance of local Detroit readership as compared to the out-of-town subscribers, since Reitzel never published receipts or other information about his local subscribers. If we subtract the known out-of-town subscribers from the estimated total circulation figures, it would appear that his local readership in the mid-1880s was no more than a fifth of his estimated circulation of 2,500–3,000 in 1887.[24]

Judging from the relatively large number of advertisements placed by local small businesses (several dozen display ads in each issue), one might assume that the local readership was more substantial, but many of these advertisers may have been admirers who used advertising as a way of supporting the paper financially. That must have been the case with out-of-town advertisers. While collectively the out-of-town subscribers represented a substantial audience, there were not enough subscribers in any one place to justify advertising from a business point of view. Many did nonetheless. The Anheuser-Busch Brewery ran a large display ad (close to a quarter-page) in every issue for years. Like many of Reitzel's readers, who formed local Arme Teufel

Table 2
Occupations of *Der arme Teufel* Subscribers, 1886

	N	%
High white collar		
Manufacturer	13	
Professional[1]	17	
Wholesale or large merchant	7	
Brewery owner	18	
Office manager, business executive,		
real estate or insurance agency proprietor	10	
Government official	3	
Misc. large proprietor[2]	4	
Total	72	26.4
Low white collar		
Small retailer[3]	38	
Saloonkeeper, restaurant or bar owner	66	
Bookkeeper, clerk, cashier	17	
Salesman, agent, notary, collector	12	
Teacher	5	
Artisanal proprietor[4]	15	
Total	153	56.0
Skilled worker[5]		
Total	37	13.6
Unskilled worker		
Total	11	4.0
Total N	273	

1. Physician, lawyer, architect, chemist (Ph.D.), editor, publisher, orchestra director, school principal or proprietor.

2. Hotel owner, meeting hall owner, recreational park proprietor.

3. Groceries, drugs, books, produce, wines, liquor, furniture, clothing, shoes, hardware.

4. Includes individuals in artisanal trades with a listed business address or a display ad; probably some of those listed under skilled workers were also self-employed.

5. Tailor, cook, draughtsman, bricklayer, polisher, engraver, lithographer, jeweler, watchmaker, cooper, weaver, armorer, frescoer, dyer, printer, cigarmaker, machinist, glassworker, roller, barber, furniture or cabinetmaker, foreman; the only one of these occupations with more than three listings was furniture and cabinetmaker with six.

Sources: *Der arme Teufel*, Nov. 28, 1885; Jan. 2, 1886; Jan. 23, 1886; Feb. 27, 1886; Apr. 10, 1886; May 1, 1886; June 19, 1886; July 31, 1886; Sept. 25, 1886; Oct. 9, 1886; Oct. 16, 1886; Oct. 23, 1886; Nov. 27, 1886; Dec. 11, 1886; Dec. 18, 1886; Dec. 25, 1886; 1886 city directories for Philadelphia, Pittsburgh, Cleveland, St. Louis, Grand Rapids, Washington, D.C., Indianapolis, Minneapolis, New York City, and Milwaukee.

clubs around the country where they met to discuss articles in the paper and to boost its circulation, these business owners must have been admirers and soulmates.

Perhaps not surprisingly, given the paper's emphasis on literature and high culture, the readership of *Der arme Teufel* was decidedly middle-class (see table 2). While in most American cities in the late nineteenth century more than three-quarters of employed Germans were in working-class occupations,[25] only about one-sixth of Reitzel's identifiable subscribers in 1886 were skilled or unskilled workers. The single largest occupational group among identifiable subscribers, saloonkeepers and restaurant owners, comprised over 24 percent of identified subscribers, more than all working-class occupations combined. Of course, given the tendency of city directories (the source for identifying occupations) to underreport workers and the likelihood that many workers patronized the bar owners who subscribed to provide reading matter for their customers, these figures may understate the working-class readership somewhat. But even making allowances for a few extra working-class readers, it seems clear that Reitzel's readership was proportionately much greater among businessmen, white-collar employees, and professionals than among industrial workers. Most of the identified workers worked in small-scale consumer crafts, hardly any in large-scale heavy industries.

Occupations, of course, give us only the barest clues to the background and worldview of Reitzel's following. The "Briefkarten" from his readers, which appeared regularly, give more insight. The letter writers were enthusiastic admirers of Reitzel. They were deeply committed to the cause of human liberation, but judging from the contents of their correspondence, like Reitzel they took far more pleasure in poring over their Goethe, Schiller, or Heine than in the ideological polemics which consumed their German brethren within the organized socialist movement. They met regularly with each other in Arme Teufel clubs or Turnvereine in Chicago, Cleveland, or Milwaukee or in little outposts of Germania like New Ulm, Minnesota, or Sauk Center, Wisconsin, seeking kindred spirits for intellectual stimulation and Gemütlichkeit. The Chicago Arme Teufel Club wrote Reitzel in 1897 to describe their celebrations for the beginning of his fourteenth year of publication: "Chicago friends celebrate the beginning of v.14 with lectures, songs, friendly hanging around . . . free drinking, and world commentary, and toasting." A Chicago saloonkeeper captured the spirit of Reitzel admirers when he advised fellow readers they would find at his establishment (named Nirwana):

Mein Bier ist gut!
Mein Wein ist klar!
And freedom beckons from afar.[26]

By the 1890s, Reitzel's writings emphasized these cultural concerns even more than in the past. Whether he wrote about nature, about religion, about history, or about literature, he still battled against hypocrisy, against ignorance, against all cultural or political Philistines, but both his choices of topics and his language displayed less immediate political engagement than they had in the late 1880s. He wrote a long serialized account of his early years in America and one of his most imaginative works—the reminiscences of a waiter who worked in a Stratford tavern next door to Shakespeare's home between 1616 and 1618, the last two years of Shakespeare's life.[27] Reitzel's Shakespeare, clearly a voice for Reitzel's own deepest concerns, rejected the superficial praise of his neighbors as he acidly condemned their provincialism and puritanical narrow-mindedness.

By 1894 Reitzel contracted the tuberculosis which had killed his mother. The disease attacked his spine and other large bones, and he became an invalid virtually confined to his bed. Yet, with the help of friends, *Der arme Teufel* still appeared weekly with perfect regularity. At least by the standards of small radical literary journals, it was enjoying ever-increasing success. Despite his illness, Reitzel continued to write with the same wry, self-deprecating wit which had always been his hallmark.

But the optimistic dreams of his youth seemed to recede ever further from reality. Many German-American socialists looked with pride and enthusiasm to the electoral rise of the German Social Democratic party as a harbinger of the socialist future. Even in America, by the late 1890s the small and poorly organized socialist movement showed signs of expansion beyond its heretofore narrow base of German émigrés. Reitzel was unimpressed. Militarism still ruled Germany, and money ruled ever more firmly in America.

In November 1897, six months before his death, inevitably prodded by the anniversary of the Haymarket executions, he looked back on the events which had marked his life. "Has it really already been ten years since the working people escorted their dead through the streets of Chicago?" Thinking back on the anger and sadness of that day, somehow one event, "which unfortunately I cannot forget," was fixed in his mind. The mourners' procession had just left the railroad station with the coffins bound for Waldheim Cemetery, when "a chap . . . like a sailor on a furlough sprang up at the head of the line brandishing with hurrahs an American flag. . . . He danced like a harlequin to the timbres of the funeral march . . . and . . . shouted 'Not a damned Dutch, not a damned Anarchist can take the flag away from me, the flag of my country.'" The marchers, fearful of police reprisal if they interfered, grimly did their best to ignore him. "When I behold the November twilight I must ask myself have ten years really flown by since that day? It seems to me that a century has passed, a century in which nothing has changed, in which only crime has been heaped upon crime and which has brought no atonement, none."

He was sick in spirit as well as body. "I shudder to look into the future. A morning must truly come, but first this horrible long night! I think about the past and see how the stepping-stones of freedom sink ever deeper in the morass." It was now twenty-five years since the Prussian monarchy had ascended to the throne of the German Empire, dashing the hopes of the revolutionary nationalists of 1848 who had sought German unification in a free state. Georg Herwegh, the revolutionary and poet who had been his mother's friend, had still sung with optimism in 1873 about the disappointed dreams of '48:

> Eighteen hundred and forty-eight,
> When the spring cracked through the ice—
> Days of February, days of March,
> Wasn't it proletarian hearts—
> Which full of hope first awakened,
> Eighteen hundred and forty-eight?!

> But we poor, sold and betrayed,
> Think of proletarian deeds,
> Still not all Marches have passed,
> Eighteen hundred and seventy-three.

Thinking of Herwegh, Reitzel wrote another verse:

> Eighteen hundred and ninety-eight,
> Do you still believe in the freedom-struggle?
> Where is the harvest of the bloody seeds,
> Where are the proletarian deeds?
> Rules not the same old evil
> Eighteen hundred and ninety-eight?[28]

Robert Reitzel died April 1, 1898. His last poem was published a few days later:

> Life is the sultry day,
> Death is the cool night,
> It grows dark already, I feel sleepy,
> The day has made me tired.

> Over my bed rises a tree,
> In which a young nightingale sings,
> She sings about true love,
> I hear it as in a dream.[29]

Reitzel's friend Martin Drescher attempted to carry on after Reitzel's death. But *Der arme Teufel* had been too much Reitzel's personal vehicle. Within two years, the subscriptions had fallen by 60 percent, and in 1900 Drescher ceased publication.[30] Reitzel's admirers still sought to publicize his work, in two posthumous collections of his writing.[31]

Despite such efforts, Reitzel's reputation barely outlived him. As Paul Buhle has argued, figures like Reitzel have received scant attention from American historians, even historians of the left, who often have not appreciated the ethnic basis of much of American radicalism or have lacked the language skills to enter the cultural worlds of the non-English-speaking population. In the generation after his death, perhaps Reitzel's reputation faded quickly because his brand of emotional and literary radicalism was out of step with the increasing dominance of "scientific" socialism over radical intellectual life. Yet for the generations of radical German émigrés who left Germany before the hegemony of Marxism, Reitzel had been more than a quixotic figure. His concerns were theirs. They too were Arme Teufels dreaming of the birth of freedom in a better world.[32]

NOTES

1. See, for example, the recent biography of Reitzel by Ulrike Heider, *Der arme Teufel*, which emphasizes Reitzel's commitment to sexual emancipation, free love, feminism, homosexual rights, and individual freedom; and also Paul Buhle's essay in this volume.

2. For a suggestive description of radical Germans in antebellum Buffalo, see David A. Gerber, *Making of an American Pluralism*, esp. pp. 196–99, 227–35.

3. Biographical information on Reitzel, in addition to Reitzel's own memoirs cited below, is taken from Heider and from Adolf Eduard Zucker, *Robert Reitzel*. For capsule accounts of the activities of Hecker, Herwegh, and Blum, see Peter N. Stearns, *Eighteen Forty-Eight*, pp. 141–42, 158.

4. Zucker, *Robert Reitzel*, p. 11.

5. "Ich liebe, weil ich lieben muss,
   ich lieb nach einem Himmelschluss,
   und wenn ich Keinen lieben kann,
   fang ich, verflucht! zu saufen an."
Robert Reitzel, "Abenteuer eines Grünen," *Des armen Teufel gesammelte Schriften*, 1:37–149, 43. The following account of Reitzel's early career in the

United States is taken from this and is cited by page number in the text. The translations are my own.

6. *Der arme Teufel*, Jan. 5, 1895.
7. Richard Oestreicher, *Solidarity and Fragmentation*, pp. 33, 43–52, 120–27.
8. *Der arme Teufel*, Dec. 6, 1884.
9. *Der arme Teufel*, Jan. 10, 17, 1885; Mar. 20, 1886.
10. *Der arme Teufel*, May 2, Dec. 12, 1885.
11. Reitzel, "Ein Protest" (speech to the Detroit protest meeting of Oct. 16, 1887), *Des armen Teufel gesammelte Schriften*, 3:117, 123.
12. A notable exception was Joseph Labadie, the editor of the Detroit *Labor Leaf*, whose defense of the Haymarket defendants and analysis of the significance of the event mirrored Reitzel's. After reading one of Labadie's "Cranky Notions" columns, Reitzel wrote, "I despair no more about the Americans." *Der arme Teufel*, Apr. 24, May 22, 1886.
13. Reitzel, "Vae Victis!" *Des armen Teufel gesammelte Schriften*, 3:91–93.
14. Reitzel, *Des armen Teufel gesammelte Schriften*, 3:109, 118.
15. Reitzel, *Des armen Teufel gesammelte Schriften*, 3:110, 127–28; Henry David, *History of the Haymarket Affair*, pp. 347–71.
16. Reitzel, *Des armen Teufel gesammelte Schriften*, 3:122, 126.
17. *Dies irae:* day of wrath, from a hymn sung in the requiem mass; *dies illa:* in Reitzel's rather idiosyncratic translation, the day of salvation.
18. David, *History of the Haymarket Affair*, pp. 382–88; Reitzel, "Dies Irae," *Des armen Teufel gesammelte Schriften*, 3:130–33.

> Blitz auf ein Wetterschlag!
> O wag es doch nur einen Tag,
> Nur einen frei zu sein!

19. Reitzel, "Am Grabe," *Des armen Teufel gesammelte Schriften*, 3:142–44.
20. Oestreicher, *Solidarity and Fragmentation*, pp. 43–50.
21. The figures for Saginaw are combined totals for Saginaw and East Saginaw, separate municipalities in 1885 but united shortly thereafter. Saginaw had a very active labor movement, was the scene of a massive lumber mill strike in 1885, and was the home of Tom Barry, a member of the Knights of Labor General Executive Board who was also elected to the Michigan legislature as a Labor Democrat in 1884. For more on Barry and description of the Saginaw valley lumber strike, see my "Limits of Labor Radicalism."
22. Heider, *Der arme Teufel*, p. 80; Zucker, *Robert Reitzel*, p. 49.
23. The weekly subscription rates, if annualized, do not come close to the claimed circulation figures. As the subscription receipts show, many subscribers supported the paper by sending in money for several years in advance. This probably explains the discrepancy.
24. *Der arme Teufel*, Dec. 3, 1887. I tabulated a total of 1272 out-of-town subscribers between May 1885 (when Reitzel first began publishing subscription receipts) and October 1886. I have not gone through these lists systematically to check for repeated names, but even a cursory examination makes it clear

Richard Oestreicher

that the proportion of renewals by people appearing earlier on my list is very small (not surprising—the time span covers only a little over a year and early in the publication's history). The total of 1272 does not include subscribers prior to May 1885 or in the period (more than a year) between the end of my tabulations and the appearance of Reitzel's circulation estimate. There is no way to estimate initial and early subscribers before May 1885, but judging from the rate of new subscriptions in 1886 there must have been well over a thousand additional new out-of-town subscribers between October 1886 and December 1887, leaving *at most* 500–600 Detroit subscribers, using the high (3000) circulation estimate. Reitzel's circulation estimate is corroborated by Karl J. R. Arndt and May E. Olson, *German-American Newspapers and Periodicals*, p. 212, who used circulation figures from the Ayer's directories of newspapers.

25. Nora Faires, "Occupational Patterns of German-Americans," esp. pp. 40–41.

26. *Der arme Teufel*, Nov. 13, 1897.

27. Reitzel, "Ein Herbst-Traum," *Des armen Teufel gesammelte Schriften*, 2: 79–119.

28. "Von trüben zu trüben Tagen," *Der arme Teufel*, Nov. 13, 1897.

> Achtzehnhundert vierzig und acht,
> Als im Lenze das Eis erkracht—
> Tage des Februar, Tage des Märzen,
> Waren es nicht Proletarierherzen—
> Die voll Hoffnung zuerst erwacht
> Achtzehnhundert vierzig und acht?!
>
> Aber wir Armen, verkeuft und verraten,
> Denken der Proletarier-Taten,
> Noch sind nicht all Märze vorbei,
> Achtzehnhundert siebzig und drei.
>
> Achtzehnhundert neunzig und acht,
> Glaubst du noch an die Freiheitsschlacht?
> Wo ist die Ernte der blutigen Saaten,
> Wo sind die Proletariertaten?
> Herrscht nicht die alte Niedertracht
> Achtzehnhundert neunzig und acht?

29. Heider, *Der arme Teufel*, p. 121.

> Das Leben ist der schwüle Tag,
> Der Tod das ist die kühle Nacht
> Es dämmert schon, mich schläfert,
> Der Tag hat mich müde gemacht.
>
> Über mein Bett erhebt ein Baum,
> Darin singt die junge Nachtigall,
> Sie singt von lauter Liebe,
> Ich hör' es sogar im Traum.

30. Martin Drescher edited *Der Herold*, the weekly organ of Detroit's Central Labor Union, from August 1897 until April 1898. During Reitzel's last few months Drescher spent every night at Reitzel's sickbed, reading to him and helping him continue to put out *Der arme Teufel*. Zucker, *Robert Reitzel*, pp. 24, 48–49.

31. Robert Reitzel, *Mein Buch* and *Des armen Teufel gesammelte Schriften*.

32. Paul Buhle, in this volume; Paul Buhle, "Jews and American Communism," esp. 9–11, 28–31. See also several of the fine studies of ethnic radicalism in *"Struggle a Hard Battle."*

Paul Buhle

Ludwig Lore and the *New Yorker Volkszeitung:* The Twilight of the German-American Socialist Press

The *New Yorker Volkszeitung* (*NYVZ*) (1878–1932) is the historical standard for American Marxist newspapers. Among those founded in the same pioneer era of the modern left, only the *Chicagoer Arbeiterzeitung* and the *Philadelphia Tageblatt* had similar staying power, and none had the prestige, intellectual leadership, or sustained national impact of the *NYVZ*. Others, such as the *Jewish Daily Forward*, the *Appeal to Reason*, or the *Daily Worker* have had larger circulations. But the *NYVZ* truly ruled American Marxist organization at various times and places. To its last days, it took a unique, essentially independent position anchored outside the socialist and Communist parties proper, in the fraternal societies and the German immigrant-based unions. Therein lay its strength and its longevity.

Only the *NYVZ* of the 1920s, i.e., after the Bolshevik Revolution, has received the attention of prestigious scholars in previous generations, and then only in the light of cold war politics. It is a measure of American historians' linguistic provincialism that only in recent years have some scholars—mostly Germans—begun to examine the paper in its own right.[1] My small contribution here is a bit of initial "revisionism" in both directions, in tune with the emerging historiography.

Theodore Draper's *American Communism and Soviet Russia* (1960),[2] long considered a standard in the field of research on the Communist party, has been challenged by a new generation of scholars who have examined many related subjects—in addition to the Communist party proper—with far greater attention to social-historical context. Leaving aside neotraditional scholars, either dogmatically Communist or anti-

Communist, most of the newer works on radicalism (or Marxism) view Communism as only one element in the picture. The writing of a more-developed history of American anarchism, socialism, labor Zionism, and Communism, labor movements and labor reforms, is well underway. By and large, these studies are not primarily "political" in the old sense of "history is past politics." Rather, following the lead of E. P. Thompson and Herbert Gutman, they have attempted the reconstruction of daily life for the groups and individuals considered. In order to do so, they have turned to the non-English-language periodicals as the single most useful source.[3]

Earlier studies of the *NYVZ* by socialist intellectuals had described it and its milieu in passing, with insight but without depth or obvious additional research. *NYVZ* writers themselves, in the various *NYVZ* anniversary issues over the decades, devoted vast quantities of prose to nostalgic reflections. (Probably the most important contribution to scholarship to this point has indeed been the reprinting of essays from the 1888, 1903, and 1928 editions, by the Labor Newspaper Preservation Project in Bremen.)[4] These "primary sources" help us greatly in understanding the autonomous history of the paper and its special role in its last days. We will see how little the phases of American Communism altered the *NYVZ* in its essence.

The *NYVZ* took the field in 1878, following a monumental fund-raising campaign among German-American workers in New York and New Jersey. From its first day to its last, it represented a constituency broadly socialist but only to a minor degree made up of members of the various left-wing parties. Its ownership lay in the *NYVZ* corporation—not in the hands of any political entity as such—and it was answerable in the final sense only to itself and its constituents. The paper's readership and financial stability rested upon the German-speaking immigrant communities of the area, predominantly working-class but also small middle class. Its back columns were filled with notices of the "Vereine und Versammlungen," the sickness-and-death-benefit societies that the Germans originated around the socialist movement, and those of the "Sozialistische Liedertafel" singing societies, the picnics, winter balls, and other such working-class entertainments. Its advertising base—physicians, patent medicine companies, local restaurants, beer and tobacco companies, and a wide range of immigrant service firms—reflected the daily lives of its readers. With a scattering of 48ers, most of these readers had immigrated as children or young adults in the 1860s or 1870s. After a final major wave in the early 1880s, the numbers of new German immigrants decreased rapidly, and the *NYVZ* readership became the *alte Genossen* (and *Genossinnen*), a generation with bittersweet feelings about old and adopted homelands, sharing their experiences, hopes, and fears together until their final days.

Their relationship with the American radical movement shifted decisively over the 1880s and 1890s, forming a pattern which remained in place through the 1920s. At the *NYVZ*'s founding, and for a decade or so after, they viewed themselves as the intellectual and spiritual vanguard of a working class on the verge of class-conscious awakening. Among dozens of radical papers founded in the wake of the 1877 railroad strike, only a handful of publications (none in English) survived. Among craft unions, German-American workers who read the *NYVZ* and its sister papers exerted a vastly disproportionate role, challenged only by the often conservative and almost invariably antisocialist Irish-Americans. Far ahead of their fellow-workers in the realm of ideas, German-Americans tended naturally to cluster among themselves, discussing socialist ideas and establishing their various fraternal and social institutions. This status placed the *NYVZ*, during the labor upswelling of 1884–86, in the ambiguous position of ideological superiority to, and at the same time, widespread physical absence from, the meteoric rise of the largely Irish-American Knights of Labor. Readers of the *NYVZ* participated in all strike activities, often leading the way. They hailed every political advance. But, as Friedrich Engels complained, they failed to lead the revolutionary column into a revived and broadened socialist movement. In the aftermath of Haymarket they faced a veritable Red Scare in which their relative cultural insularity proved their abiding strength. Following Henry George's mayoral campaign, which they had supported even to the extent of funding an English-language organ, they saw that the grandest hopes of coalition with other groups could go to smash, leaving them wholly dependent upon their own self-created durability.

What lessons could be drawn from these experiences? They took the cautious approach, determined to nurture what resources they possessed—above all the *NYVZ* itself. By the late 1890s, the Socialist Labor party, which had never attained a national membership of more than 20 percent of the *NYVZ*'s readership, became (via its national executive ruling body meeting in New York City) more the organ of the *NYVZ* than vice versa. In 1889, the *NYVZ*-dominated NEC suspended the national German-language organ as too critical of unions, and in effect subjected the entire SLP to a *coup de main*.[5]

A decade later, responding to the dual-unionist strategies of English-language socialist leader Daniel DeLeon, the *NYVZ* virtually repeated the maneuver. They had initially welcomed DeLeon, as well as the

People, an English-language weekly, which served as DeLeon's mouthpiece. They did not foresee that DeLeon would accuse them of bureaucratic conservatism and threaten to overthrow their plan of union consolidation and patient propaganda. Some socialists bolted rather quickly, including a Jewish group which established a daily Yiddish socialist paper, the *Forward,* almost overnight exceeding the *NYVZ* in readership and journalistic innovation. The *NYVZ* waited until 1899, challenging DeLeon for SLP leadership and then sponsoring a rival SLP which would merge into the new Socialist party. Meanwhile, with the steady growth of the immigrant left, the *NYVZ* was only one paper among dozens in various non-English languages. At the opening of the new century, the hegemony of the *NYVZ* and the German proletarian element it represented on the left had definitely been transcended.[6]

German speakers had already adapted themselves to this new reality. The entrance of new Jewish immigrants and native-born Americans during the 1890s permitted a sense of ethnic collectivity, both precursor and counterpart to the mass-based and mature "American" movement the *Volkszeitung* had long awaited. Their unabashed reverence (like that of the Jewish radicals) for Eugene Debs, leader of the unified socialist movement, symbolized their acceptance of a narrower gauge for their own special identity. The role of this aging group of craftsmen and their families can hardly be overestimated, however. According to Charles Leinenweber, as late as 1916 they remained the largest single group in New York City Socialist membership ranks.[7]

Their status among the ethnic socialist press has other features as well. In general, the *NYVZ* early gained and long sustained a reputation for literary quality unsurpassed in the radical press. Jewish radicals, it is fair to say, had to *develop* their Yiddish political-literary style. Germans had only to build upon the *Vormärz* and the classic German literary tradition, serializing from past and current German works. The *NYVZ* editors and staff writers included some of the most prestigious, talented immigrant radical intellectuals. To mention only a few is sufficient: Adolf Douai, famed pedagogue, former abolitionist editor and novelist, and an early leader of the American socialist press; Sergius Schewitsch, charismatic public lecturer (the only German-American who could speak with great facility to English-language audiences) and colorful journalist; and Hermann Schlüter, an early historian of American socialism, with the detailed *Erste Internationale in Amerika* (1911) among other works to his credit.[8]

The *NYVZ*'s final leading editor, Ludwig Lore, was, like several of his precursors, a German Jew. A university graduate, well-tempered in the German Socialist movement before his immigration to the United

States in 1903, he had (unlike most of his *NYVZ* predecessors) a rich political life as an intellectual and activist outside the German sector. Along with distinguished Marxist economist Louis Boudin and the first ideologue of American Communism, Louis C. Fraina, Lore also edited the *Class Struggle* (1917–19), a journal which bridged the gap between the left of the Socialist party and the mainstream of American Communism.[9]

But it was within the German Socialist Federation, and the *Volkszeitung*, that Lore's influence was greatest. As a typical *NYVZ* intellectual, he manifested his influence with careful regard to his constituency's inclinations but without much regard for prevailing orthodoxies. The aging—in many cases quite aged—German-American socialists of 1919 wanted a "pure socialism." They believed they had found it in Communism, and they had a great deal of difficulty understanding the factional wrangling that preceded and followed the break with the Socialist party. They were altogether willing to be "Communists"; they thought highly of the Russian Revolution. They did not expect to be leaders of the emerging left movement. But they were adamantly against losing their own special identity and the right to conduct their own collective affairs in their own fashion, as they had done under previous party regimes.[10]

Theodore Draper rightly says that the Communist leaders in the United States resented the power of ethnic leaders and ethnic institutions outside ostensible party discipline. Of course, Socialist party leaders (including a future leading Communist or two) had likewise resented such power, as had Socialist Labor party leaders before them. The invective that Communist functionaries threw at Lore and at the Germans had a parallel in Daniel DeLeon's day. But the rhetoric had changed. And the critics had the unprecedented (if for them vicarious) prestige of an accomplished revolution in Russia behind their demands. These leaders attempted to seize all ethnic institutions during the 1920s, and they earned for their movement mainly the widespread disaffection (in many cases, disaffiliation) of long-standing fraternal activists. But even among ideological deviants, Lore and the *NYVZ* were sui generis.[11]

In the first place, the *NYVZ* had more the feel of a tabloid magazine than a newspaper. My interviews with free-lance writers and Federated Press representatives who wrote for or visited Lore confirm that this format suited his personality and approach. He was a jolly man whose political and aesthetic inclinations fit no prescribed categories. If he enjoyed a particular writer, in any of the many languages he could understand, he ordered translations made, or did them himself. He printed classics galore, but he also went out of his way to encourage young artists. He did not, personally, have any great immediate hopes for the dramatic transformation of the United States. Rather, the *NYVZ* set itself to create an enjoyable publication for the aging reader, whose main political activities centered around fraternal, support, and leisure activities. Unlike the other immigrant papers whose editors had to battle for left positions (likewise readership) against social democratic or conservative elements in their own communities, the *NYVZ* already had all the readers it would ever require. Lore needed to hold onto them, through chains of loyalty and the charms of literary excellence.[12]

An average issue of the *NYVZ* in the early 1920s, then, featured news from Europe (especially Germany). For a time, it had special correspondents in Germany (among them, Max Baginsky, a veteran anarchist), and prided itself on being the only German-language U.S. paper with such direct, thorough coverage of the homeland. Reports from Russia and Eastern Europe—so long as the *NYVZ*'s affiliation with Communism persisted—came directly from the Comintern services, supplemented by serializations of Lenin and others. On the other hand, news about and official endorsement by characteristically German union locals of waiters, cigarmakers, brewers, and butchers remained prominent in the back pages (again, very differently from most other Communist papers), part of the usual description of club, society, and union activities. The *NYVZ* relegated American events, aside from trade-union news, largely to the writers of the decidedly left but also politically independent Federated News Service. Was this a Communist paper in anything but name? Lore himself clearly thought so, and the readers expressing themselves agreed. The paper endlessly justified its separation from the Socialist party, even when it offered a strange variety of reasons. The socialists (as revealed in their 1920 election campaign) failed to oppose prohibition, for one thing! The socialists were old-fashioned (a remarkable charge from users of a literary style fading in Germany). The socialists' concept of unity was only appearance, since its mentality was dominated by "kleinbürgerlichen Schlacken," petit bourgeois schlock which had nothing in common with the class struggle.[13]

The principal argument—perhaps inevitably a European one—was aimed not at American socialists but at the parties of the Second International. They had betrayed socialism in voting war credits; and they (most obviously the German party) had supported the repression of postwar revolutionary tendencies. "Had it not been for 'Democratic' Socialism, we would have had a Soviet Europe Today!" as one of Lore's editorials put the matter. And the lesson followed: "The danger is too great, that one day, when the time comes, the American proletariat, will hand over to Capital the 'great unity movement' of the working-class and be betrayed. The example of Europe alarms and terrifies."[14] It was within the perspective of eventual revolutionary challenge to American capitalism—an argument that could be read as fundamentally pessimistic about the ability of the American working class to take matters in hand—that the embrace of American Communism made good sense to the *NYVZ*'s traditions. Communism, successful in Russia despite all obstacles, had established the pattern for the future. One could not be left behind politically. The *NYVZ* naturally carried the public news of American Communism as the saga of the struggle in the United States.

And yet . . . form and content conflicted, sometimes wildly. Like his readers, Lore was a million miles from "Socialist Realism." Even in the era of "literary NEP (New Economic Policy)," most Communist publications (the Yiddish *Freiheit*, likewise very literary, was a partial exception) placed limits upon the types of contributors and contributions permitted. Lore regularly exceeded the literary license taken by the early *New Masses*, clearly billed as a nonparty publication. He published the Wobbly poet Covington Hall and the feminist science fiction writer Miriam Allen DeFord, also reprinting Jack London, Guy de Maupassant, and many others. In politics, Lore preferred the pre-1919-style left, feminist-ultraradical Sylvia Pankhurst, anarchist Gustav Landauer, Rosa Luxemburg's companion Paul Frölich, and he probably published more Trotsky than any American newspaper (including the Trotskyist press) managed to make available for a decade. The paper also retained the best women's column in a left U.S. newspaper.[15]

In other ways, the *NYVZ* set itself off from the contemporary Communists. Perhaps the most touching feature (certainly for the historian, but also likely for the contemporary reader) was the loving obituary, the tribute to long decades of faithful struggle. Karoline Ott, for instance, was lauded as "eine treue, hingebungsvolle Proletarierin," perhaps the highest compliment from a movement which believed ardently in its rank-and-filers.[16] The most outstanding quality, manifest in the occasional special issues, was the historical sense of self, of immigrant memories both from old Germany—now vanished but still dear to memory—and from nineteenth-century America, equally long gone. Another striking feature, in our perspective from the 1990s, is the increasingly "green" character of nature lore. The "Friends of Nature, Inc." (a hiking and nature-appreciation society, with its main camp in Midvale, New Jersey) came to dominate an increasing amount of space during the 1920s, the descriptions of past and forthcoming hikes a veritable manifesto on the eternal qualities which socialists should strive to understand.[17]

In essence, then, the *NYVZ* of the 1920s overlaid Communist interpretation of developments abroad, and a generally Communist policy at home, upon the long-standing structure and assumptions of the newspaper's milieu, and upon Lore's literary tastes. From a strictly political point of view, it was a Communist paper. But any sort of deconstruction, let alone an attempted historical reconstruction of the average *NYVZ* loyalist's "reading" of the paper, would take us in a very different direction. No one could describe the *NYVZ* as postmodern, yet its extraordinary layering, its sets of assumptions from different historic periods or different geopolitical circumstances, render it an artifact with multiple meanings.

Evolution of the *NYVZ* continued against the background of fierce internal conflict in the 1920s American Communist movement, dragging the *NYVZ*, against the will of its editor and readers, into the mire. Draper portrays one dimension of the conflict between Lore and the Communist leaders with some accuracy, but without a sense for the larger symbolic issues which were at stake. For the *NYVZ* veteran, the struggle for political, electoral socialism in the United States had taken decades of self-sacrifice and many reversals. Readers of the paper had never been happy with the "underground" mentality of the early Communist movement, because they viewed hyperrevolutionary rhetoric as the worst possible response to repression. The formation of a legal Workers party in 1922, and the beginnings of a political campaign structure (minimal though it was), encouraged them greatly.

On the other hand, they drew the line at subordinating left politics to the agenda of the American petite bourgeoisie, fearing the prospect of fusion—the reform strategy that they had combated throughout the history of the socialist movement. Since their own unhappy experience with Henry George's United Labor mayorality campaign in 1886, they had viewed fusion as the onset of virtual treason. They therefore resisted, along with many other formerly socialist ethnic activists, the prospect of Communist identification with a farmer-labor party in 1924. Lore himself hammered away at the Wisconsin Socialist party leader Victor Berger for suggesting an arrangement with Progressive Robert La Follette. Behind that polemic lay discomfiture with an entire mode of activity that had been adopted, with Lenin's approbation, in an effort to locate the mainstream of American life. In Draper's account, Comintern wrangling over the farmer-labor party strategy not only wrecked the American Communists' initial following in the

Paul Buhle

Chicago Federation of Labor and among farmers from Wisconsin to the Dakotas but also exposed the overriding difference between Lore and other Communist leaders: he could not be forced to take discipline. As a closer study of California ethnic Communists reveals, Lore actually articulated a feeling widespread among established ethnic entities. Resistance against the farmer-labor strategy did not have to be whipped up, as in Draper's account; it did have to be articulated, and the *NYVZ* took the lead in this context.[18]

Framed by such subtleties, the larger differences in style and substance began to grow more evident. German-Americans had always worked within the existing unions, in many cases had founded the organizations. But they had almost invariably, within these mostly German, AFL, or independent organizations, disdained to hide their political affiliations. To the German-American worker, even a Republican one, "socialism" was not a strange concept and generally no cause for panic. But to many of the immigrant and native-born workers who would make up the bulk of the successful industrial movement in the 1930s (for which earlier prewar, wartime, and immediate postwar labor activism had been a rehearsal), socialism was an alien idea which community religious leaders and other trusted "respectables" condemned. Toward them (and, in many cases, as protection against the outside world), Communist factory workers increasingly adopted the pose of militants who ostensibly reported and acted upon immediate grievances. The *NYVZ* had always opposed dissimulation. As in the case of the proposed farmer-labor policies, its readers wanted to be socialists openly and proudly, without evasions or reservations.[19] Outside particular ethnic pockets, the days of this old-fashioned political approach had ended, and the Communists had merely adapted (or maladapted) to the new situation. Electoral socialism, save at the local level, would not make a comeback on the pre-1920 model, in any hands. The need for alliances eventually led both Communists and most socialists (albeit as individuals) into New Deal, American Labor party, or (in Minnesota) Farmer-Labor party arrangements. The labor upsurge of the mid- and late 1930s that resumed in the latter days of World War II and ended only with the political division of CIO ranks also took place with "militant" leadership (Communist, socialist, Trotskyist, etc.) which rightly judged itself, at candid moments, as incapable of giving political education to the mass of workers. Leadership substituted for the autodidact's learning, displaced by commercial entertainment in an increasingly all-encompassing popular culture.[20]

Lore's reluctance to take political orders reinforced the paper's image as a renegade publication. His well-known personal fondness for Trotsky led him to become the whipping boy during the party's offensive against language federation indiscipline (and proto-Trotsky-ist or feared proto-Trotskyist indiscipline) in general. In 1925, the party brought Lore up on charges in front of its German Language Federation board, and when the Germans refused to expel Lore, arranged for changes in the board to make his expulsion inevitable.[21]

The subsequent history of the *NYVZ* offers much food for thought. The German Language Federation indeed expelled Lore, but they thereby lost the *NYVZ* and nearly all of its supporters, i.e., whatever remained of German-American Marxism. The Communists attempted several weekly German-language papers. Each was unsuccessful. Not even a stream of newer German refugees could add life to this ghost-apparatus.[22]

The perspective of the writers in the Golden Jubilee 1928 *NYVZ* anniversary issue is most instructive. They charted the split with sections of the 1889 SLP, with DeLeon in 1899, and with the wartime Socialist party in 1919; the recent split with the Workers' (Communist) party shared the historical stage of political tragedy. In each case, the *NYVZ* had struggled *for its own existence* and for the correct balance in leadership of its constituency, neither too opportunistic or too sectarian. In one case, they had been persuaded and forced to leave an organization (the Socialist party) which had ceased to represent the working class; in the other three, they could not permit political hotheads, out of tune with American life and with immigrant radicalism, to destroy the *NYVZ*'s hard-won institutional gains and unique standing with the German-American working class.[23]

To be sure, the tone of the *NYVZ* shifted, and not only politically. By the end of the 1920s, the *NYVZ* unquestionably lost some of its political tone, and became rather more of a "socialistic" labor and culture paper with a full page of wire-service photos and some other ostensibly nonpolitical matter like local radio listings. Lore's literary tastes, now completely unshackled, became more daring. Walt Whitman, André Gide, Boccaccio, and Flaubert's *Madame Bovary* now appeared in the weekly *Vorwärts*. News of Europe took on an avant-garde character, as in "Karl Kraus gegen Theodor Wolff: Eine kleine Berliner Sensation."[24]

On a purely political level, the paper urged support of Norman Thomas's socialist mayoral candidacy and spoke in such comradely terms as "Wir Sozialisten." Lore himself frankly wished for a choice somewhere between socialism and Communism, like Britain's Independent Labour party, although no such choice existed in America. He and the *NYVZ* shared political space, in that sense, with a number of prominent political refugees from American Communism, such as

J. B. S. Hardman, editor of the Amalgamated Clothing Workers' important weekly paper, *Advance*. Lore sought, vainly—especially as the Communist movement passed into an ultrasectarian phase—to carve out a space in which activists of various backgrounds and generations could work with socialists, Communists, and others on specific projects, in the name of a larger labor-radical unity.[25]

For its own part, the paper maintained a remarkable equanimity. Indifference toward the curses of current American Communist leaders could be compartmentalized (as it often was by immigrants of all kinds) from negative conclusions about the Soviet Union, at least for a time. The Soviet Union, whatever its many faults, deserved defense. The Communist-oriented labor and fraternal institutions in the United States deserved support. At the level of the International Workers Order (formed by a split from the Jewish Workmen's Circle) and the International Labor Defense—both Communist-led but with a great deal of leeway and considerable benefits to the foreign-born community in particular—the *NYVZ* printed notices of meetings which even the expelled and deplored Lore himself continued to address! The Communists, in various phases, might to their own disadvantage move sharply away from such mixed milieux, then sharply back again. The *NYVZ* community knew where it stood.[26]

In any case, the institutions around the *NYVZ* continued to function past their Communist phase. The sickness-and-death-benefit societies, the singing societies, the German-based union locals, the "Deutsch-Amerikanischer Fussball-Bund," and the nature-walk societies might well have lost a handful of the more determined (or younger) comrades to the rigors of Leninism. But the institutions and the basic spirit continued, as embodied in the anniversary issues and in the *Pionier Volks-Kalender*, which had appeared for nearly a half-century. The Communists surely had lost more by far than they gained in limiting the loose arrangement.

The historical experience of the *NYVZ*, Lore noted, had been far from a steady advance, from victory to victory. The workers' movement of 1928, he lamented, was perhaps less well organized than that of 1898. But the task had been the same all along, whatever the political rhetoric: organization of all the working classes, no matter what their immediate affiliations, into one class-conscious mass. The *NYVZ* had kept the faith. And so—we must say too—it had.[27]

NOTES

I wish to acknowledge the financial assistance, for research specifically in German-American sources, of the New Jersey Historical Commission and the American Council of Learned Societies; and the National Endowment for the Humanities, for its generous funding of oral history and research into immigrant radicalism. This essay reflects insights worked out in less detail in *Marxism in the United States*.

1. See, for example, the entry by Dirk Hoerder on the *NYVZ* and separate entries by Carol Poore on fraternal and social activities of nineteenth-century German-American socialists, in the *Encyclopedia of the American Left*. Also see Carol Poore, *German-American Socialist Literature*.

2. The new edition of *American Communism and Soviet Russia* seeks, like Draper's earlier attacks upon the most prominent of young radical historians of American Communism, to seal off precious scholarly turf. Ironically, we meant the old man no harm and indeed have paid frequent tribute to his hard research work and to his personal encouragement in his (and our) younger days. The "Commissar" (as Draper was known among his *New Masses* associates of the 1930s), victim of bad habits acquired long ago, has lost friends and scholarly credibility when he might otherwise have celebrated the new generation he helped bring into being.

3. Draper's generation of scholars—with the partial exception of Jewish historians working in Yiddish materials—essentially applied ideological generalities to particular cases, ignoring contradictory evidence. No more than William Z. Foster's *History of the Communist Party, USA* did Draper, or Lewis Coser and Irving Howe, or for that matter such younger scholars as James Weinstein, interest themselves particularly in subjecting broad generalities to closer scrutiny. See Foster's *History of the Communist Party, USA*, easily the worst of the accounts; and see the best of the farmer-labor episode, James Weinstein, *Decline of Socialism in America*. Among the many Yiddish-language scholars writing in English we can count Melech Epstein, Irving Howe, and Moses Rischin; among those in Yiddish, I. Sh. Hertz, Kalmon Marmor, A. Sh. Sacks, and a number of less-remembered students of anarchism and labor Zionism.

4. *Glimpses of the German-American Press*, which also contains an important essay on the Chicago socialist press by Renate Kiesewetter, is certainly the most important resource yet available in the field.

5. Some of this is drawn from my own attempt at a balanced account in *Marxism in the United States*; see also the unfavorable and not entirely inaccurate criticism of *NYVZ* insularity and high-handedness in the 1889 events, in Rudolph Katz, "With DeLeon since '89," the official DeLeonist, SLP account.

6. Ira Kipnis, a doctrinaire historian with little feeling for cultural questions, nevertheless offers the most detailed account of the splits and fusions in *American Socialist Movement*, chaps. 1–6.

7. Charles Leinenweber, "Urban Socialism."

Paul Buhle

8. See Poore, *German-American Socialist Literature,* and her accompanying German-language anthology of the writers, *Deutsch-amerikanische sozialistische Literatur,* for discussion of and samples from some of the writers named. On women's activities see Mari Jo Buhle, *Women and American Socialism,* and a valuable essay by Ruth Seifert, "Portrayal of Women in the German-American Labor Movement," drawing mostly on the *NYVZ,* 1901–3.

9. See Draper, *Roots of American Communism,* chap. 8, for an unsurpassed account of the politics and importance of *Revolutionary Age.*

10. See my account of this mentality in *Marxism in the United States,* chaps. 3–4.

11. Draper's lengthy treatment in *American Communism and Soviet Russia* is frequently insightful, but burdened by his own intellectual agenda, and by his lack of access to (or interest in) the non-English-language sources. I have excluded here Draper's treatment of Lore as faction-fighter in the 1920s Communist party because it does not bear directly upon the *NYVZ* and because Lore's intentions and motivations remain a mystery. Did he believe that he could intervene to help guide the party through troubling days that might pass? Evidently. His own role in the intrigues is, however, out of character, and many veterans of the day later admitted that the frenzy of internecine warfare turned idealism in upon itself.

12. See my interviews with Martin Birnbaum and Harvey O'Connor, in the Oral History of the American Left archives, Tamiment Library, New York University. I am grateful for the recollections of the late Yiddish poet Martin Birnbaum, who achieved his first publication in the mid-1920s *NYVZ* and who recalled to me the literary brilliance of the paper and of its editor. Birnbaum had been especially struck by the translation of the Yiddish humorist and essayist, Moshe Nadir, into German. Much of this interview was published as "Poetry in the 1930s," in *Cultural Correspondence,* #9 (1979). O'Connor, whose job was to collect overdue fees from the *NYVZ* to the Federated Press, regaled me about his meetings with Lore.

13. Editorial, "Debs und Steadman," *NYVZ,* May 22, 1920; Viktor Klotzman, "Aus unserem Leserkreise: Einigkeit—im Princip oder zum Schein," *NYVZ,* Apr. 23, 1920.

14. Editorial, "Debs und die Einigung aller Sozialismus," *NYVZ,* Apr. 24, 1923. Punctuation as in original [trans. eds.].

15. The introduction of an English-language section, made up mostly of Federated Press features, added a sort of Wobbly literary sensibility, closer to the IWW's contemporary *Industrial Pioneer* than to any existing Communist publication.

16. "Karoline Ott," *NYVZ,* May 2, 1920.

17. This subject has just been scrutinized by a group of young scholars. See the "Nature Friends" entry in *Encyclopedia of the American Left* and the collection of interviews in the Oral History of the American Left archives.

18. See Draper, *American Communism and Soviet Russia,* chap. 7, on "Bolshevization," which Draper unfortunately fails to connect with Lore and the

NYVZ; Gustav Landauer, "Briefe aus der deutschen Revolution," *NYVZ,* Dec. 16, 1923; "The Workers Party und die Mittelklasse," *NYVZ,* Jan. 17, 1924; "National Konvention der Deutschen Sprachgruppe," *NYVZ,* Nov. 30 and Dec. 6, 1924.

19. Best seen retrospectively in Lore, "Nach fünfzig Jahren," *NYVZ,* Nov. 29, 1928.

20. Editorial, "Sozialisten sein—oder nicht sein, das ist die Frage," *NYVZ,* Dec. 5, 1924.

21. At this point, historiographically speaking, Lore and the *NYVZ* disappear from *American Communism and Soviet Russia.* One would not know that the *NYVZ* continued as an independent socialist daily until 1932, and (amid the rapidly advancing old age of its constituents) managed to appear weekly until 1944, when the hated Nazis had at last been defeated. Draper, of course, did not write a history of the American left but of American Communism and not so much of American Communism as of its leaders. Some account of Lore, the *NYVZ,* and its successor, the *Neue Volkszeitung,* can be found in Robert E. Cazden, *German Exile Literature in America.* See also Joachim Radkau, *Deutsche Emigration.*

22. Interview with Martin Birnbaum. See Cazden, *German Exile Literature in America,* and Cazden, "Bibliography of German-American Communist Newspapers."

23. Lore, "Nach fünfzig Jahren."

24. "Karl Kraus gegen Theodor Wolff," *NYVZ,* Nov. 23, 1929; see also, for example, "Aus der Arbeiterbewegung," *NYVZ,* Nov. 19, 1928; "Deutsch-Amerikanischer Fussball-Bund," *NYVZ,* Nov. 20, 1928. *Pionier Volks-Kalender* advertisements continued during the latter part of each year for next year's calendar, marked with traditional workers' holidays, birthdays of great heroes (like saints' days), and essays on various subjects.

25. Editorial, "Vom Tage," *NYVZ,* Nov. 27, 1929. I examine the yearning for a third, noncommunist, and nonsocialist force in some detail in my dissertation, "Marxism in the US," chaps. 3–4.

26. Editorial, "Eine neue Welle des roten Terrors," *NYVZ,* Oct. 30, 1929. The United Front styles are abundant in this period.

27. Lore, "Nach fünfzig Jahren."

Dirk Hoerder

The German-American Labor Press and Its Views of the Political Institutions in the United States

This essay will survey the development of the German-American labor press from the 1840s to the 1940s, analyze its opinions about U.S. political institutions in the 1880s, and detail the experience of one editor, who worked in America from 1910 to 1923, to illuminate the everyday problems of labor journalists. The term "labor press" includes all union periodicals, social democratic, socialist, anarchist, and communist papers, local and regional labor papers, and publications of workers clubs, whether in newspaper or magazine format. The first identifiable German-American labor periodicals appear in the 1840s, publications of the utopian socialists. Unlike the thinking of some nineteenth-century British unions, no German-language periodicals seem to have advocated a return of skilled workers or miners to agrarian pursuits. And unlike the concepts of some American groups, embodied for a time in the ideology of the Knights of Labor, no explicit producer ideology seems to have existed among German labor migrants in the 1880s and after, though from the 1840s to the 1870s it was advocated in Weitling's *Republik der Arbeiter* and by pro-labor radical democratic 48er journalists. The German-American labor press did not link the struggle of workers to that of small farmers, little shopkeepers, and the like—to those groups in the social hierarchy which are sometimes called the lower middle class, sometimes the independent proletariat. In the case of migrants from eastern and southern Europe, there was only a small middle-class migration—a few 48ers, farmers, priests, journalists, and entrepreneurs. Thus their middle-class publications, whether religious or nationalist, had to accommodate their views to a working-class readership (though this does not imply that the writers took a class position). The German community, on the other hand, was sufficiently heterogeneous that different audiences could be and were addressed.[1] Connections between the German middle-class and labor press appeared briefly when some disenchanted 48ers turned to more radical viewpoints and then reappeared eighty years later when refugees from Nazi Germany came to the United States.

It should also be noted here that the classification of German migrants as belonging to the "old immigration" is misleading: the "old"-"new" dichotomy between immigrants from western and northern Europe and those from southern and eastern Europe was introduced with racist overtones. It implied that the former became farmers, the latter workers, and assumed the changeover to have occurred in the late 1880s. However, Germans and Scandinavians continued to migrate in large numbers in the first half of the 1890s and most of them were skilled or unskilled workers. On the other hand, Eastern Europeans had come since the 1840s and included farmers. In this essay I distinguish between settlement (agrarian) and labor (urban) migration instead.

The German-Language Labor Press: A Survey

The development of the German-American labor press is closely related to early labor migration from the 1840s and to the massive out-migration of the period from 1879 to 1893.[2] Three groups of political refugees played a particularly important role among the editors and journalists: the refugees of the failed revolution of 1848–49, the socialists and anarchists expelled between 1878 and 1890 under the antisocialist law, and the émigré opponents of Nazi rule between 1933 and 1945. Though the political emigrants were numerically insignificant when compared to the whole of German settlement and labor migration, they took a decisive role in the development of the labor press as particularly outspoken members of the community. The 48ers and early socialists gave a distinct appearance to Phase I of the labor and radical press (1844–69). Socialist, anarchist, and union publications marked Phase 2 (1870–1902). Phase 3 (1903–29) was characterized by a consolidation of the existing press but also by a decline of new ideas and new periodicals. A final phase (1930–45) represented a different radical press: antifascist and antiwar. Much of it was not labor-oriented. Since its early beginnings this press was concentrated in areas that were to remain the centers of labor and left German publishing activities in North America: in the north, Sheboygan, Wisconsin, Detroit, Toronto, Syracuse, and Boston marked the borders. In the

Dirk Hoerder

south it ran from Baltimore along the southern border of Pennsylvania and the Ohio River to St. Louis, and in the west from St. Louis via Davenport to Milwaukee. Publishing outposts were New Orleans, San Antonio and Hallettsville in Texas, San Francisco, Omaha and Kansas City, as well as Winnipeg and Edmonton in Canada.[3]

The *formative period* of the labor press from the 1840s to the 1860s included publications of radical artisans, 48ers and their predecessors, of the first Marxists arriving in the United States, and of a number of local workingmen's organizations. Active participation of many of them in the Civil War resulted in a decrease of periodical publications during the 1860s. While classification is always to some degree arbitrary, the more than sixty periodicals first published during these years may be divided into the press of 48ers and freethinkers sympathetic to labor, of advocates of early or utopian socialism, and of middle-class reformers addressing workers (twenty-three titles). Sixteen titles were issued by local workers' clubs, twenty-four advocated social democratic, socialist,[4] and general labor principles. Many of these periodicals were relatively short-lived.

Phase 2, from the 1870s to the turn of the century, was the *dynamic period* of the German-American labor press. The influence of early socialism and utopian communism had come to an end. Workers' clubs on a citywide basis were replaced by organizations of more continuity and broader influence. Socialist ideas began to play a larger role, a development that reached other immigrant groups only later. Economic growth and recessions, labor's organizational achievements as well as its increased exploitation, and the influx of labor migrants from Germany contributed to the burgeoning of the labor press. Political exiles under the antisocialist law provided capable editors. While contemporaries and those historians limiting themselves to political theory and labor organization have criticized the sectarianism of the German-American socialists, a reading of the major German-language labor newspapers reveals their strong predisposition to come to terms with the new society. Nevertheless some political exiles continued to look back and hope for a return, and considerable energies of German-American socialists were directed to the support of the embattled German Social Democratic party in the 1880s and into the 1890s.[5] Some leaders of the Socialist Labor party did engage in dogmatic debates followed by party splits, but most socialists noted that in the new society experience was the best teacher.

Accordingly the German-American socialist and workers' movement had integrated into the English-language mainstream labor

movement or into the English-speaking socialist parties by about 1900.[6]
Of the more than 120 periodicals established during Phase 2, only one
was a socialist Turner paper and one a free-thought periodical. Local
and general labor periodicals accounted for seventeen titles, socialist,
Workingmen's party, and Socialist Labor party publications for thirty-
seven. When (modest) election successes were stolen from socialist
candidates and when class war was propagated from the top down in
the wake of the 1877 national railroad strike, anarchist thought temporarily gained influence (twenty-one titles). The social democratic, municipal socialism, and Socialist party press also made its debut (seven
titles). Throughout the period trade-union periodicals (thirty titles)
achieved impact and continuity. The average duration of publication
for each new title was—with the exception of most of the anarchist
press—considerably longer than in the formative period.[7]

In addition to the variety and number of publications, the most
significant achievement of Phase 2 was the establishment of a "core
press": twenty-one periodicals, founded mainly in the 1870s and 1880s,
which lasted for more than twenty years. By total years of publication,
the core press accounted for about half of the periodicals available during this phase, for about three-quarters in Phase 3 (1903–29), and for
about one-third in Phase 4 (1930–45). It represented the whole spectrum of the German-American labor press from free-thought, Turner,
and anarchist to union, social democratic, and socialist publications.
The periodicals lasting less than twenty years show the vivacity of
German-American reform, labor, and left movements, reflect remnants of the personal journalism of the 1840s and 1850s as well as
doctrinal differentiation, and reflect the many courageous attempts to
establish periodicals in smaller towns. The core of the labor movement
is represented by the long-lived periodicals.

Phase 3 from 1903 to the beginning of the Great Depression was
a period of limited continuity but also of stagnation and decline. The
core press and several other publications continued into this period,
but a dramatic decline in the founding of new periodicals is registered as well as a decline in total numbers of periodicals published.
This development has its roots in the 1890s, when the influx of new
migrants ended, as the German-American labor movement passed its
apogee as an ethnic movement and began to integrate into the English-
language multiethnic organizations. Until 1929 only sixteen new labor
periodicals were founded, including one Catholic labor-union paper,
a syndicalist-oriented one, and a Communist party paper. This accen-
tuated the fact that German-American workers—by now often second

generation—had acculturated and were underrepresented among unskilled workers. The geographical expansion of places of publication
noted for Phase 2 is replaced by a sharp contraction.

Only two additions to the core press are registered for these three
decades. Both emphasized cultural and recreational aspects of the
movement. Several periodicals were organs of ethnically based mutual
benefit organizations that still fulfilled an economic, social, and recreational function. World War I further reduced the number of labor
periodicals, capping a trend of a decade and a half.

During the last phase of German-American publishing, from the
Depression through World War II, the core press declined to seven
publications by 1930 and to one by 1945. The periodicals of the early
1930s marked the brief emergence of a Canadian-German labor movement, while in the United States the labor press restricted itself to reports on working-class culture in the German-American ethnic group.
The appearance of the *Kampfsignal* marked the transition from cultural
periodicals on the left to antifascist publications. From that period,
German-American social democratic, socialist, Communist, and non-
aligned left periodicals opposed Nazi ideology and dictatorship and
became fundamentally different in character from the earlier immigrant labor press. They were joined in this struggle by many publications of non-working-class intellectuals.

While earlier a tendency to partial publication in English was ob-
servable, these new periodicals were published exclusively in German,
addressing themselves to other exiles in North America or Europe as
well as to the German resistance movement. After 1941 many publications were concerned intensively with plans for a postwar Germany.

After the war, a few German-language and left periodicals continued to be published or were newly established. They remained marginal and provided a somewhat undistinguished ending for a once important element of the North American ethnic labor press. In the century from the 1840s to the 1940s about 250 labor periodicals appeared
(of a total of about five thousand German-language periodicals). Only
the Jewish and the Italian labor presses were similarly significant in
numbers, the latter, because of a large number of ephemeral anarchist
publications, had less impact.[8]

The Labor Press Views "Democratic" Society

The view German immigrants held of the new society varied
greatly according to their social position. The letters of settlers in the

first half of the nineteenth century generally show people content with having left behind the arrogance of German officials, with escaping the swarms of tax, tithe, and other collectors. Artisans emphasized that when asking for a job they did not have to cringe, they did not even have to take their caps off. The letters included references to the quick work pace, to problems with "strange" farming methods, to difficulties in gaining a foothold in commerce, but the basic theme was: by hard work any individual can make his or her own way.[9] This positive image was grafted onto an earlier positive view dating from the "age of bourgeois-democratic revolution" when the new American state became the model for many reformers and revolutionaries in Europe[10] and has taken deep root in historians' studies as well.

This view of the American experience totally neglects the condition into which labor migrants were cast and which determined their opinion of the new society. Several authors have recently pointed out that by the 1880s, letters from workers to their families and villages painted a very realistic image of "oppression," that is, exploitation, in America.[11] A reading of the labor press in many European countries shows that workers could adequately gauge their chances—or the lack of them—from the regular reporting about conditions in America: social and economic differences were as large as in Europe. This is being conceded—if somewhat reluctantly—by economists and some historians.[12] It is worth noting that the highly critical attitude of organized labor toward conditions in the United States was shared by German diplomats looking from the top down. Rarely did they see anything positive in turn-of-the-century America, in fact many called the United States a country where money ruled, a plutocracy.[13]

The initial hypothesis for my research was that German outmigrants assumed that in the United States, the job and destination conditions would be better, if only slightly. It was assumed that the constant police presence at workers' meetings in Germany under the antisocialist law created a feeling of totalitarian surveillance, while the aid given by ward heelers of the Democratic—and more rarely of the Republican—party created a feeling of having at least extra-institutional access to some benefits of the system. For the top level the hypothesis assumed limited paternalism in Germany—social security legislation—and intolerant rejection of all of labor's demands in the United States as evidenced in the judgments handed down by the Supreme Court and other higher courts in all matters of labor legislation and labor struggles. A detailed reading of the *New Yorker Volkszeitung* (*NYVZ*) proved the first part of the hypothesis wrong. A detailed reading of Supreme Court opinions revealed a more deep-seated and more openly espoused class consciousness by the majority of the judges than expected.

"Amerika ist kein neues Land mehr," the *NYVZ* complained in 1881. Statistics, often provided by the state bureaus of labor, were marshaled to show the low standard of living which workers had to accept and the high degree of exploitation to which they were subjected. Working conditions differed little from those in Germany. Violence exerted by the monopolies against strikers was worse than the policeman's club in Germany; corruption was worse than in Czarist Russia; the work pace was faster than in Great Britain.[14] Democratic and republican ideals were but a veil to hide the reality of wage slavery. Adolf Douai quoted the former governor and senator from New York, William H. Seward: "The entire difference between you (the slaveholders) and us (the free-soil people) is that you own your workers, and we rent them." Wage slavery became the dominant theme and from this it is obvious that workers would not experience the new world turned old as a testing ground for republican ideals, a beacon of liberty.[15] Indeed, when the Statue of Liberty was dedicated in October 1886, a gift of the French people in memory of the centennial of the Declaration of Independence, the *NYVZ* noted: "Freedom's Symbol. Unveiled by the Rich and the Aristocrats. The Wage Slaves are Allowed to Stand By." The "rich" and the "aristocrats" were described in the text as idlers, exploiters, a hypocritical bourgeoisie "living in luxury screaming hurrah according to their understanding of freedom."[16]

Workers had different experiences with liberty. Few of them shared in the benefits distributed by ward heelers, more came in contact with the ever-present police. The days of the revolutionary period were gone—when a few constables had looked after the proper conduct of the people; when the people rioted to bring back into the fold the wealthy, i.e., the merchants, the powerful, the few officials who had overstepped the norms set by community standards. Half a century later the Boston police, faced with an increasing number of indigent and unemployed, had opened soup kitchens on their own initiative. A full century later the police forces in American cities had been transformed into instruments of one class, the higher bourgeoisie, to suppress another class, the workers, with the lower bourgeoisie left in the middle, sometimes siding with workers, particularly in smaller towns where a feeling of community was preserved, sometimes siding with the higher-ranking people, usually in the larger towns. After the railroad workers' uprising in 1877, the police were reinforced by the heavily armed National Guard, an army to quell internal uprisings. In addition there were several private police and paramilitary organizations, like the Pinkertons and the coal and steel police.[17] Many historians of migration specializing in the cultures of origin find little difference between repression in the Czarist, Habsburg, or Prussian empires and in the United States. While no detailed comparative studies have yet been undertaken, the impression prevails that the savage police attack on the unemployed in New York's Tompkins Square in 1874 may be comparable to European police violence, while incidents on the scale of the Ludlow massacre have no counterparts in European relations between industry or government and labor. Kaiser Wilhelm II's dictum that social democrats were "vaterlandslose Gesellen" found its parallel in the persecution of socialists from Haymarket to the Red Scare, as Attorney General A. Mitchell Palmer and other prosecutors labeled radicals as "un-American," as "seditious aliens."[18]

An analysis of the *NYVZ*'s reporting of New York police activities between 1886 and 1892 shows that at least for the readers of this paper it was common knowledge that the police were corrupt (the personal property of police officers was contrasted with their official pay), brutal in everyday affairs (attacks on citizens with no class motivation), and partisan (siding with capital during strikes).[19] In the latter case the *NYVZ* called the officers "Bestie Polizist," "offizielle Rowdies," "Banditen der Kapitalmacht." Police Inspector McKellar was quoted as having said, "You god-damned socialists are reponsible for all this turmoil. . . . The best thing to do would be to smash all your skulls."[20] It might be said that from the viewpoint of workers two kinds of criminals existed, those operating privately for their personal gain and those paid by government (or in some cases industry) and operating for both their private gain and to preserve the class society.

Can the reporting of the *NYVZ* be considered to yield a realistic picture of police activities? Few of its charges were taken up by the English-language press of New York. The foreign-language press was not read by the hegemonic society, the grievances of the immigrants not taken seriously. On the other hand, police brutality did annoy native English speakers and criticism of it can be found in English-language papers.[21] In 1894, the official "Lexow Committee" substantiated almost all the charges that the *NYVZ* had raised against the police since they began publishing in 1878, with the exception, of course, of the paper's position on the class struggle. A comparison of the reporting of the *NYVZ* with that of the *New York Times* demonstrates that both sides accepted the role of the police as a mainstay of middle-class power and politics. Police clubs are used with "alacrity," strikers are lectured by mayors to subdue their pride, or, directly to the point:

"The law-abiding people of the United States will regret, not that three or four of the Scranton rioters were killed, but that the rifles of the volunteer company charged with the protection of property did not do more execution." [22]

Moving from the level of lawlessness in law enforcement—from Wickersham—to the attitude of the *NYVZ* to the political system as a whole, the viewpoint was equally clear. President Garfield's inauguration was decribed as "Carneval des Grosskapitalismus." [23] Legislation applying "criminal conspiracy laws" to workers' organizations met with harsh criticism and was called class legislation in the interests of one class, a class that was variously called bourgeois, money lords, capitalist, or the moneyed aristocracy. [24] Historians hostile to the concept of class as a category for analyzing society might charge that such statements were overblown rhetoric. At the other end of the spectrum, though, the Supreme Court judges in commencement speeches and court opinions talked about the war between classes (as the previous war had been one between sections) and saw it as their role to oppose the "march of the 60 million" toward a more equal distribution of property and opportunity. [25] Class rhetoric may not have been as common as in Europe and probably boundaries between classes were less rigid, but class consciousness was voiced from many sections of the population, it was not a foreign import. The Knights of Labor developed their class analysis from an analysis of labor's position in American society, while the Supreme Court in the Income Tax cases followed bourgeois ideology, particularly the interests of large capital, when using the concept of class war.

To combat this tendency, the German immigrants as well as those of different ethnic backgrounds fused their social democratic thought with the social republicanism of American workers as expressed by the Knights of Labor and striking workers. They referred to an internationally recognized body of thought about equal rights stemming both from the American Declaration of Independence and from the French Revolution. In an article entitled "Why Continue to Celebrate the Fourth of July?" published in 1881, the *NYVZ* emphasized that it was a great achievement for the American Revolution to have demanded independence by declaring that "all humans are born with equal rights" ("dass alle Menschen gleiche angeborene Rechte haben") and that a people has the right to change its constitution and its government, when these violate the principle of equality and of the Bill of Rights ("dass ein Volk das Recht habe, seine Verfassung und Regierung zu wechseln, wenn diese die gleichen Menschenrechte verletze"). Such principles, however, had become a thing of the past. The wealthy descendants of the republic, whom Andrew Carnegie proudly called an aristocracy of the dollar, liked to stay in Europe and to marry into aristocracy. There, workers also observed a turnaround in class norms. Hungarian, German, Slovak, and other workers in Budapest witnessed the arrival of marriage candidates and ridiculed the socially exclusive aristocrats who forgot all distinctions of rank when rich American citizens came to their doors.

While historians and sociologists have emphasized the difference between feudal and bourgeois upper classes, workers at the turn of the century witnessed an aristocracy and a capitalist class merge into each other through marriage and capital transfer. This whole class was, as native and immigrant workers in the United States bitterly charged, no longer responsible to the laws. It imported wage slaves from all over the world and bribed the legislatures and civil servants. Immigrant upstarts like the (German-American) brewery bosses emulated the American top class: modern dukes and small despots; the railroad magnates conducted themselves like the old European powers. Nevertheless the *NYVZ* did not recommend abolishing the Fourth of July. Rather it demanded a return to first principles. Those who fought for independence from Great Britain in 1776 had vowed to fight for it or to perish; they did not want to live as slaves. Now the struggle had to go on: free men had been turned into wage slaves by the dominance of a capitalist class which had turned the American republic into a modern sort of feudalism.[26]

Having outlined the criticism of the political (and economic) system of the United States as voiced in the *NYVZ*, which as part of the core press can be taken as representing a cross section of opinions of socialist-oriented workers, we should now ask, what chances for an improvement did the workers see? Apart from a brief period when election frauds stole success at the polls from many socialist candidates in municipal elections and when in consequence a substantial section of the politically active German-American workers turned to anarchism and to armed resistance against police and Pinkerton violence, the German-American socialists shared the liberal-republican tradition stemming from the American and French revolutionary heritage, as Hartmut Keil has pointed out.[27] While some socialist thinkers debated American society in terms of a strict Marxist analysis, the vast majority of the socialists decided to use accepted institutional channels to promote their view of social republicanism:[28] the polls and the unions. The struggle for a different economic system in the future receded against

Dirk Hoerder

short-term gains. Their efforts yielded only limited results: working-men's parties and municipal socialism did gain a foothold in many cities but not on a nationwide scale.

The hopes for victory at the polls were diminished not only by the limited voter response but also by massive election frauds and by reactionary Supreme Court rulings that declared unconstitutional any legislative gains labor made. The socialists and some committed liberals had to realize, as did the Knights of Labor earlier, that they were the only ones in the system who took democratic rules seriously. This certainly contributed to the bitterness of their rhetoric, and it also led some activists to withdraw or to view the system with cynicism. I have argued elsewhere that, given the high incidence of migration, notwithstanding warnings from disillusioned immigrants and all of the accurate information available to those who still chose to come, and given bitter experiences in the United States, migration was not a move toward a better society but rather an attempt to take one's future out of the hands of "fate," out of a predetermined course in the old country, into one's own hands. Kerby Miller has put forward a similar argument for Irish migrants.[29] Migration became a secular religion: a determination not to wait for a better life after death, not to wait for the results of class struggle leading to better conditions in one's society of birth, but rather to move away, i.e., to an industrializing area in Europe, North America, or elsewhere in the world, to realize limited improvements in personal conditions, and if necessary continue the struggle for societal improvement there. Moving off when conditions became intolerable gave many migrants, according to their own accounts, a feeling of independence, of dignity. If power relationships prevented any fighting back, out-migration was the last resort to show discontent.[30] Similarly, if power relationships in a "democratic" society could nullify election successes, a move to anarchism or a withdrawal into cynical contempt for the new society was a logical response. Those who continued the struggle had more and more difficulty explaining to themselves and their followers why they should harbor any hopes for an improvement in conditions, as the columns of the German-American labor press show.

Case Study of a Labor Editor[31]

Josef Jodlbauer, social democratic deputy in the Diet (Landtag) of Styria, Austria, migrated to the United States in 1910. His reasons were personal: a broken marriage and a child with his new companion. He did not go toward something better, he left rigid and confining social norms.

He harbored no illusions about the new society, as he made clear in his autobiography; he merely saw a chance to earn a living and to remain active in the movement. But he soon had to realize that even a person as well informed about the new society as he was did harbor illusions. The persecution of all those who did not subscribe to the capitalist system and its parliamentary and police branches forced him to return to Austria in 1923. His illusions, his hopes, and his struggles may be taken as representing the experience of many activists who aspired to change, to improve the system from within, who did not believe the official rhetoric about the rights and the rule of the people but who attempted to use those rights the laws gave them.

On arrival, passing the Statue of Liberty, he felt the symbol misplaced: he knew all the details about the Haywood, Moyer, Pettibone trial, which definitely did not square with any concept of liberty. His only reason to absolve the American people from hypocrisy was the fact that the statue had been a gift of the French people and had not been erected by the American people themselves. "In less than fifty years it has become very dilapidated through rust. But it is not yet as brittle as what the Americans call freedom!" (p. 14).

Looking for a job, he visited the office of the *NYVZ* and found the staff—in 1910—somewhat superannuated. Viewed from Europe, socialism in the United States seemed to be a factor of some influence ("beachtenswert"), and he wrongly assumed that this was the reason why the First International's central office had been transferred to Philadelphia in 1870. Though it came to a quick demise, Jodlbauer had his own positive image of the past: in the 1870s more than twenty dailies claiming to follow socialist principles had been published in the United States. This had been a time when nobody could even have thought of publishing a truly socialist paper in Austria. In addition, more than one million workers in the United States were organized in unions, and their strikes aroused interest all over the world (pp. 19–20).

Disappointed with the *NYVZ*, he began to look halfheartedly for a job in his trade as a baker or in any other manual employment, but his hopes to continue working as an editor remained unabated. The editors of the *NYVZ* bypassed him whenever there was an opening. Jodlbauer assumed that they hired Germans only, no Austrians. A position at the *Philadelphia Tageblatt* was not suited to his capabilities and he did not consider the *Tageblatt* a socialist paper. In addition, working conditions were miserable. A lucrative offer to change sides and join the staff of the Hearst-owned *New York Journal* meant "unlimited opportunities" and agreeable working conditions, but, unwilling to sell out his principles, he turned it down (pp. 26–30).

Finally he began to work as a "master mechanic" at the Singer sewing machine factory in Elizabeth, New Jersey. For a brief time he wrote articles for the *NYVZ*, but soon realized that imported notions of socialism did not fit the situation of American workers. He decided to study statistical and background materials about the United States, and as a result his lectures were well attended (pp. 40–41). When he attempted to discuss social security legislation with workers of his factory, he was well aware that under section 23 of the Austrian press law this might have led to arrest; trusting the doctrine of freedom of press, speech, and assembly in the United States, he went ahead, and was summarily arrested and sentenced for littering the street with handbills. So much for the laws and the Bill of Rights.

When it was suggested that he tour the country to agitate for socialism, he felt that the conservative wing of the party merely wanted to have him out of town—he was now working in New York City— but accepted the proposition because a prospective editor (his hope!) of a major German-American labor periodical should know more of the new country than downstate New York and the surrounding areas (p. 59). He was lecturing in New England when the textile workers' strike of 1912 began and experienced the "terrorism" against strikers, worse than anything he had ever witnessed in Austria (p. 64). Citizens of the most free and democratic country of the world armed against workers; public institutions used the whole repressive apparatus established since the 1880s to mistreat the immigrants in every way possible (pp. 64, 111–12).

In 1912 he became editor of the Cleveland *Echo,* a socialist weekly started in 1911 but financially ruined by the beginning of 1912. Jodlbauer succeeded in reestablishing a sound basis for the paper, became secretary of Local 19 of the Bakers' Union, and reported as critically about the machinations of the union's leadership as about the country's political leadership. His position as editor was difficult, because he was Austrian, not German; because his opinions not only conflicted with the middle-class press but were also voiced rather uncompromisingly; because in many cases larger periodicals had faster access to information while he had merely the background knowledge to interpret the materials. Jodlbauer threw a little light on the composition of the German-language ethnic community: one side was made up of older immigrants from Germany, assimilated and middle-class oriented ("verbürgerlicht"); the other part consisted of recent arrivals, mainly proletarians from Austria, Hungary, the Baltic areas, even from Syria "and from God only knows where." The established section of the ethnic community played a self-assumed leadership role, but in Jodlbauer's opinion it was nothing but the tail end of the Democratic or Republican parties. To reach all groups of new arrivals, he had to limit his writing style to a "basic German," consisting of no more than a few hundred words. As long as he did not touch on questions of broad interest, his work as editor received little notice beyond that of the readership. He was placed in the limelight or rather on the pillory when he deviated from accepted majority opinion in emotionally charged situations. For example, when the "Titanic" sank, he noted that probably it was not the iceberg that should be faulted but the White Star Line's demand for speed. Angry readers and other members of the German ethnic community besieged him, pointed out that he was no German anyway but a "Pollack," and asked repentance for exposing the German-American community to the hostility of the new society. When an Italian-language paper supported his argument, the ethnic slur was changed, he now was called "Spagettifritzi" (pp. 72–74, 76).

The next problem arose when two policemen were killed on duty while looking for "suspicious foreigners" ("verdächtige Ausländer"). The incident was used to begin a broad anti-alien campaign to arouse class hatred among all bourgeois groups, regardless of ethnicity, against all impoverished foreigners. While he supported a decent pension for the families of the two policemen, he opposed a public burial, arguing that the incident was a work accident ("Betriebsunfall") like thousands of others and that efforts should be made to procure support for all victims of work accidents. He used the example of a number of workers who had been killed when enlarging the waterworks in Lake Erie and whose families had received no support. "Why do we say we live in a country of equality, when such differences are maintained?" he asked (pp. 78–79). Even the (socialist) administrative board of the paper felt that this was going too far. When a former AFL official admitted having been an employers' agent, Jodlbauer was told in advance by union officials, knowing his outspoken manners, to keep quiet. As might be assumed, he did not heed the advice. He knew corruption and double-dealing when he saw it (pp. 102–3).

His demands for equality went far—even from the perspective of his contemporaries including his socialist comrades. When Archduke Ferdinand was assassinated in Sarajevo, Jodlbauer merely noted that socialists definitely did not support the death penalty, but that by Aus-

Dirk Hoerder

trian law people used to be hanged for lesser crimes. On the question
of war, socialists were split into class-conscious and patriotic groups.
Jodlbauer, belonging to the former, decided to remain somewhat aloof
from the Cleveland *Echo* because otherwise the factional struggles
would cause the periodical to fail. His deep mistrust of the American
democratic system led him to propose organizing the Socialist party,
of which he was the German Ohio state organizer, into groups of
ten, which could operate secretly should the government use the war
situation to institute severely repressive measures. His suggestion was
rejected as coming from someone who grew up in the Austrian police
state (pp. 124, 192). The repressive measures of the government in the
winter of 1919–20 justified his suspicions. The continuous harassment,
the antiradical campaigns which to Jodlbauer were always anti-alien
campaigns, and the brutality of the police, Chamber of Commerce
vigilantes and other thugs, and officials of the Department of Justice
(as described in the autobiography) seemed to be different only in degree from earlier Russian pogroms and the later SA-terror. Jodlbauer
ascribed the political success of the government and the capitalist class
over their workers to a policy of divide and conquer, of bread and cir-
cuses. The workers had been made to believe by the government, the
press, and the AFL unions that they had no distinct political interests
of their own. It was merely accepted that workers would have their
own support organizations for illness and death. Since they were ad-
mittedly less well off than others in the United States and since no
one else paid their bills for doctors, medication, and burial, it was
the advantage a free worker had to be self-sufficient in these respects.
Still following Jodlbauer's argument, all efforts to unionize workers
had been imported in the cultural baggage of migrant laborers, but
the American organizations were turned into craft unions that were
closer to medieval guilds than to modern labor unions (p. 188).[32] Anyone who did not accept fate, who did not mindlessly accept whatever
the ruling circles decided, was designated a "radical," thus becoming
an outlaw, no longer a part of the community. Any kind of violence
and terror could be used against the "radical." The imprisonment of
Eugene Debs in 1918 on charges of sedition; a policeman's attack on
Jodlbauer's pregnant wife; the burning of the Socialist party files; and
hundreds of other incidents served to confirm his notion of America.

By 1923, at the age of forty-six, the difficulty of securing a job—
his radical opinions were well known—and the constant threats to
his life (including those from union thugs), as well as internal splits
among the U.S. left, and despair over the possibility for change in the
United States, prompted his to return to Europe. His rationale was

that of the quintessential labor migrant: we will find something better than death. On the other hand, his wife provided a rationale similar to the labor migrants who decided to stay: she had gotten used to new surroundings and new friends (pp. 268ff.).

Judging from his autobiography, Jodlbauer was no revolutionary. He and the labor press in general never counseled one-sided reliance on the ballot but with few exceptions remained within the framework set by the Constitution, the laws, and very importantly the Declaration of Independence. Like many of its immigrant workers' readership, the labor press took the liberty of condemning some means of exploitation and some governmental measures as inconsistent with the "first principles" of the American people.

Jodlbauer, like many of the German-American labor editors, had considerable difficulty reaching middle-class German immigrants. This press remained class-based, with ethnicity relegated to the second rank. The *Echo* reflected the experience of those labor migrants among the German-Americans who came during the period of the so-called new immigration. In fact, a part of its "German" readership came from areas eastward of the German national territories in Europe. The *Echo* is a typical example of the German-American labor press surveyed above, since it was neither one of the short-lived radical or local publications nor part of the core press. It provided information and critical comments about American political institutions on a sophisticated level, a sophistication shared by many activists of the German-American labor movement. Its pragmatism and strong emphasis on U.S. unions and socialist parties also made clear that German-American workers had become part of the American labor movement.

NOTES

1. The standard bibliography for the German-American press is Karl J. R. Arndt and May E. Olson, *Deutsch-amerikanische Zeitungen und Zeitschriften;* for the German-American labor press see Anne Spier, "Germans." For the labor press of other ethnic groups see Christiane Harzig and Dirk Hoerder, eds., *Press of Labor Migrants.*

2. The periodization has been developed on the basis of research done by Anne Spier.

3. Anne Spier, "Germans," fig. 3.

4. This category includes periodicals with free-thought tendencies or affiliation with the Turners or the International Workingmen's Association.

5. Dirk Hoerder and Hartmut Keil, "American Case and German Social Democracy."

6. This was demonstrated by both the research project "A Social History

of the German Workers of Chicago, 1850–1910" (Universität München, Hartmut Keil and John B. Jentz, directors) and the "Labor Newspaper Project" (Universität Bremen, Dirk Hoerder, director).

7. See table, "Length of Publication," in Dirk Hoerder, "The Press of Labor Migrants from Western and Central Europe: Introduction," p. 218.

8. Ida C. Selavan, "Jews," and Annamaria Tasca, "Italians."

9. "Amerika ist ein freies Land."

10. Günter Moltmann, Atlantische Blockpolitik im 19. Jahrhundert; American and European Revolutions; Impact of the American Revolution Abroad. A less well researched "plebeian" or "Jacobin" tradition developed from the French Revolution.

11. John H. M. Laslett, "America before and after Emigration"; Lars-Goeran Tedebrand, "Image of America among Swedish Labor Migrants."

12. Jeffrey Williamson and Peter Lindert, American Inequality; Hartmut Kaelble, Historical Research on Social Mobility; Peter R. Shergold, Working-Class Life.

13. "Plutokraten und Sozialisten."

14. NYVZ, Feb. 14, 20, July 1, 1881, May 6, 24, 1887.

15. NYVZ, Jan. 28, 1888.

16. NYVZ, Oct. 29, 1886, quoted in Hartmut Keil, "Ambivalent Identity."

17. Dirk Hoerder, " 'Mobs, a Sort of Them at Least, Are Constitutional' "; Joseph J. Holmes, "National Guard of Pennsylvania"; Jeremiah P. Shalloo, Private Police; Sidney L. Harring, Policing a Class Society.

18. This idea has been debated by scholars cooperating in the Labor Migration Project at the University of Bremen. Studies of the Russian labor movement by U.S. scholars confirm this impression. The German-language social democratic newspaper Volkstimme published in Budapest between 1894 and 1924 does indicate a comparable level of repressive violence as well as a higher level of gendarme brutality against the rural population.

19. Thomas Weber, "Berichterstattung der 'New Yorker Volkszeitung.' "

20. NYVZ, Apr. 24, 1886.

21. James F. Richardson, New York Police, p. 193.

22. New York Times, Aug. 2, 1877.

23. NYVZ, Mar. 2, 1881.

24. NYVZ, Mar. 4, 1882.

25. Income Tax cases, expression used by Joseph H. Choate, counsel for plaintiff, accepted by judges; quoted in Louis B. Boudin, Government by Judiciary, 2 vols. (New York, 1932), 2:219, 223–33.

26. NYVZ, July 4, 1881.

27. Keil, "Ambivalent Identity," cf. n. 16.

28. Paul Krause, "Labor Republicanism and 'Za Chlebom' "; Richard Schneirov and John B. Jentz, "Social Republicanism and Socialism."

29. Dirk Hoerder, "German Immigrant Workers' Views of 'America' "; Kerby A. Miller, "Golden Streets, Bitter Tears" (forthcoming in Dirk Hoerder

and Horst Roessler, eds., *Distant Magnets: Expectations and Realities in the Immigrant Experience*).

30. Jacquelyn Dowd Hall, Robert Korstad, and James Leloudis, "Cotton Mill People," pp. 249, 260, 267.

31. The following section is based on the manuscript autobiography of the Austrian social democrat Josef N. Jodlbauer, "13 Jahre in Amerika" [1910–1923], written in March 1948, 278 pages. I am grateful to Dr. Herbert Steiner, Vienna, for drawing my attention to the unpublished manuscript in his possession and for permission to use a photocopy for this essay. I am presently looking for a publisher for a translated, abridged, and annotated version of this important autobiography. Citations are given by manuscript page number in the text.

32. This paraphrases the German text.

Moses Rischin

Envoi

I

Like no other non-English-speaking group in nineteenth-century America, German immigrants played a central role in the creation of the American labor movement. As David Brody has reminded us, trade-union structure and policy may have been based on English models, but American labor philosophy was derived largely from German sources.[1] Yet for many obvious reasons the German-American role has been slighted—in part at least because, unlike the Irish who into the third and fourth generation accounted for a disproportionately high percentage of the officers of the American Federation of Labor (as did those of British origin, and subsequently those of Russian-Jewish origin), the German-American subculture did not produce an equivalent cadre of prominent union leaders to give symbolic recognizance to the German role. Of the seventy-eight of the 150 late-nineteenth-century labor leader sample identified by ethnic origin by Warren Van Tine, only five were German; in the subsequent generation, of 120 identified by ethnic origin (of a sample of 200 business unionists), only seven were of German parentage and only one was a German immigrant.[2] Equally telling has been the commitment to Americanization and self-dissolution fostered by the German-American labor ideology, so that inquiries into the most emphatically expressive German-American labor institutions seemed, at least until recent years, gratuitous, even as a study of process.

On these grounds alone, a volume like this one takes on unusual import. For the first time, it makes vividly apparent the role of the German-American radical press during the last half of the nineteenth and the first decades of the twentieth century and opens the way to an understanding of a sector of American life that has eluded historians heretofore.

Essential to a comprehension of the role of the German-American radical press is an appreciation of the extraordinary volume, variety, and complexity of the great German immigration and its historic timing. At three critical junctures in the course of nearly half a century, German immigration crested to the accompaniment, both in Germany and in the United States, of political turbulence and ideological ferment that demanded to be heard. In the first period, between 1847 and 1854, German immigration averaged over 100,000 annually, second only to the Irish of the great famine years; in the second, between 1865 and 1874, German immigration mounted to 110,000 annually, running ahead of all others; and in the third, between 1881 and 1892, the record total of 1,700,000 German immigrants, or about 140,000 annually, was without compare in the whole history of immigration before the twentieth century. After that the great German migration subsided with an abrupt finality. So much was this so that Walter Kamphoefner noted that in the early years of the twentieth century, of all immigrants, Germans were the least likely to travel abroad or to enter the United States more than once. The story of German-America clearly had reached a new stage, impelling a German savant to put forth the famous question—"Why is there no socialism in the United States?"— clearly pointed at German-America, which historians have continued to debate ever since. From the German laborer's diet of "potatoes and alcohol" up the rungs of the German-American workman's Algeresque ladder to "roast beef and apple pie" was not quite Werner Sombart's answer to the question he posed.[3] But whether the German historical sociologist knew it or not, by the early years of the twentieth century, German-American workmen in particular were abundantly represented among the charter members of the American Federation of Labor. In an ever more sharply stratified and bureaucratized multiethnic industrial America, German-American workmen had rounded a corner, had acquired a privileged American place, and had attained a new equilibrium.

In the preceding half-century, no other major ethnic group in America had encountered the full brunt of the forces of modernity —nationalism, liberalism, industrialism, and socialism—both in its country of origin and its country of adoption—with the swirling intensity of German-America. Massively settled in virtually all of America's great cities, German immigrants were more heavily and diversely colonized in the skilled crafts than were members of any other ethnic group. Moreover, the succession of worldwide depressions which simultaneously struck the world's two leading industrializing countries with unmatched force and severity, coincided with the German migration to America. In Germany the rise and suppression of socialism and in the United States an unprecedented labor upheaval would give the German-American radical press a sense of historic immediacy not quite shared by others less directly implicated.

Already, in the mid-nineteenth century, when American workmen expanded their ranks to encompass an ever more varied multiethnic fellowship, German immigrants were the first to test American labor's capacity for fraternity. Infused with the French, the German, and the wider international revolutionary élan of the 1840s, as one historian has emphasized, German immigrants totally transformed the Anglo-American workmen's world, most notably of metropolitanizing New York, the nation's greatest industrial city.

By the Civil War years, in Chicago no less than in New York, as John Jentz has demonstrated, and in so many other cities as well, the formidable German presence contributed to the emergence of the first bona fide interethnic labor movement in the world. However episodic, then and for a generation thereafter, the German-American labor movement would occupy an integral place in labor's ranks. "Given the immigrant basis of so much of America's urban and industrial work force after 1850 and the influence of German-America on so many other foreign language speaking immigrants, this link was arguably the true tap-root of the American labor movement," contends Stanley Nadel. Samuel Gompers' tribute to New York of the 1860s and 1870s as "the cradle of the labor movement," his assertion that the labor-veteran-led German-American socialist organizations constituted the most "virile and resourceful" segment of the New York labor movement, and the influence of the originally bilingual American Federation of Labor further testify to the centrality of the German role in New York City. In Chicago, Bruce Nelson sees its flourishing labor movement at the turn of the century as the triumphal heir of labor's most shattering defeat. Within a decade, the Haymarket tragedy and Waldheim, inseparable from German-American labor, had catalyzed the fusion of two antagonistic "republicanisms," the one homegrown or Anglo-American, the other "imported, almost alien," heterogeneous and continental but dominantly German, enabling Chicago to challenge London for the honor of "trade union capital of the world."[4]

II

It is these tumultuous decades in American labor history which found special cause and voice in the German-American radical press and which the contributors to this volume elucidate with freshness, authority, and originality. To highlight the nature of the topic, I shall comment mainly on the essays by Hartmut Keil, Ken Fones-Wolf and Elliott Shore, Ruth Seifert, and Paul Buhle. Since these four essays are representative of the larger contours of our theme, reflective of the volume's four-part design, and suggestive of the major strengths and minor weaknesses of this undertaking, I trust my remarks may have some significance.

No historian has studied the German-American labor movement in the United States so diligently and so imaginatively as has Hartmut Keil. Clearly, his profile of German-American radical editors is a product of his long-term commitment, his virtual immersion in the files of the German-American radical press, and his association with the monumental bibliographical project calendaring the whole immigrant labor press that long absorbed the energies and talents of Dirk Hoerder and his associate Christiane Harzig.[5]

Keil's study, as well as Hoerder's landmark work, make all too apparent the fact that there has been a major blind spot, not only in the scholarship on the German-American press, which heretofore focused almost exclusively on the pre-Civil War era and especially on the 48ers, but even in the latest biographical dictionaries of American labor, reform, and radicalism, where the German-American presence goes virtually unrecorded.[6]

Keil's profile of the editors of the German-American radical press in its golden age between 1850 and 1910 is therefore a pioneer effort that promises to recast our understanding not only of the German-American labor subculture but of American labor as a whole. The circumstances that led to the "juvenescence" of German-American journalism, as Keil puts it, synchronizing as it did with the greatest migration in all of German history, are spelled out with great sensitivity and discrimination. If pre-Civil War journalism was primarily personal, the later radical press, as Keil makes evident, depended on a wide labor network to sustain it. Keil is especially thorough in analyzing for the first time the wide range of personalities who comprised the corps of editors and journalists, exiles like their predecessors, of the German-American radical papers and providing us with detailed data identifying the provenance of some two hundred of them. Most importantly, Keil reminds us that the editors of the German-American radical press were emissaries of a German social democratic tradition that sharply distinguished them from their German-American competitors. In addition to emulating German labor institutions, editors of the radical press in the United States kept abreast of developments on both continents, engaged in a perennial interchange of copy with their colleagues in Europe, and often not only visited back and forth but shifted from one editorial post to another on either side of the Atlantic.

Most important, radical editors, unlike their counterparts of the larger German immigrant press, were committed on principle to the Americanization of their readers that was inseparable from their socialist and cosmopolitanizing mission. They perforce, therefore, had not only to witness the decline of a prideful classic German literary culture to which they were pledged but to address an English-reading public as well, which led them to issue and distribute a great number of English-language publications. Since labor organization was given priority over cultural maintenance, Keil concludes, the ethnic and ideological marginality of the German-American radical press combined to divest it of its readership and its staying power to a far greater extent than was true of the other German-American newspapers.

Yet Keil has insisted elsewhere that despite the erosion of the German-language press and the ascendancy of the second generation, the "German working-class culture did not disappear without a trace into a homogeneous middle-class culture but contributed to an American working-class culture differing in significant ways from the norms and values of the hegemonic society."[7] But Keil leaves it at that and does not go beyond to analyze or portray the impact of a residual German-American labor subculture on the American labor scene in the opening decades of the twentieth century.

In response perhaps to John Higham's plea that labor and ethnic historians surmount their parochialisms, two scholars have collaborated to produce a case study of the interplay between class and ethnicity based on a fine-grained analysis of the German-American and general press of Philadelphia. In their essay Ken Fones-Wolf and Elliott Shore demonstrate how German-American workingmen responded to the dilemma created by the conflict between their economic self-interest and class fealties and their ethnic group loyalties.

In this intricate paper the authors chose to focus on three kinds of newspapers, those committed to ethnic solidarity at many different levels, those engaged in modifying immigrant culture to accommodate the individualistic drives of their readers in a dynamic economy, and those committed to working-class unity. Inevitably, Fones-Wolf and Shore's study becomes a study in irony, for they show how in

1872, in the absence of a pro-labor German newspaper, workingmen turned to the general press for support. By contrast, in 1886, the very existence of a radical pro-labor German newspaper proved politically self-defeating, for it only intensified persistent ideological and ethnic differences within the ranks of labor.

Fones-Wolf and Shore do not carry their study of the German press into the 1890s and beyond, nor do they portray the relations between German workmen and others, except obliquely. One wonders whether the survival rate for labor unions and workmen's societies twenty years and older in Philadelphia in 1900 was any greater than New York City's 19 percent, what proportion were German, and what sectors of the labor world continued to be ethnoculturally German.[8] To what extent did the German-American socialist heritage, upon merging with an Anglo-American ideology of republican constitutionalism and millennial Christianity, continue to inform the labor ethos? Along what lines did a changing economy and technology and the immigrants coming predominantly from southern and eastern Europe drastically alter labor's ethnic composition, create a new set of relationships, and contribute as well to the consolidation of an ethnically stratified labor force?[9] A portrayal of these changes as they were reflected in Philadelphia's German-American and general press in the first two decades of the twentieth century, as ingenious in its design as the one for the earlier decades, would enhance our understanding of the labor dynamics of an ethnocultural urban America and of the role of the press as interpreter, mediator, and partisan.

Ruth Seifert's careful study of the woman question, based primarily on an examination of the women's page of the *New Yorker Volkszeitung* between 1900 and 1914, although it holds few surprises, is an important one. Since German-American socialists, like their German counterparts, showed little spirit for diverting their energies away from the socialist struggle in which both men and women shared, the cause of women's emancipation remained peripheral. Except for a few fleeting voices, in these years the airing of women's problems, it would seem, was almost as uncongenial to the German socialist press, as it was to the larger German-American press and to the Social Democracy and the trade unions in Wilhelmine Germany.[10]

Seifert's paper would have been even more valuable had the woman question been placed in a larger American ethnocultural context. By doing so, Seifert might have viewed the woman question along with prohibition, immigration restriction, and other social issues that contributed to the apparent standoff between an older and a newer America in the opening decades of the twentieth century and that compromised the role of the socialists. Surely the conflict between socialist German-America and progressive Anglo-America would make even more intelligible the modest acknowledgment of women's problems by members of a patriarchal culture responding to a genuine sense of siege.[11]

Surprisingly, America's most important German socialist newspaper has yet to find its historian. Even recently published biographical encyclopedias of labor, of the left, and of reform make no place for *New Yorker Volkszeitung* editors Alexander Jonas, Adolf Douai, Sergius Schewitsch, and Hermann Schlüter, while the *Biographical Dictionary of the Left* grants its last editor, Ludwig Lore, no more than a brief sketch. Thus far, all we have had, and most valuable indeed, thanks to the publication program of the Labor Newspaper Preservation Project in Bremen, are reprints of the tenth (1888), twenty-fifth (1903), and fiftieth (1928) anniversary issues of the *Volkszeitung*.

Paul Buhle's paper therefore is especially welcome. A close study of the *New Yorker Volkszeitung* in the aftermath of World War I and the Russian Revolution, when the whole nineteenth-century socialist tradition appeared to have entered upon a final parting of the ways, provides a rare opportunity for genuine stocktaking. Here for the first time, Buhle leads us to believe, we will learn about a newspaper which more than any other had "the prestige, intellectual leadership," and "sustained national impact" that placed it at the hub of German-American socialist culture and of the German-American labor movement. Most importantly, we are led to anticipate that for the critical thirteen-year period upon which Buhle has focused, he will elaborate in precise historical detail on the provocative assertions that he makes in his opening statement: "The *Volkszeitung*" to its last days, "truly ruled American Marxist organization. . . . It took a unique, essentially independent position anchored outside the Socialist and Communist movements proper, in the fraternal societies and the German-immigrant-based unions. Therein lay its strength and its longevity."

Regrettably Buhle has not gone much beyond the *Volkszeitung*'s fiftieth anniversary issue, and a few others, to inform his vision of the changing role of that newspaper. If the *Volkszeitung* was indeed the stellar journal that he insists that it was, then surely a careful, critical, and detailed appraisal of its contents from 1917 to 1930 would have shown beyond a doubt that the paper's "reputation for literary quality unsurpassed in the radical press" had genuine merit and that the *Volkszeitung* was indeed the culmination of fourscore years of German-American cultural idealism. A review of the editors' approach to cultural, political, labor, social, and international affairs and issues, as well as reader response, would have demonstrated what it meant to be a German-American socialist in such portentous times as World War I, the German and Russian revolutions, the Red Scare, the era of Prohibition, and the age of Weimar, Hitler, and Stalin.[12] A precise and textured portrait of "the brilliant dusk of German-American socialism," if it indeed was that, as recorded in the *Volkszeitung*, would vindicate Buhle's claims, do justice to his best insights, and make a major contribution to our understanding of an important era and newspaper which he is singularly equipped to delineate.

III

In sum, the distinctive virtues of the contributions to this volume are attributable to the intensity of their focus and their authors' scrupulous, almost compulsive, reliance upon the files of the German-American radical press. Their weakness, naturally, is the obverse of their strength—simply put, their exclusivity: their failure to relate the German-American radical press to the American, the other ethnic, and the nonradical German-American newspapers. Whatever the reason for this limitation, also left untold is the wider influence of the German-American radical press. Clearly, the press, labor movement, and related supportive German-American social and cultural institutions cut a wide swath, for it was they who served as models for other ethnic groups. Even Bruce Nelson, who gives considered attention to the non-German radical press, makes only passing note of the relationship between the Chicago German newspapers and their Czech, Polish, Lithuanian, Danish, Italian, and general American counterparts.

Three disparate examples perhaps may be suggestive of the extended impact of the German-American labor culture, both early and late, and lines of further research that might be pursued. The first illustrates its relationship to another ethnic group; the second relates to the role of the social democratic press in combating totalitarianism; and the third points to the little studied connections in the twentieth century between the generations.

Often remarked but little explored has been the role which the German-American labor movement played in nurturing its early Jewish analogue. The adoption of German terms such as *Gewerkschaften* for trade unions, *Genossen* for party members, and *Sektions* for party branches, no less than the Yiddish equivalents of the German in the titles of newspapers and in everyday nomenclature, was inevitable. The patterning of the United Hebrew Trades on the model of the United German Trades and the Workmen's Circle on the Arbeiter Kranken and Sterbe Kasse was no less so. The aid extended to the founders of the first Yiddish socialist weekly, no less than the appropriation of the whole universalistic German socialist frame of discourse, was taken as a matter of course.[13] The dynamics of that German-Jewish relationship, however, have yet to be explored.

At an entirely different level is the need to relate the German-American socialist press to Hitlerian Germany, to the American labor movement, and to the German Resistance. In 1932, upon the demise of the last German-American social democratic daily, the *New Yorker Volkszeitung* was succeeded by the *Neue Volkszeitung*, which became German-America's leading anti-Nazi weekly. Staffed primarily by political refugees, it has yet to be afforded its proper place within the German-American socialist tradition.[14]

Finally, German-American labor's finest hour has gone unnoticed. Surely a singular contribution to the enhancement of labor's role in mid-twentieth-century America has been attributed to the remarkable Reuther brothers—Roy, Victor, and most notably, Walter—whose vision of the labor movement was conditioned by the total commitment of their German immigrant father to the socialist dream of social justice. "Reuther's idealism and inventiveness were products of the American working-class experience, a creative adaptation of social democratic perspectives to American conditions and realities, manifested not only in words, but also in the daily lives of millions," one of Walter Reuther's biographers has written. A second has gone so far as to call Reuther "the most exciting and influential trade unionist" of his time "because he defined the outer limits of liberalism's social and economic agenda."[15] Yet it is the invisible role of Reuther's father's generation, Valentine's generation, that needs the attention of historians if the fuller implications for American life of the continuing legacy of the German-American socialist experience is to be understood.

Thus far, not surprisingly, the initiative for the advancement of our knowledge of German-American labor including the history of the German-American radical press has in great part come not from American but from German historians, initially interested primarily in their own history, especially the history of German immigration. The result in the 1980s has been the publication of an extraordinary corpus of historical works that for the first time illuminate the German, no less than the German-American, labor experience.[16]

It is to be hoped that American historians will now redress the balance, further extending and broadening our understanding by asking questions that will go beyond the scholarship generated thus far. The effective utilization of the German-American radical press, no less than the newspapers of other ethnic groups and the general press, as well as diverse sources not readily accessible to German historians, ought to carry the story a step further. By making the multiethnic, interethnic, and cross-cultural parameters of the German-American labor experience intelligible as they have not been heretofore, American historians are in a position to extend the boundaries of our knowledge in serendipitous ways that will further cosmopolitanize our understanding of the emergent American and modern world, no less than the history of American labor.

NOTES

1. David Brody, "Labor," pp. 611–12.

2. See David Montgomery, "Irish and the American Labor Movement," pp. 205–6; Pitrim Sorokin, "Leaders of Labor," p. 390; Moses Rischin, "Jewish Labor Movement in America," p. 241; Robert L. Mikkelsen, "Immigrants in Politics," pp. 292–93; Warren R. Van Tine, *Making of the Labor Bureaucrat*, pp. 9, 19–20, 29, 185–86.

3. See Patricia M. Hocking and G. T. Husbands, eds., *Why Is There No Socialism in the United States?* pp. 105–6, 121; Peter R. Shergold, *Working-Class Life*, pp. 8–9, 224–30.

4. Stanley Nadel, "From the Barricades of Paris," pp. 47–50, 54–55, 74–75; Bruce C. Nelson, *Beyond the Martyrs*, pp. 238–39, 242.

5. *Immigrant Labor Press in North America.*

6. *Biographical Dictionary of American Labor Leaders; American Reformers;* and *Biographical Dictionary of the Left.*

7. Hartmut Keil, "German Immigrant Workers in Nineteenth-Century America," 1:203; Keil, "German Working-Class Radicalism," pp. 86–90; also see *German Workers' Culture in the United States.*

8. John Higham, "Current Trends in the Study of Ethnicity." See Moses Rischin, *Promised City*, pp. 172–73; Ellen Skerrett, "Development of Catholic Identity," pp. 128–29.

9. See e.g. Shergold, *Working-Class Life*, pp. 54–55; Rischin, *Promised City*, pp. 184–85.

10. Werner Thonnessen, *Emancipation of Women*, pp. 70–71; Richard Evans, *Feminist Movement in Germany*, pp. 3ff., 175ff., 265ff.; Jean H. Quataert, *Reluctant Feminists*, pp. 93–94, 228ff.

11. Frederick C. Luebke, *Bonds of Loyalty*, pp. 68, 99; James H. Timberlake, *Prohibition and the Progressive Movement*, pp. 96–99; Alan P. Grimes, *Puritan Ethic and Woman Suffrage*, pp. 130–33.

12. See Carl E. Schorske, *German Social Democracy*, pp. 285–330; Richard Breitman, *German Socialism and Weimar Democracy*; and Lewis J. Edinger, *German Exile Politics.*

13. Rischin, *Promised City*, pp. 150–51, 176–77; also see Stanley Nadel, "Jewish Race and the German Soul," pp. 19–22.

14. "Foreign Language Press in New York," typescript, on deposit in the Columbia School of Journalism Library, 1941, p. 411; Robert E. Cazden, *German Exile Literature in America*, pp. 29–38; and Franz Osterroth, *Biographisches Lexikon des Sozialismus*.

15. John Barnard, *Walter Reuther*, pp. 1–17, 117, 214; Nelson Lichtenstein, "Walter Reuther and the Rise of Labor-Liberalism," p. 310; see also Irving Howe and B. J. Widick, *UAW and Walter Reuther*, pp. 187–92 and Irving Bernstein, *Turbulent Years*, pp. 502, 556–59.

16. Irmgard Steinisch, "Studies of American Labor History in West Germany," pp. 531–32.

Hartmut Keil

Appendix: List of Editors/Journalists of German-American Radical Papers, 1865–1914[1]

Appel, George W. *Hammer*, Philadelphia (1886–?)
Bachmann, Charles G. *Deutsch-Amerikanische Buchdruckerzeitung*,
   Philadelphia (1873–76)
Backhofen, Charles *Arbeiterzeitung*, Erie (1892)
Backstein, G. *California Arbeiterzeitung* (1887–93)
*Baginski, Max *Vorbote* (1894–?), *Chicagoer Arbeiter-Zeitung* (1894–
   1907?), *Sturmglocke* (1896), *Freiheit* (1907–10), *Internationale
   Arbeiter-Chronik* (1914)
Baginski, Richard *Buffaloer Arbeiterzeitung* (1897)
Ballin, Hans *Amerikanische Turnzeitung*, Milwaukee (1910)
*Bartel, Heinrich [1874–after 1954] *Neuengland Staaten Volkszeitung*,
   Lawrence, Mass. (1906), *Chicagoer Arbeiter-Zeitung* (1906–11),
   Sheboygan Volksblatt (1909–16), *Milwaukee Vorwärts* (1911–32), *Das
   freie Wort*, Milwaukee (1933–54)
Bechtold, Heinrich C. *Michigan Arbeiterzeitung* (1888–92?), *Chicagoer
   Arbeiter-Zeitung, Fackel*, Chicago (1889–95)
Berandun, J. *Freidenker*, Milwaukee (1908–13)
*Berger, Victor Louis [1860–1929] *Wisconsin Vorwärts* (1894–98?)
*Biedenkapp, Georg [1843–1924] *Der Tramp*, New York (1888; 1901–2?)
Biron, Michael [1832–?] *Freidenker* (1872–74), *Milwaukee'r Sozialist*
   (1877), *Vorwärts* (1878), *Arbeiterzeitung* (1879–80), *Milwaukee*

---

* = more detailed information available
# = left Germany 1878–90
Place of publication may vary according to date of publication.

Journal (1880–81), *Arminia,* Milwaukee (1882?–1906), *Lucifer,* Milwaukee (1882?–1906) *Milwaukee Volkszeitung* (?–1892)

Blatz, Valentin *Milwaukee'r Arbeiterzeitung* (1889), *Wahrheit,* Milwaukee? (1889–1910)

Block, George A. *NYVZ* (1881–?), *Deutsch-Amerikanische Bäcker-Zeitung* (1885–89)

Blumhardt, Charles *Buffalo Tribüne* (1876)

Boehm, Ernst *Brauerzeitung,* Cincinnati (1888)

*Boppe, Carl Hermann [1842–99] *Newarker Post* (1874–75), *Freidenker,* Milwaukee (1877–99), *Deutsch-Amerikanische Turnzeitung* (1885–99)

Brandt, H. *California Freie Presse* (1879–80)

Braun, Charles *Hammer,* Philadelphia (1882–89)

Briesen, Julius v. *NYVZ*

Brucker, Joseph [1849–1921] *Milwaukee'r Sozialist* (1875–78), *Chicagoer Sozialist* (1876–79), *Volkszeitung,* Chicago (1877), *Freidenker,* Milwaukee (after 1895)

Brunnemann, Carl *Volksstimme des Westens, Sonntagsblatt,* St. Louis (1877–80)

Bunge, Martin L. D. *Amerikanische Turnzeitung,* Milwaukee (1913–17)

*Carl, Conrad *(Neue) Arbeiter-Zeitung,* New York (1873–75)

*#Christensen, Jens L. [1856–?] *Chicagoer Arbeiter-Zeitung, Vorbote, Fackel* (1888–89)

*Conzett, Conrad [1848–97] *Vorbote* (1874–78), *Chicagoer Arbeiter-Zeitung* (1876–80)

Cuno, Theodor [1847–1934] *NYVZ* (1880?–)

Currlin, Albert *Chicagoer Arbeiter-Zeitung* (1889?), *Arbeiterstimme,* Chicago (1889), *California Arbeiterzeitung* (1890?–91), *Volkszeitung der Pacific-Küste,* San Francisco (1891–94)

Damm, Peter *Carriage and Wagon Workers Journal,* Chicago (1899–1904)

Darkow, Martin *Philadelphia Tageblatt*

Daut, Carl *Arbeiterzeitung,* Philadelphia (1869?–)

Degen, Robert *NYVZ* (1878–?), *Deutsch-Amerikanische Bäckerzeitung* (1889)

Detmers, F. *Cincinnati Zeitung* (1888–89)

Deuss, Edmund *Volksblatt Sheboygan* (1905), *Wisconsin Vorwärts* (?–1911)

*Dietzgen, Joseph [1828–88] *Sozialist* (1885), *Chicagoer Arbeiter-Zeitung, Vorbote* (1886–88)

*Douai, Adolf [1819–88] *Arbeiter-Union* (1868–70), *NYVZ* (1878–88)

Dreifuss, Adolf *Neues Leben* (1907–10), *Chicagoer Arbeiter-Zeitung* (?–1919), *Vorbote* (?–1924)

*Drescher, Martin [1863–1920] *Herold,* Detroit (1897–98), *Der arme
Teufel* (1898–1900), *Wolfsaugen,* St. Louis (1900–1901), *Mephisto*
(1901–?), *Chicagoer Arbeiter-Zeitung* (1901–7?), *Zigeuner* (1902),
Milwaukee Vorwärts

Drexler, Adolph *Buffaloer Arbeiterzeitung* (1892–93)

Dreyer, Theodor *Herold,* Detroit (?–1918)

Ebel, Ernst *Neues Leben,* Chicago (1902?–10?), *Tageblatt,* San Francisco
(1902?–6?)

Eckhart, Emil C. *Laterne,* Buffalo (1880)

Emrich, Henry *Möbel-Arbeiter Journal,* New York (1883–?)

Ende, Heinrich *Ohio Volkszeitung,* Cincinnati (1876–78?), *Emancipator?*
(1877), *Arbeiter am Ohio* (1877–79), *Pionier*

Ferle, Max *Deutsch-Amerikanische Fleischerzeitung,* Brooklyn (1904)

Fernitz, Gustav *Neue Zeit,* Louisville (1877–78)

*Fischer, Adolf [1863–87] *Anarchist,* Chicago (1886)

Fleck, Willibald *Amerikanische Turnzeitung,* Milwaukee (1910–13)

Forker, Max *Buffaloer Arbeiterzeitung* (1889–1900)

*Franz, Jacob L. [1846–1902] *Philadelphia Tageblatt* (1878–82), *NYVZ*
(1882–96), *Brauerzeitung* (1886–1900)

*#Fritzsche, Friedrich Wilhelm [1825–1905] *Philadelphia Tageblatt, Ham-
mer* (1882–?)

Fuchs, Jacob *Herold,* Detroit (1897)

Geissler, Ludwig A. *Hammer,* New Orleans (1876)

Gragorovius, Rudolph *NYVZ* (1901–?)

Grossmann, Maximilian [1854–?] *Freidenker,* Milwaukee (1883–84)

Grossmann, Rudolf *Zeitgeist,* New York (1901), *Fackel* (1902–?)

*Grottkau, Paul [1846–98] *Vorbote, Chicagoer Arbeiter-Zeitung* (1878–80;
1881–84; 1888), *Milwaukee'r Arbeiter-Zeitung* (1886–88), *California
Arbeiter-Zeitung* (1891?–?)

Grunzig, Julius [1855–?] *NYVZ* (1890–91)

Haecker, Friedrich *Philadelphia Tageblatt*

Haefelin *Arbeiterfreund,* McKeesport, Penn. (1884–85)

Haller, Frederic *Progress,* New York

Hartung, Urban *Herold,* Detroit (1911–?)

Hass, Peter *Arbeiterzeitung,* Philadelphia (1869?–?)

*#Hasselmann, Wilhelm [1844–?] *Amerikanische Arbeiterzeitung,* New
York (1886)

Hecht, Julius *Buffaloer Arbeiterzeitung* (1892–?)

Heins-Heuryot, A. *Volksanwalt Cincinnati* (1897)

*Heinzen, Karl [1809–80] *Pionier* (?–1879), *Freidenker* (1880)

*#Hepner, Adolf [1846–1923] *NYVZ* (1883–84?), *Philadelphia Tageblatt,
St. Louis Tageblatt* (1888–97)

Herbrand, Louis *Brauerzeitung* (1886–88)

Hickler, Simon *Milwaukee'r Arbeiterzeitung* (1888), *Chicagoer Arbeiter-Zeitung* (1889–90), *Vorbote* (1889–94), *Milwaukee Volkszeitung* (1890?)

Hirschberger, Anton *Volksblatt Sheboygan* (1901–?)

Hoehn, G. A. *Chicagoer Arbeiter-Zeitung* (1890–94), *Tageblatt-Abendpost, St. Louis* (1897–98), *Arbeiterzeitung St. Louis* (1898–1910–1931?)

Hoffmann, Charles *Buffaloer Arbeiterzeitung* (1887–88, 1891)

Hohmann, Charles F. *Deutsch-Amerikanische Bäckerzeitung*, Chicago (1908–?)

Holler, Joseph *NYVZ* (1878–?)

Huhn, Heinrich *Freidenker* (1899–1908), *Amerikanische Turnzeitung*, Milwaukee (1901?–8?)

Hunger, Jakob *Milwaukee'r Arbeiterzeitung* (1889), *Volkszeitung Milwaukee* (1890–92), *Wisconsin Vorwärts* (?–1911)

*#Ibsen, Karl *Deutsch-Amerikanische Bäckerzeitung*, Chicago (1889–91), *Clevelander Volksfreund* (1893–?)

Isaak, A. *Das freie Wort*, New York (1907)

Jahn, M. P. *Arbeiterzeitung Erie* (1893–95)

*Jonas, Alexander [1834–1912] *Arbeiterstimme* (1877–78), *NYVZ* (1878–1912)

Joos *Arbeiterfreund*, McKeesport, Penn. (1884–85)

Kahler, H. *Philadelphia Tageblatt*

Kaufmann, Adolf *Herold*, Detroit (?–1898)

*#Keitel, August [1844–93] *Clevelander Volksfreund* (1886–92)

*Kleist, Carl *Wisconsin Vorwärts* (?–1911)

*Klings, Carl [1846–?] *Der Deutsche Arbeiter* (1869–70), *Vorbote*, Chicago (1874)

Koberlein, Anton *Zukunft*, Philadelphia (1884–85)

Koberstein, Paul *Buffalo Tribüne* (1876–78), *Arbeiterstimme am Erie* (1878), *Philadelphia Tageblatt*

Koch, Hans *Der Strom*, New York (1910), *Anti-Autoritär*, New York (1911)

Koppel, Richard *Clevelander Volksfreund* (1908?–18)

Kraemer, L. T. *Freiheit*, New York

Kurzenknabe, Ernst *Brauerzeitung* (1888–96)

Lange, E. *Parole*, St. Louis (1884–85)

*Landsberg, Dr. Wilhelm *Arbeiter-Union*, New York (1868)

Lehmann, August *Biene*, Holyoke, Mass. (1894–1918)

Liebig, Dr. Edward *Chicagoer Arbeiter-Zeitung, Vorbote* (1880–81)

Liess, Emil *San Francisco Tageblatt* (1894–99), *Vorwärts der Pacific Küste* (1911)

Loebel, Oscar *Volksblatt Sheboygan* (1895–1901?)

Lore, Lily *NYVZ*

*Lore, Ludwig [1875–1942] *NYVZ*

*#Lossau, Paul *Philadelphia Tageblatt, NYVZ* (1881–?)

Ludwig, Otto *Volksstimme des Westens*, St. Louis (1877–80)

*Lyser, Gustav [1841–1909] *Sozial-Demokrat* (1874–75), *Milwaukee'r Sozialist* (1875), *Leuchtkugeln*, Milwaukee (1876), *Die rothe Laterne*, Milwaukee (1876), *Fackel*, Chicago (1879–80), *Bahnbrecher der Zukunft*, Chicago (1886)

Mauer, Nic. *Anarchist*, New York (1891–?)

Mayer, A. *Parole*, St. Louis (1885)

Meier, Ernst A. *Cincinnatier Zeitung* (1886–?)

*#Milke, Friedrich [1845–?] *Deutsch-Amerikanische Buchdrucker-Zeitung* (1883–86)

Miller, Hugo *Gewerkschaftszeitung* (1879–80), *Deutsch-Amerikanische Buchdrucker-Zeitung*, New York and Indianapolis (1886–1926)

*#Most, Johann [1846–1906] *Freiheit*, New York (1879–1906), *Buffaloer Arbeiterzeitung* (1897–98)

Mostlar, August *Brauerzeitung* (1906–17)

Mostler, Joseph *Buffaloer Arbeiterzeitung* (1897, 1898–99), *Buffalo Herold* (1897–98), *Neuengland Staaten Volkszeitung*, Lawrence, Mass. (?–1906)

Mueller, Gus *Volksanwalt Cincinnati* (1891?–94)

Mueller, Jakob *Hammer*, New Orleans (1876)

Mueller, Otto *California Freie Presse* (1879–80)

Neuhauser, Carl *Arbeiter-Freund*, Wheeling (1865–76)

Newald, E. *Herold*, Detroit (1893?–97)

*Otto-Walster, August [1834–98] *Sozial-Demokrat, Arbeiterstimme*, New York (1876–77), *Volksstimme des Westens*, St. Louis (1877–80)

Price, George M. *Buffaloer Arbeiterzeitung* (1887)

Rahnmlow, G. *Anti-Autoritär*, New York (1911)

Rahn, Gustav A. *Volkszeitung Milwaukee* (1890)

Rappaport, Philip

Reifgraber, Joseph J. *Parole*, St. Louis (1884, 1886)

*#Reimer, Otto [1841–?] *NYVZ*

*Reitzel, Robert [1849–1898] *Der arme Teufel*, Detroit (1884–98)

Rinke, Otto *Kämpfer*, St. Louis (1896)

Roepke, O. *Gewerkschaftszeitung*, New York (1880–81)

Romm, Julie *NYVZ* (?–1919)

*#Rosenberg, Wilhelm Ludwig [1850–193?] *Fackel*, Chicago (1880–84), *Sozialist*, New York (1885–89), *Vorwärts* (1892–?), *Cincinnati Tageblatt* (1895–96), *Echo*, Cleveland (1911)

Ruhbaum, Rudolph *Arbeiterfreund*, Chicago (1874)
Saltiel, Robert *Neues Leben*, Chicago (1905–7)
Savary, Carl *Vorwärts*, Newark (1877–79)
Schaefer, John *NYVZ* (1878–?)
Schaefli, Gustav A. *Amerikanische Turnzeitung*, Milwaukee (1908)
*Schewitsch, Sergius [1848–?] *NYVZ* (1878–90)
*#Schiele, Friedrich [1848–?] *Cincinnatier Zeitung* (1886–?)
*Schilling, Robert [1843–1922] *Coopers Journal* (1870–75), *Reformer*,
    Milwaukee (1880–?), *Milwaukee Volksblatt* (1882–90?)
*#Schlüter, Hermann [1851–1919] *NYVZ* (1890–1919)
Schmidt, Joseph *Deutsch-Amerikanische Bäckerzeitung*, Chicago
    (1903–8)
Schmidt, Karl *Freiheit*, New York
Schneider, Charles *Carriage and Wagon Workers Journal*, Chicago
    (1904–6)
Schneppe, Carl *NYVZ*
Schudel, John *Deutsch-Amerikanische Bäckerzeitung*, Chicago (1897–
    1903)
Schulze, Moritz *Freiheit, Chicagoer Arbeiter-Zeitung* (1887–88, 1890–94)
Schultze, W. M. *Hammer*, Philadelphia (1886)
*Schumm, Georg *Pionier* (1874), *Libertas*, Boston (1888)
Schwab, Justus H. *Freiheit*, New York (1882)
*Schwab, Michael [1853–98] *Vorbote, Chicagoer Arbeiter-Zeitung* (1884–
    86)
Sigel, Hermann [1840–94] *Milwaukee'r Sozialist* (1878), *Vorwärts*
    (1878–79)
Silz, Max *Volksanwalt Cincinnati* (1894–98?)
Soubron, Otto [1846–?] *Amerikanische Turnzeitung*, Milwaukee (1909)
Sozing, W. *California Freie Presse* (1881–?)
*Speyer, Carl *Gewerkschaftszeitung*, New York (1879–81), *Carpenter*,
    Indianapolis (1904?–?)
Speyer, George J. *Gewerkschaftszeitung*, New York (1880–81)
*Spies, August [1855–87] *Vorbote, Chicagoer Arbeiter-Zeitung* (1884–86)
*Starke, Rudolf *Arbeiter-Union*, New York (1869–70), *(Neue) Arbeiter-
    Zeitung*, New York (1873–75)
Steichmann, H. *Herold*, Detroit (1898–1905)
Steiner, Robert *Arbeiterzeitung Belleville* (1884), *Chicagoer Arbeiter-
    Zeitung* (1890–94), *Arbeiterzeitung St. Louis* (1899), *Buffaloer
    Arbeiter-Zeitung* (1916)
*#Stoehr, Max [1849–?] *Tageblatt St. Louis* (1888?–97?), *St. Louis Tageblatt-
    Abendpost* (1897–98)

*Strasser, Adolf *Cigar Makers Official Journal* (1877–?), *Gewerkschafts-zeitung*, New York (1879–80)

Tagwerker, Joseph *Nebraska Arbeiterzeitung* (1899)

Tiecke, Louis *Hammer*, Philadelphia (?–1886)

Timmermann, Claus *Parole*, St. Louis (1885–86), *Anarchist*, St. Louis (1889–95), *Brandfackel*, New York (1893–95), *Sturmvogel*, New York (1897–99)

Trautmann, William *Brauerzeitung* (1900–1905)

*#Vahlteich, Julius [1839–1915] *Chicagoer Freie Presse* (1883), *Illinois Volks-zeitung* (1884–85), *Tageblatt St. Louis* (1891), *NYVZ* (1901–8), *Chicagoer Arbeiter-Zeitung* (after 1910)

Vogt, Hugo *Vorwärts*, New York (1878–?)

Vossberg, A. *Arbeiterstimme*, New York (1875–76)

Walter, Ernst *Buffaloer Arbeiterzeitung* (1888–?)

Weber, Maurice *Sattler und Wagenbauer*, Chicago (1891?–1904?)

Wegener, Ernst *Solidarität*, New York (1906–16)

Weier, Ernest A. *Cincinnati Zeitung* (1886–87)

Weigel, John P. *Brauerzeitung* (1905–6)

Weil, Jean *Deutsch-Amerikanische Buchdrucker-Zeitung*, New York (1876–83)

Weisman, Henry *Deutsch-Amerikanische Bäcker-Zeitung*, New York (1891–97)

*Weiss, Samuel [1861–97] *Buffaloer Arbeiter-Zeitung* (?–1891), *Arbeiter-zeitung Erie* (1891), *The People*

Wendt, F. W. *Parole*, St. Louis (1885)

*#Werner, Ludwig *Philadelphia Tageblatt* (1879–1926)

Willig, Jakob *Volksanwalt Cincinnati* (1889–91), *Cincinnatier Zeitung* (1890–95)

Winnen, Jakob *Vorbote*, Chicago (1874)

Winter, Georg *Arbeiterstimme* (1877), *NYVZ*

Wytzka, J. *Metallarbeiter*, New York (1888)

NOTE

1. Based on Karl J. R. Arndt and May E. Olson, *German-American Newspapers and Periodicals,* and Dirk Hoerder and Christiane Harzig, eds., *The German-American Radical Press* (forthcoming).

Selected Bibliography

Abbot, Carl. *Boosters and Businessmen: Popular Economic Thought and Urban Growth in the Antebellum Middle West*. Westport, Conn.: Greenwood Press, 1981.

America and the Germans: An Assessment of a Three-Hundred Year History. Edited by Frank Trommler and Joseph McVeigh. 2 vols. Philadelphia: University of Pennsylvania Press, 1985.

The American and European Revolutions, 1776–1848: Socio-Political and Ideological Aspects. Edited by Jaroslaw Pelenski. Iowa City: University of Iowa Press, 1980.

American Reformers. Edited by Alden Whitman. New York: H. W. Wilson Co., 1985.

"Amerika ist ein Freies Land": Auswanderer schreiben nach Deutschland. Edited by Wolfgang Helbich. Darmstadt: Luchterhand, 1985.

Arndt, Karl J. R., and Olson, May E. *German-American Newspapers and Periodicals, 1732–1955: History and Bibliography = Deutsch-amerikanische Zeitungen und Zeitschriften, 1732–1955: Geschichte und Bibliographie*. Heidelberg: Quelle and Meyer, 1961; 2d rev. ed., New York: Johnson Reprint Corp., [1965].

———. *The German Language Press of the Americas, 1732–1968: History and Bibliography*. Munich: Verlag Dokumentation, 1973.

Avrich, Paul. *The Haymarket Tragedy*. Princeton: Princeton University Press, 1984.

Bade, Klaus J. *Vom Auswanderungsland zum Einwanderungsland?: Deutschland, 1880–1980*. Beiträge zur Zeitgeschichte, vol. 12. Berlin: Colloquium, 1983.

Barnard, John. *Walter Reuther*. Boston: Little, Brown & Co., 1983.

Barrett, James B. "Unity and Fragmentation: Class, Race, and Ethnicity on Chicago's South Side, 1900–1922." In *"Struggle a Hard Battle": Essays on*

Working-Class Immigrants, edited by Dirk Hoerder. DeKalb: Northern Illinois University Press, 1986.

Bergquist, James Manning. "The Political Attitudes of the German Immigrant in Illinois, 1848–1860." Ph.D. Dissertation, Northwestern University, 1966.

Bernstein, Charles Iver. "The New York City Draft Riots of 1863 and Class Relations on the Eve of Industrial Capitalism." Ph.D. Dissertation, Yale University, 1985.

Bernstein, Irving. *The Turbulent Years.* Boston: Houghton Mifflin, 1969.

Biographical Dictionary of American Labor Leaders. 2d ed. Edited by Gary M. Fink. Westport, Conn.: Greenwood Press, 1974.

Biographical Dictionary of the Left. Edited by Bernard Johnpoll and Harvey Klehr. Westport, Conn.: Greenwood Press, 1986.

Bjorklund, Oddvar. *Marcus Thrane: Socialist Leder i et Utland.* Oslo: Tiden, 1970.

Börnstein, Heinrich. *Fünfundsiebzig Jahre in der Alten und Neuen Welt: Memoiren eines Unbedeutenden.* 2 vols. Leipzig: O. Wigand, 1881. Reprint. New York: Peter Lang, 1986.

———. *The Mysteries of St. Louis.* Edited by Steven Rowan and Elizabeth Sims. Chicago: Charles H. Kerr, 1990.

Breitman, Richard. *German Socialism and Weimar Democracy.* Chapel Hill: University of North Carolina Press, 1981.

Bridges, Amy. *A City in the Republic: Antebellum New York and the Origins of Machine Politics.* New York: Cambridge University Press, 1984.

Brody, David. "Labor." In *Harvard Encyclopedia of American Ethnic Groups,* edited by Stephan Thernstrom. Cambridge: Harvard University Press, 1980.

Brooks, Frank. "Industrialization and Radical Ideology: Labor, Revolution and Anarchism in the Thought of Dyer D. Lum." Ph.D. Dissertation, Cornell University, 1988.

Brückner, Peter, and Ricke, Gabriele. "Über die ästhetische Erziehung des Menschen in der Arbeiterbewegung." In *Das Unvermögen der Realität,* edited by Peter Brückner et al. Berlin: K. Wagenbach, 1974.

Bruncken, Ernst. *German Political Refugees in the U.S. during the Period from 1815–1860.* Reprint. San Francisco: R. & E. Research Associates, 1970.

Bubenick, Rudolf. *Dějiny Čechů v Chicagu.* Chicago: Naekladem Vlastnim, 1939.

Bubnys, Edward. "Nativity and the Distribution of Wealth: Chicago 1870." *Explorations in Economic History* 19 (1982): 101–9.

Buchanan, Joseph. *The Story of a Labor Agitator.* New York: Outlook Co., 1903.

Buchstein, Frederick. "The Anarchist Press in American Journalism." *Journalism History* 1 (Summer 1974): 43–45, 66.

Buhle, Mari Jo. *Women and American Socialism.* Urbana: University of Illinois Press, 1982.

Buhle, Paul. "German Socialists and the Roots of American Working-Class Radicalism." In *German Workers in Industrial Chicago, 1850–1910: A Comparative Perspective,* edited by Hartmut Keil and John B. Jentz. DeKalb: Northern Illinois University Press, 1983.

———. "Jews and American Communism: The Cultural Question." *Radical History Review* #23 (Spring 1980): 9–33.

———. "Marxism in the U.S., 1900–1940." Ph.D. Dissertation, University of Wisconsin, 1975.

———. *Marxism in the United States*. London: Verso Books, 1987.

Burgard, Roswitha, and Gaby Carsten. *Die Märchenonkel der Frauenfrage: Friedrich Engels and August Bebel*. Berlin: Sub Rosa Frauenpresse, 1981.

Cale, Edgar Barclay. *The Organization of Labor in Philadelphia, 1850–1870*. Philadelphia: University of Pennsylvania Press, 1940.

Čapek, Tomáš. *Padesát Let Českého Tisky v Americe*. New York: "Bank of Europe," etc., 1911.

Cazden, Robert E. "Bibliography of German-American Communist Newspapers in the U.S., 1933–1945." *Internationale wissenschaftliche Korrespondenz zur Geschichte der deutschen Arbeiterbewegung* 5 (Dec. 1967): 39–41.

———. *German Exile Literature in America, 1933–1950*. Chicago: American Library Association, 1970.

———. *A Social History of the German Book Trade in America to the Civil War*. Columbia, S.C.: Camden House, 1984.

Clinton, Catherine. *The Other Civil War: American Women in the Nineteenth Century*. New York: Hill and Wang, 1984.

Cohn, Norman. *Warrant for Genocide: The Myth of the Jewish World-Conspiracy and the Protocols of the Elders of Zion*. New York: Harper & Row, 1967.

Commons, John R., et al. *Documentary History of American Industrial Society*. 10 vols. New York: Russell & Russell, 1958.

Commons, John R., et al. *History of Labour in the United States*. 4 vols. New York: Macmillan, 1918–35.

Concise History of the Great Trial of the Chicago Anarchists in 1886. Edited by Dyer D. Lum. 1888. Reprint. New York: Arno Press, 1969.

Conzen, Kathleen. *Immigrant Milwaukee, 1836–1860*. Cambridge: Harvard University Press, 1976.

Cooper, Jerry M. *The Army and Civil Disorder: Federal Militia Intervention in Labor Disputes, 1887–1900*. Westport, Conn.: Greenwood Press, 1980.

Crosscurrents: Writings of German Political Emigrés in Nineteenth-Century America. Edited by Patricia A. Herminghouse. New York: Peter Lang, 1986.

Danielsen, Jens-Bjerre. "The Early Danish Immigrant Socialist Press." In *Essays on the Scandinavian-North American Radical Press*, edited by Dirk Hoerder. Bremen: Labor Newspaper Preservation Project, Universität Bremen, 1984.

David, Henry. *The History of the Haymarket Affair: A Study in the American Social-Revolutionary and Labor Movements*. New York: Russell & Russell, 1958.

Dell, Floyd. "Socialism and Anarchism in Chicago." In *Chicago: Its History and Its Builders*, edited by J. Seymour Currey. 5 vols. Chicago: S. J. Clarke Pub. Co., 1912. Vol. 2: 361–405.

Deutsch-amerikanische sozialistische Literatur, 1865–1900: Anthologie. Edited by Carol Poore. Berlin: Akademie-Verlag, 1987.

Dietzgen, Eugene. "Joseph Dietzgen: A Sketch of His Life." In Joseph Dietzgen, *Some of the Philosophical Essays on Socialism and Science, Religion, Ethics, Critique-of-Reason and the World at Large*. Chicago: Kerr and Co., 1914.

Dobert, Eitel W. *Deutsche Demokraten in Amerika: Die Achtundvierziger und ihre Schriften*. Göttingen: Vandenhoeck & Ruprecht, 1958.

[Douai, Adolf]. "Bericht über den Fortgang der sozialistischen Bewegung: Amerika." *Jahrbuch für Sozialwissenschaft* 1 (1879): 186–91.

Dowe, Dieter. "Einleitung." In *Bibliographie zur Geschichte der deutschen Arbeiterbewegung, sozialistischen und kommunistischen Bewegung von den Anfängen bis 1863*, edited by Dieter Dowe. Bonn: Verlag Neue Gesellschaft, 1976.

Draper, Theodore. *American Communism and Soviet Russia*. New York: Viking Press, 1960. Rev. ed. New York: Vintage Books, 1986.

———. *The Roots of American Communism*. New York: Viking Press, 1957.

Dubofsky, Melvyn. *When Workers Organize: New York City in the Progressive Era*. Amherst: University of Massachusetts Press, 1968.

Edinger, Lewis J. *German Exile Politics: The Social Democratic Executive Committee in the Nazi Era*. Berkeley: University of California Press, 1956.

Ely, Richard. *The Labor Movement in America*. New York: T. Y. Crowell & Co., 1886.

Encyclopedia of the American Left. Edited by Mari Jo Buhle, Paul Buhle, and Dan Georgakas. New York: Garland Pub., 1990.

Engberg, Jens. *Til Arbejdet! Liv Eller død! Louis Pio og Arbejderbevaegelsen*. Copenhagen: Gyldendal, 1979.

Essays on the Scandinavian-North American Radical Press. Edited by Dirk Hoerder. Bremen: Labor Newspaper Preservation Project, Universität Bremen, 1984.

Evans, Richard. *The Feminist Movement in Germany, 1894–1933*. London: Sage Pub., 1976.

———. *Sozialdemokratie und Frauenemanzipation im deutschen Kaiserreich*. Berlin: J. H. W. Dietz, 1979.

Failure of a Dream?: Essays in the History of American Socialism. Edited by John H. M. Laslett and Seymour Martin Lipset. Berkeley: University of California Press, 1974.

Faires, Nora. "Occupational Patterns of German-Americans in Nineteenth-Century Cities." In *German Workers in Industrial Chicago, 1850–1910: A Comparative Perspective*, edited by Hartmut Keil and John B. Jentz. DeKalb: Northern Illinois University Press, 1983.

Flexner, Eleanor. *Century of Struggle: The Woman's Rights Movement in the United States*. Cambridge: Harvard University Press, 1966.

Foner, Eric. *Free Soil, Free Labor, Free Men: The Ideology of the Republican Party before the Civil War*. New York: Oxford University Press, 1970.

———. "Why Is There No Socialism in the United States?" *History Workshop* 17 (Spring 1984): 57–80.

Fones-Wolf, Ken. *Trade-Union Gospel: Christianity and the Labor Movement in Industrial Philadelphia, 1865–1915.* Philadelphia: Temple University Press, 1989.

Formation of the Workingmen's Party of the United States, 1876. Edited by Philip Foner. New York: American Institute for Marxist Studies, 1976.

Foster, William Z. *History of the Communist Party, USA.* New York: International Publishers, 1952.

Fricke, Dieter. *Die deutsche Arbeiterbewegung, 1865 bis 1914: Ein Handbuch über ihre Organisation und Tätigkeit im Klassenkampf.* Berlin: Verlag Das europäische Buch, 1976.

Friedrich, Cäcilie, editor. *Kalendergeschichten.* Berlin: Akademie-Verlag, 1975.

Gerber, David A. *The Making of an American Pluralism: Buffalo, New York, 1825–1860.* Urbana: University of Illinois Press, 1989.

German Workers' Culture in the United States, 1850–1920. Edited by Hartmut Keil. Washington: Smithsonian Institution Press, 1988.

German Workers in Chicago: A Documentary History of Working-Class Culture from 1850 to World War I. Edited by Hartmut Keil and John B. Jentz. Urbana: University of Illinois Press, 1988.

German Workers in Industrial Chicago, 1850–1910: A Comparative Perspective. Edited by Hartmut Keil and John B. Jentz. DeKalb: Northern Illinois University Press, 1983.

Germans for a Free Missouri: Translations from the St. Louis Radical Press, 1857–1862. Edited and translated by Steven Rowan. Columbia: University Press of Missouri, 1983.

Glimpses of the German-American Radical Press. Edited by Dirk Hoerder and Thomas Weber. Bremen: Labor Newspaper Preservation Project, 1985.

Goedsche, Herman (Sir John Retcliffe, pseud.). *Biarritz.* Berlin: Verlag von E. S. Liebrecht, 1868.

Goldberg, Judith Lazarus. "Strikes, Organizing, and Change: The Knights of Labor in Philadelphia, 1869–1890." Ph.D. Dissertation, New York University, 1985.

Grimes, Alan P. *The Puritan Ethic and Woman Suffrage.* New York: Oxford University Press, 1967.

Grossmann, Atina. *The New Woman, The New Family, and the Rationalization of Sexuality: The Sex Reform Movement in Weimar Germany, 1928–1933.* Ann Arbor: University Microfilms, 1984.

Gutman, Herbert. "Alarm: Chicago and New York, 1884–1889." In *The American Radical Press, 1880–1960,* edited by Joseph Conlin, vol. 2. Westport, Conn.: Greenwood Press, 1974.

————. "Labor in the Land of Lincoln: Coal Miners on the Prairie." In *Power and Culture: Essays on the American Working Class,* edited by Ira Berlin. New York: Pantheon, 1987.

Gutman, Herbert, and Berlin, Ira. "Class Composition and the Development of the American Working Class." In *Power and Culture: Essays on the American Working Class,* edited by Ira Berlin. New York: Pantheon, 1987.

Habenicht, Jan. *Dějiny Čechů v Americkych.* St. Louis: Hlas, 1910.

Selected Bibliography

Hall, Jacquelyn Dowd; Korstad, Robert; and Leloudis, James. "Cotton Mill People: Work, Community, and Protest in the Textile South, 1880–1940." *American Historical Review* 91 (1986): 245–86.

Hanagan, Michael. *The Logic of Solidarity: Artisans and Industrial Workers in Three French Towns, 1871–1914.* Urbana: University of Illinois Press, 1980.

Harring, Sidney L. *Policing a Class Society: The Experience of American Cities, 1865–1915.* New Brunswick, N.J.: Rutgers University Press, 1983.

Harzig, Christiane, and Hoerder, Dirk, eds. *The Press of Labor Migrants in Europe and North America, 1880s-1930s.* Bremen: Labor Migration Project, Universität Bremen, 1985.

The Haymarket Affair and the Trial of the Chicago Anarchists, 1886. Edited by John Kebabian. New York: H. P. Kraus, 1970.

Heider, Ulrike. *Der arme Teufel: Robert Reitzel vom Vormärz zum Haymarket.* Frankfurt: Elsten, 1986.

Heiss, Christine. "German Radicals in Industrial America: The Lehr- und Wehr-Verein in Gilded Age Chicago." In *German Workers in Industrial Chicago, 1850–1910: A Comparative Perspective,* edited by Hartmut Keil and John Jentz. DeKalb, Ill.: Northern Illinois University Press, 1983.

Herminghouse, Patricia. "Radicalism and the 'Great Cause': The German-American Serial Novel in the Ante-Bellum Era." In *America and the Germans: An Assessment of a Three-Hundred Year History,* edited by Frank Trommler and Joseph McVeigh, vol. 1. Philadelphia: University of Pennsylvania Press, 1985.

Higham, John. "Current Trends in the Study of Ethnicity in the United States." *Journal of American Ethnic History* 2 (Fall 1982): 5–15.

Hildebrandt, Günther. *Die Paulskirche in der Revolution 1848/49.* Berlin: Verlag der Nation, 1986.

Hirsch, Carl. *Die Parteipresse: Ihre Bedeutung und Organisation.* Leipzig: Druck und Verlag der Genossenschafts-Buchdr., 1876.

Hirsch, Susan E. *Roots of the American Working Class: The Industrialization of the Crafts in Newark, 1800–1860.* Philadelphia: University of Pennsylvania Press, 1978.

Hlaváček, Francis. "Zlomky českého počátečního hnutí dělnického v Americe." In *Rocenka Americkych Delnickych Listu.* Cleveland: Tiskem uniové tiskarny Amer. děl. listů, 1924.

Hocking, Patricia M., and Husbands, G. T. *Why Is There No Socialism in the United States?* London: Macmillan, 1976.

Hoerder, Dirk. "German Immigrant Workers' Views of 'America' in the 1880s." In *In the Shadow of the Statue of Liberty,* edited by Marianne Debouzy. Saint-Denis: Presses Universitaires de Vincennes, 1988.

——. " 'Mobs, a Sort of Them at Least, Are Constitutional': The American Revolution, Popular Participation, and Social Change." *Amerikastudien* 21 (1976): 289–306.

——. "The Press of Labor Migrants from Western and Central Europe: Introduction." In *The Immigrant Labor Press in North America,* edited by Dirk

Hoerder and Christiane Harzig, vol. 3. Westport, Conn.: Greenwood Press, 1987.

Hoerder, Dirk, and Harzig, Christiane. *"Why Did You Come?"—Proletarian Mass Migration: Research Report, 1980–1985.* Bremen: Universität Bremen, 1986.

Hoerder, Dirk, and Keil, Hartmut. "The American Case and German Social Democracy at the Turn of the Twentieth Century, 1878–1907." In *Why Is There No Socialism in the United States? Pourquoi n'y a-t-il pas de Socialisme aux Etats-Unis?*, edited by Jean Heffer and Jeanine Rovet. Paris: Ed. de l'Ecole des Hautes Etudes en Sciences Sociales, 1988.

Hoerder, Dirk, and Roessler, Horst, eds. *Distant Magnets: Expectations and Realities in the Immigrant Experience.* New York: Holmes and Meier, forthcoming.

Hofacker, Erich P. *German Literature as Reflected in the German-Language Press of St. Louis prior to 1898.* St. Louis: Washington University Studies, Language and Literature (New Series, no. 16), 1946.

Holmes, Joseph J. "The National Guard of Pennsylvania: Policemen of Industry, 1865–1905." Ph.D. Dissertation, University of Connecticut, 1971.

Howe, Irving and Widick, B. J. *The UAW and Walter Reuther.* New York: Random House, 1949.

Huffines, Marion L. "Language-Maintenance Efforts among German Immigrants and Their Descendants in the United States, 1960–1980." In *America and the Germans,* edited by Frank Trommler and Joseph McVeigh, vol. 1. Philadelphia: University of Pennsylvania Press, 1985.

Ickstadt, Heinz, and Keil, Hartmut. "A Forgotten Piece of Working-Class Literature: Gustav Lyser's Satire of the Hewitt Hearing of 1878." *Labor History* 20 (Winter 1979): 127–40.

The Immigrant Labor Press in North America, 1840s-1970s: An Annotated Bibliography. 3 vols. Edited by Dirk Hoerder and Christiane Harzig. Westport, Conn.: Greenwood Press, 1987.

The Impact of the American Revolution Abroad. Washington, D.C.: Library of Congress, 1976.

In the Shadow of the Statue of Liberty. Edited by Marianne Debouzy. Saint-Denis: Presses Universitaires de Vincennes, 1988.

Kaelble, Hartmut. *Historical Research on Social Mobility: Western Europe and the USA in the Nineteenth and Twentieth Centuries.* New York: Columbia University Press, 1981.

Kamman, William Frederic. *Socialism in German American Literature.* Philadelphia: Americana Germanica Press, 1917.

Kargau, E. D. *St. Louis in früheren Jahren. Ein Gedenkbuch für das Deutschtum.* St. Louis: A. Wiebusch & Sohn Printing Co., 1893.

Katz, Rudolph. "With DeLeon since '89." In *Daniel DeLeon: The Man and His Work.* New York: Socialist Labor Party, 1918.

Kaufman, Stuart Bruce. *Samuel Gompers and the Origins of the American Federation of Labor, 1848–1896.* Westport, Conn.: Greenwood Press, 1973.

Kawaguchi, Lesley Ann. "The Making of Philadelphia's German-America: Ethnic Group and Community Development, 1830–1883." Ph.D. Dissertation, UCLA, 1983.

Kebabian, John, S., ed. *The Haymarket Affair and the Trial of the Chicago Anarchists, 1886.* New York: H. P. Kraus, 1970.

Keil, Hartmut. "An Ambivalent Identity: The Attitude of German Socialist Immigrants toward American Political Institutions and American Citizenship." In *In the Shadow of the Statue of Liberty,* edited by Marianne Debouzy. Saint-Denis: Presses Universitaires de Vincennes, 1988.

———. "Chicago-Projekt: Lebensweise und Kultur der deutschen Arbeiterschaft Chicagos zwischen 1850 und dem Ersten Weltkrieg." *Amerikastudien* 29 (1984).

———. "Deutsche sozialistische Einwanderer in den USA im letzten Drittel des 19. Jahrhunderts: Lebensweise und Organisation im Spannungsfeld von Tradition und Integration." Habilitation Thesis, University of Munich, 1985.

———. "German Immigrant Workers in Nineteenth Century America: Working-Class Culture and Everyday Life in an Urban Industrial Setting." In *America and the Germans,* edited by Frank Trommler and Joseph McVeigh, vol 1. Philadelphia: University of Pennsylvania Press, 1985.

———. "The German Immigrant Working Class of Chicago, 1875–1890: Workers, Labor Leaders, and the Labor Movement." In *American Labor and Immigration History, 1877–1920s: Recent European Research,* edited by Dirk Hoerder. Urbana: University of Illinois Press, 1983.

———. "German Working-Class Radicalism in the United States from the 1870s to World War I." In *"Struggle a Hard Battle": Essays on Working-Class Immigrants,* edited by Dirk Hoerder. DeKalb: Northern Illinois University Press, 1986.

———. "Knights of Labor, the Trade Unions, and German Socialists in Chicago, 1870–1890." In *Impressions of a Gilded Age,* edited by Marc Chenetier and Rob Kroes. Amsterdam: Amerika Instituut, Universiteit van Amsterdam, 1983.

Kellner, George Hellmuth. *The German Element on the Urban Frontier: St. Louis, 1830–1860.* Columbia: University of Missouri Press, 1973.

Kiesewetter, Renate. "Die Institution der deutsch-amerikanischen Arbeiterpresse in Chicago: Zur Geschichte des *Vorboten* und der *Chicagoer Arbeiterzeitung,* 1874–1886." In *Glimpses of the German-American Radical Press,* edited by Dirk Hoerder and Thomas Weber. Bremen: Labor Newspaper Preservation Project, 1985.

———. "Die Institution der deutsch-amerikanischen Arbeiterpresse in Chicago: Zur Geschichte des *Vorboten* und der *Chicagoer Arbeiterzeitung,* 1874–1886." M.A. Thesis, Ludwig-Maximilians-Universität, 1982.

Kipnis, Ira. *The American Socialist Movement, 1897–1912.* New York: Columbia University Press, 1952.

Kleppner, Paul. *Cross of Culture: A Social Analysis of Midwest Politics, 1850–1900.* New York: Free Press, 1970.

Koehn, Birgit; Milz, Helga; et al. "Verlässliche Frauenspersonen und Luxusdamen: Anknüpfungspunkte für eine emanzipatorische Frauenpolitik." In *Geschlechterverhältnisse und Frauenpolitik,* edited by Projekt Sozialistischer Feminismus. Berlin: Argument-Verlag, 1984.

Krause, Paul. "Labor Republicanism and '*Za Chlebom'* ": Anglo-Americans and Slavic Solidarity in Homestead." In *"Struggle a Hard Battle,"* edited by Dirk Hoerder. DeKalb: Northern Illinois University Press, 1986.

Kruszka, Waclaw. "Gazeciarstwo Polskie w Ameryce." In *Historya Polska w Ameryce,* 13 vols. Milwaukee: Drukiem Spoeki Wydawniczek Kuryera, 1905–8.

Labor Migration in the Atlantic Economies. Edited by Dirk Hoerder. Westport, Conn.: Greenwood Press, 1985.

Land ohne Nachtigall. Deutsche Immigranten in Amerika, 1777–1886. Edited by Rolf Weber. Berlin: Der Morgen, 1981.

Laslett, John H. M. "America before and after Emigration: Scottish Miners' Views of the U.S. through the Columns of the *Glasgow Sentinel,* 1850–1876." In *The Immigrant Labor Press in North America,* edited by Dirk Hoerder and Christiane Harzig. Westport, Conn.: Greenwood Press, 1987.

Laurie, Bruce. *Working People of Philadelphia, 1800–1850.* Philadelphia: Temple University Press, 1980.

Laurie, Bruce, and Schmitz, Mark. "Manufacture and Productivity: The Making of an Industrial Base, Philadelphia, 1850–1880." In *Philadelphia: Work, Space, Family, and Group Experience in the Nineteenth Century,* edited by Theodore Hershberg. New York: Oxford University Press, 1981.

Laurie, Bruce; Hershberg, Theodore; and Alter, George. "Immigrants and Industry: The Philadelphia Experience, 1850–1880." In *Philadelphia,* edited by Theodore Hershberg. New York: Oxford University Press, 1981.

Lavinskas, Frank. *Amerikos Lietuviu Lakrasciai, 1879–1955.* New York, 1955.

Le Blanc, Paul. "Revolutionary Socialism in America, 1877–1887." Seminar paper, University of Pittsburgh, 1979.

Leinenweber, Charles. "Urban Socialism." Unpublished monograph in the author's possession, 1978.

Levine, Bruce C. "Free Soil, Free Labor, and Freimänner: German Chicago in the Civil War Era." In *German Workers in Industrial Chicago, 1850–1910,* edited by Hartmut Keil and John B. Jentz. DeKalb: Northern Illinois University Press, 1983.

————. "Immigrant Workers, 'Equal Rights,' and Anti-Slavery: The Germans of Newark, New Jersey." *Labor History* 25 (Winter 1984): 26–52.

————. " 'In the Spirit of 1848': German-Americans and the Fight over Slavery's Expansion." Ph.D. Dissertation, University of Rochester, 1980.

Lexikon sozialistischer deutscher Literatur. The Hague, 1973; pirated printing of an earlier edition (Halle [Saale]: Verlag Sprache und Literatur, 1963).

Lichtenstein, Nelson. "Walter Reuther and the Rise of Labor-Liberalism." In *Labor Leaders of America,* edited by Melvyn Dubofsky and Warren Van Tine. Urbana: University of Illinois Press, 1987.

Lilienthal, Meta. *Dear Remembered World.* New York: R. R. Smith, 1947.

———. *From Fireside to Factory.* New York: Rand School of Social Science, 1916.

———. *Women of the Future.* New York: Rand School of Social Science, 1916.

Loeher, Franz. *Geschichte und Zustände der Deutschen in Amerika.* 2d ed. Göttingen: G. H. Wigand, 1855.

Luebke, Frederick C. *Bonds of Loyalty: German-Americans and World War I.* DeKalb: Northern Illinois University Press, 1974.

Lunardini, Christine A. *From Equal Suffrage to Equal Rights: Alice Paul and the Woman's Party, 1910–1928.* New York: New York University Press, 1986.

Mahaim, Annik; Holt, Alix; and Heinen, Jacqueline. *Frauen und Arbeiterbewegung: Deutschland vor 1919, Russische Revolution, Spanischer Bürgerkrieg.* Frankfurt: ISP Verlag, 1984.

Marx, Karl, and Engels, Friedrich. *The German Ideology.* Edited by R. Pascal. New York: International Publishers, 1947.

Marx, Karl, and Engels, Friedrich. *Werke.* 43 vols. Berlin: Dietz, 1964–.

Marzolf, Marion. *The Danish-Language Press in America.* New York: Arno Press, 1979.

Mikkelsen, Robert L. "Immigrants in Politics: Poles, Germans, and the Social Democratic Party of Milwaukee." In *Labor Migration in the Atlantic Economies,* edited by Dirk Hoerder. Westport, Conn.: Greenwood Press, 1985.

Miller, Kerby A. "Golden Streets, Bitter Tears: The Irish Image of America during the Era of Mass Migration." In *Distant Magnets: Expectations and Realities in the Immigrant Experience,* edited by Dirk Hoerder and Horst Roessler. New York: Holmes and Meier, forthcoming.

Moltmann, Günter. *Atlantische Blockpolitik im 19. Jahrhundert: Die Vereinigten Staaten und der deutsche Liberalismus während der Revolution von 1848/49.* Düsseldorf: Droste Verlag, 1973.

Montgomery, David. *Beyond Equality: Labor and the Radical Republicans, 1862–1872.* New York: Viking, 1967.

———. "The Irish and the American Labor Movement." In *America and Ireland 1776–1976,* edited by David N. Doyle and Owen Dudley Edwards. Westport, Conn.: Greenwood Press, 1980.

———. "Nationalism, American Patriotism, and Class Consciousness among Immigrant Workers in the United States in the Epoch of World War I." In *"Struggle a Hard Battle,"* edited by Dirk Hoerder. DeKalb: Northern Illinois University Press, 1986.

Mott, Frank Luther. *American Journalism: A History, 1690–1960.* 3d ed. New York: Macmillan, 1962.

Na'aman, Shlomo. *Demokratische und soziale Impulse in der Frühgeschichte der deutschen Arbeiterbewegung der Jahre 1862/63.* Wiesbaden: F. Steiner, 1969.

Nadel, Stanley. "From the Barricades of Paris to the Sidewalks of New York:

German Artisans and the European Root of American Labor Radicalism." *Labor History* 30 (Winter 1989): 47–75.

——. "Jewish Race and the German Soul in Nineteenth Century America." *American Jewish History* 77 (Sept. 1987): 19–22.

Nagiel, Henryk. *Dziennikarstwo Polskie w Ameryce*. Chicago: Naktadem Kom. Cent. Obeslania Wystawylwowskieg Przez Polonie Amerykanska, 1894.

Nagler, Jörg. *Fremont contra Lincoln: Die deutsch-amerikanische Opposition in der Republikanischen Partei während des amerikanischen Bürgerkrieges*. Frankfurt am Main: Peter Lang, 1984.

Naturalismus-Debatte, 1891–96. Edited by Norbert Rothe. Berlin: Akademie-Verlag, 1986.

Nelson, Bruce C. *Beyond the Martyrs: A Social History of Chicago's Anarchists, 1870–1900*. New Brunswick, N.J.: Rutgers University Press, 1988.

——. " 'We Can't Get Them to Do Aggressive Work': Chicago's Anarchists and the Eight-Hour Movement." *International Labor and Working Class History* 29 (Spring 1986): 1–13.

Obermann, Karl. *Joseph Weydemeyer, Ein Lebensbild, 1818–1866*. Berlin: Dietz, 1968.

Oestreicher, Richard. "The Limits of Labor Radicalism: Tom Barry and the Knights of Labor." Paper presented at the Knights of Labor Centennial Symposium, Newberry Library, Chicago, 1979, in author's possession.

——. *Solidarity and Fragmentation: Working People and Class Consciousness in Detroit, 1875–1900*. Urbana: University of Illinois Press, 1986.

Offermann, Toni. *Arbeiterbewegung und liberales Bürgertum in Deutschland: 1850–1863*. Bonn: Verlag Neue Gesellschaft, 1979.

Omi, Michael, and Winant, Howard. *Racial Formation in the United States from the 1960s to the 1980s*. New York: Routledge & Kegan Paul, 1986.

Osada, Stanislaw. *Prasa i Publicystyka Polska w Ameryce*. Pittsburgh: "Pittsburczanina," 1930.

Osterroth, Franz. *Biographisches Lexikon des Sozialismus*. Vol. 1, *Verstorbene Persönlichkeiten*. Hannover: Dietz, 1960.

Park, Robert E. *Immigrant Press and Its Control*. New York, 1922.

Parsons, Albert. *Anarchism: Its Philosophy and Scientific Basis as Defined by Some of Its Apostles*. Chicago, 1889.

Perlman, Selig. "Upheaval and Reorganization." In John R. Commons, *History of Labour in the United States*, vol. 2. New York: Macmillan, 1918–35.

Pierce, Bessie Louise. *From Town to City, 1848–1871*. Vol. 2 of *A History of Chicago*. New York: A. A. Knopf, 1940.

Pio, Louis. *Den Lille Amerikaner. En Forer op Tølk for Skandinaverne i Amerika*. Chicago, 1879–80. Translated in Jens-Bjerre Danielsen, "The Early Danish Immigrant Socialist Press." In *Essays on the Scandinavian-North American Radical Press*, edited by Dirk Hoerder. Bremen: Labor Newspaper Preservation Project, Universität Bremen, 1984.

——. *Til de skandinaviske Arbejdere i Amerika*. Chicago, 1877.

Pitzer, Elisabeth. "Bürgerliche Presse und Arbeiterpresse im Wandel: Deutsch-amerikanische Tageszeitungen am Ende des 19. Jahrhunderts, dargestellt am Beispiel von 'Illinois Staatszeitung' und 'Chicagoer Arbeiterzeitung.'" M.A. Thesis, Ludwig-Maximilians-Universität, 1980.

"Plutokraten und Sozialisten": Berichte deutscher Diplomaten und Agenten über die amerikanische Arbeiterbewegung, 1878–1917. Edited by Dirk Hoerder. Munich: Saur, 1981.

Polišenský, Josef. "Český podíl na předhistorii Prvního máje." In *Začiatky českej a slovenskej emigrácie do USA*, edited by Miloš Gosiorovský. Bratislava: Slovenske Akadémie Vied, 1970.

Poore, Carol. *German-American Socialist Literature, 1865–1900.* Bern: Peter Lang, 1982.

Quataert, Jean. "The German Socialist Women's Movement, 1848–1918: Issues, Internal Conflicts and the Main Personages." Ph.D. Dissertation, UCLA, 1974.

———. *Reluctant Feminists in German Social Democracy, 1885–1917.* Princeton: Princeton University Press, 1979.

Rachleff, Peter. *Black Labor in the South: Richmond, Virginia, 1865–1890.* Philadelphia: Temple University Press, 1984.

Radkau, Joachim. *Die deutsche Emigration in den USA: Ihr Einfluss auf die amerikanische Europapolitik 1933–1945.* Düsseldorf: Bertelsmann Universitätsverlag, 1971.

Reitzel, Robert. *Des armen Teufel gesammelte Schriften.* 3 vols. Detroit, 1913.

———. *Mein Buch.* Edited by Martin Drescher. Detroit, ca. 1900.

Richardson, James F. *The New York Police: Colonial Times to 1901.* New York: Oxford University Press, 1970.

Rischin, Moses. "The Jewish Labor Movement in America: A Social Interpretation." *Labor History* 4 (Fall 1963): 227–47.

———. *The Promised City: New York's Jews, 1870–1914.* Cambridge: Harvard University Press, 1977.

Robertson, Priscilla. *An Experience of Women: Pattern and Change in Nineteenth Century Europe.* Philadelphia: Temple University Press, 1982.

Robinson, Thomas. "Chicago Typographical Union #16: Fifty Years of Development." Ph.D. Dissertation, University of Chicago, 1925.

Roediger, David. "Ira Steward and the Anti-Slavery Origins of American Eight-Hour Theory." *Labor History* 27 (Summer 1986): 410–26.

Rohner, Ludwig. *Kalendergeschichte und Kalender.* Wiesbaden: Athenaion, 1978.

Ross, Steven Joseph. "Workers on the Edge: Work, Leisure, and Politics in Industrializing Cincinnati, 1830–1890." Ph.D. Dissertation, Princeton University, 1980.

———. *Workers on the Edge: Work, Leisure, and Politics in Industrializing Cincinnati, 1788–1890.* New York: Columbia University Press, 1985.

Rowan, Steven. "The Cultural Program of Heinrich Boernstein in St. Louis, 1850–1861." *In Their Own Words* (Venice) 3 (1986): 187–206.

Ruge, Arnold, and Marx, Karl, eds. *Deutsch-französische Jahrbücher*. 2d rev. ed. with introduction by Joachim Höppner. Leipzig: Reclam, 1981.

Ruge, Clara. *On the Road. Drama in One Act*. New York: Modern Library, 1913.

——. *Raub. Soziales Drama*. New York: Modern Library, 1917.

——. *Die Wiederkehr, ein Drama aus der Kriegszeit*. New York: Modern Library, 1916.

Ryan, Mary P. *Womanhood in America: From Colonial Times to the Present*. New York: New Viewpoints, 1983.

The Samuel Gompers Papers. Vol. 2: *The Early Years of the American Federation of Labor*. Edited by Stuart Kaufman. Urbana: University of Illinois Press, 1987.

Sanderson, John P. *Republican Landmarks: The Views and Opinions of American Statesmen on Foreign Immigration*. Philadelphia: J. B. Lippincott & Co., 1856.

Schaack, Michael. *Anarchy and Anarchists*. Chicago: F. J. Schulte, 1889.

Schenda, Rudolf. *Die Lesestoffe der kleinen Leute*. Munich: Beck, 1976.

——. *Volk ohne Buch: Studien zur Sozialgeschichte der populären Lesestoffe, 1770–1910*. Frankfurt am Main: V. Klostermann, 1970.

Schlüter, Hermann. "Die Anfänge der deutschen Arbeiterbewegung in New York und ihre Presse." *New Yorker Volks-Zeitung*, 25th Anniversary Edition, Feb. 21, 1903, pp. 8–12.

——. *Die Anfänge der deutschen Arbeiterbewegung in Amerika*. Stuttgart, 1907. Edited by Carol Poore. New York: Peter Lang, 1984.

Schmidt, Walter. *Wilhelm Wolff: Kampfgefährte und Freund von Marx und Engels, 1846–1864*. Berlin: Dietz, 1979.

——. *Wilhelm Wolff: Sein Weg zum Kommunisten, 1809–1846*. Berlin: Dietz, 1963.

Schneirov, Richard. "The Knights of Labor in the Chicago Labor Movement and in Municipal Politics, 1877–1887." Ph.D. Dissertation, Northern Illinois University, 1984.

Schneirov, Richard, and Jentz, John B. "Social Republicanism and Socialism: A Multi-Ethnic History of Labor Reform in Chicago, 1848–1877." Unpublished paper, 1985.

Schorske, Carl E. *German Social Democracy, 1905–1917: The Development of the Great Schism*. New York: Cambridge University Press, 1955.

Schraepler, Ernst. *Handwerkerbünde und Arbeitervereine 1830–1853: Die politische Tätigkeit deutscher Sozialisten von Wilhelm Weitling bis Karl Marx*. Berlin, 1872.

Seifert, Ruth. "Bebel Revisited: Die Konstruktion des Weiblichen in der frühen Sozialdemokratie." Unpublished manuscript.

——. "The Portrayal of Women in the German-American Labor Movement." In *German Workers' Culture in the United States, 1850 to 1920*, edited by Hartmut Keil. Washington: Smithsonian Institution Press, 1988.

Selavan, Ida C. "Jews." In *The Immigrant Labor Press in North America*, edited by

Dirk Hoerder and Christiane Harzig, vol. 2. Westport, Conn.: Greenwood Press, 1987.

Seller, Maxine S. "Defining Socialist Womanhood: The Women's Page of the *Jewish Daily Forward* in 1919." *American Jewish Historical Society Quarterly Publication* 76 (June 1987): 416–38.

Shalloo, Jeremiah P. *Private Police: With Special Reference to Pennsylvania.* Philadelphia: American Academy of Political and Social Science, 1933.

Shefter, Martin. "Trade Unions and Political Machines: The Organization and Disorganization of the American Working Class in the Late Nineteenth Century." In *Working-Class Formation: Nineteenth-Century Patterns in Western Europe and the United States,* edited by Ira Katznelson and Aristide Zolberg. Princeton: Princeton University Press, 1986.

Shergold, Peter R. *Working-Class Life: The "American Standard" in Comparative Perspective, 1899–1913.* Pittsburgh: University of Pittsburgh Press, 1982.

Skerrett, Ellen. "The Development of Catholic Identity among Irish Americans in Chicago, 1880–1920." In *From Paddy to Studs,* edited by Timothy J. Meagher. Westport, Conn.: Greenwood Press, 1986.

Smith-Rosenberg, Carroll. *Disorderly Conduct: Visions of Gender in Victorian America.* New York: A. A. Knopf, 1985.

Sochen, June. *Movers and Shakers: American Women Thinkers and Activists, 1900–1970.* New York: Quadrangle, 1973.

Sorokin, Pitrim. "Leaders of Labor and Radical Movements in the United States and Foreign Countries." *American Journal of Sociology* 22 (Nov. 1927): 382–411.

Sozialistische Arbeiterpartei von Nord-Amerika, *Offizielles Protokoll der 3. National-Konvention . . . abgehalten vom 24 Dezember 1879 bis 1 Januar 1880.* Detroit, 1880.

Sperber, Manes. *Die vergebliche Warnung.* Vienna: Europaverlag, 1975.

Spier, Anne. "Germans." In *The Immigrant Labor Press in North America,* edited by Dirk Hoerder and Christiane Harzig. Westport, Conn.: Greenwood Press, 1987.

Stearns, Peter N. *Eighteen Forty-Eight: The Revolutionary Tide in Europe.* New York: Norton, 1974.

Štědronský, František. *Zahraniční krajanské noviny, časopisy a kalendáře.* Praze: Národní Knihovna, 1958.

Steinisch, Irmgard. "Studies of American Labor History in West Germany." *Labor History* 29 (Fall 1988): 531–41.

"Struggle a Hard Battle": Essays on Working-Class Radicalism. Edited by Dirk Hoerder. DeKalb: Northern Illinois University Press, 1986.

Suhrbur, Thomas J. "Ethnicity in the Formation of the Chicago Carpenters Union, 1855–1890." In *German Workers in Industrial Chicago, 1850–1910,* edited by Hartmut Keil and John B. Jentz. DeKalb: Northern Illinois University Press, 1983.

Sylvis, James C. *The Life, Speeches, Labors, and Essays of William H. Sylvis.* Philadelphia: Claxton, Remsen, & Haffelfinger, 1872.

Tasca, Annamaria. "Italians." In *The Immigrant Labor Press in North America,* edited by Dirk Hoerder and Christiane Harzig, vol. 3. Westport, Conn.: Greenwood Press, 1987.

Tedebrand, Lars-Goeran. "The Image of America among Swedish Labor Migrants." In *The Immigrant Labor Press in North America,* edited by Dirk Hoerder and Christiane Harzig. Westport, Conn.: Greenwood Press, 1987.

Thonnessen, Werner. *The Emancipation of Women.* London: Pluto Press, 1973.

Timberlake, James H. *Prohibition and the Progressive Movement, 1900–1920.* Cambridge: Harvard University Press, 1963.

Tolzman, Don Heinrich. *German-Americana: A Bibliography.* Metuchen, N.J.: Scarecrow Press, 1975.

Tomlins, Christopher L. *The State and the Unions.* New York: Cambridge University Press, 1985.

Trautmann, Frederic. *The Voice of Terror: A Biography of Johann Most.* Westport, Conn.: Greenwood Press, 1980.

Vagts, Alfred. "Heinrich Boernstein, Ex- and Repatriate." *Bulletin of the Missouri Historical Society* 12 (1955–56): 105–27.

Van Tine, Warren R. *The Making of the Labor Bureaucrat: Union Leadership in the United States, 1870–1920.* Amherst: University of Massachusetts Press, 1973.

Vorwärts. Unveränderter Neudruck. Edited by Walter Schmidt. Leipzig: Zentralantiquariat, 1975.

Wagner, Maria. "The Representation of America in German Newspapers before and during the Civil War." In *America and the Germans,* edited by Frank Trommler and Joseph McVeigh, vol. 1. Philadelphia: University of Pennsylvania Press, 1985.

Weber, Thomas. "Die Berichterstattung der 'New Yorker Volkszeitung' hinsichtlich der örtlichen Polizei im Zeitraum von 1886–1892." Unpublished state examination thesis, Universität Bremen, 1985.

Weeks, Jeffrey. "Foucault for Historians." *History Workshop* 14 (Autumn 1982): 106–19.

Weinstein, James. *The Decline of Socialism in America, 1912–1925.* New York: Monthly Review Press, 1967.

Wilentz, Sean. "Against Exceptionalism: Class Consciousness and the American Labor Movement." *International Labor and Working Class History (ILWCH)* 26 (Fall 1984): 1–24 [with rejoinders in *ILWCH* 27 by Nick Salvatore, Michael Hanagan, and Steven Sapolsky, and response by Wilentz in *ILWCH* 28].

Williamson, Jeffrey, and Lindert, Peter. *American Inequality: A Macroeconomic History.* New York: Academic Press, 1980.

Wilpert, Gero von. *Sachwörterbuch der Literatur.* 4th ed. Stuttgart: A. Kroener, 1964.

Wist, Johannes. "Den Norsk-Amerikanernes Presse, II: Pressen efter Borgerkrigen." In *Norsk-Amerikanernes Festskrift, 1914*, edited by Johannes Wist. Decorah, Iowa: Symra Co., 1914.

Wittke, Carl. *Against the Current: The Life of Carl Heinzen*. Chicago: University of Chicago Press, 1945.

———. *The German Language Press in America*. Lexington: University of Kentucky Press, 1957.

———. *Refugees of Revolution: The German Forty-Eighters in America*. Philadelphia: University of Pennsylvania Press, 1952.

———. *The Utopian Communist: A Biography of Wilhelm Weitling, Nineteenth-Century Reformer*. Baton Rouge: Louisiana State University Press, 1950.

Zeitgenossen von Marx und Engels: Ausgewählte Briefe aus den Jahren 1844–1852. Edited by Kurt Koszyk and Karl Obermann. Assen: Von Gorcum, 1975.

Zucker, Adolf Eduard. *Robert Reitzel*. Philadelphia, 1917.

Zucker, Adolf Eduard, ed. *The Forty-Eighters: Political Refugees of the German Revolution of 1848*. New York: Columbia University Press, 1950.

Notes on Contributors

PAUL BUHLE has been a writer, editor, oral historian, publisher, translator, activist, and intellectual organizer over the past quarter-century. Ph.D. from the University of Wisconsin (1975), he has been director of the Oral History of the American Left at Tamiment Library, New York University, since 1976 and has taught U.S. history at the Rhode Island School of Design since 1986. His books include: *Marxism in the United States, C. L. R. James: The Artist as Revolutionary, Working Lives: An Oral History of Rhode Island Labor,* and (with Mari Jo Buhle), *The Concise History of Woman Suffrage.*

JAMES P. DANKY, Newspapers and Periodicals Librarian, State Historical Society of Wisconsin, has authored/compiled over thirty reference works, bibliographies, and monographs on the radical press, women, and minorities. He is working on a national bibliography of African-American newspapers and periodicals.

KEN FONES-WOLF has a Ph.D. from Temple University and has written extensively on labor and Philadelphia history. His most recent publication is *Trade Union Gospel,* and he is currently at the West Virginia and Regional History Collection at West Virginia University.

DIRK HOERDER teaches North American social history at the University of Bremen, Germany. He has directed several projects on labor migration from Europe, including Eastern Europe, to North America. He has published *"Struggle a Hard Battle": Essays on Working-Class Immigrants, Labor Migration in the Atlantic Economies,* and jointly with Christitiane Harzig the three-volume bibliography *The Immigrant Labor Press in North America, 1840s to 1970s.*

JOHN B. JENTZ took his Ph.D. from the Graduate Center of the City University of New York, where he worked extensively with Eric Foner and Herbert G. Gutman. He has taught and worked in Germany, first on a Fulbright-Hays lectureship and then as a member of the Chicago Project based at the America Institute of the University of Munich. He has been Director of the Newberry Library's Family and Community History Center and is currently an assistant professor at Northern Illinois University and a lecturer at Northwestern University's University College. He has published extensively on nineteenth-century American social, labor, and immigration history and particularly on Germans in Chicago and the Midwest.

HARTMUT KEIL teaches U.S. social and cultural history at the America Institute of the University of Munich. His research fields include labor and working-class history, German immigration, and German-American radicalism, and political ideologies. He worked at the University of Wisconsin in Madison as an ACLS fellow (1975–76) and at the Smithsonian Institution's National Museum of American History (1984–85). From 1979 to 1988 he directed the Chicago Project on German immigrant workers. His publications include a collection of hearings from the McCarthy era, a documentary history of German workers in Chicago, and collections of essays on the German-American labor movement.

BRUCE C. NELSON teaches in the Department of History at Central Michigan University. He is the author of *Beyond the Martyrs: A Social History of Chicago's Anarchists, 1870–1900* and has begun a book manuscript entitled "Religion, Irreligion, and Chicago's Working Class in the Gilded Age."

RICHARD OESTREICHER, associate professor at the University of Pittsburgh, received his Ph.D. from Michigan State University in 1979. He is the author of *Solidarity and Fragmentation: Working People and Class Consciousness in Detroit, 1875–1900* and is working on a book on the working class in the United States in the nineteenth century.

CAROL POORE received her Ph.D. from the University of Wisconsin in 1979. She is associate professor of German at Brown University and author of *German-American Socialist Literature 1865–1900;* editor of

Deutsch-amerikanische sozialistische Literatur 1865–1900, Anthologie; and has also written articles on the literature of the German Democratic Republic, Peter Weiss, Heinar Kipphardt, and metaphors of illness in modern German literature.

MOSES RISCHIN, professor of history at San Francisco State University, is a past president of the Immigration History Society. His books include: *The Promised City: New York's Jews 1870–1914, The American Gospel of Success, Immigration and the American Tradition,* and *Grandma Never Lived in America: The New Journalism of Abraham Cahan.* He is completing a biography of Abraham Cahan (1860–1951), the noted editor of the *Jewish Daily Forward,* the nation's most successful and longest-lived socialist newspaper.

STEVEN ROWAN studied at the University of Washington (B.A., 1965) and Harvard University (A.M., 1966; Ph.D., 1970) before taking a position in the History Department of the University of Missouri-St.Louis. He taught at King's College London in 1975–76, and he has received fellowships from the NEH, the Humboldt Foundation, and the University of Missouri Weldon Spring Fund. In 1988–89 he was at the Institute for Advanced Study, Princeton. Among his articles and books are *Germans for a Free Missouri: Translations from the St. Louis Radical Press, 1857–1862* and *Ulrich Zasius: A Jurist in the German Renaissance, 1461–1535,* and an edition of Henry Börnstein's *Mysteries of St. Louis.*

RUTH SEIFERT received her B.A. in Liberal Arts at Temple University in 1975, and her M.A. in Political Science, Philosophy and American History at the University of Munich in 1981. From 1981 to 1988 she did research in projects in the fields of American immigration history, political sociology, and industrial sociology. She now works at the German Armed Forces Institute for Social Research in Munich.

ELLIOTT SHORE received his Ph.D. from Bryn Mawr College and is the librarian at the Institute for Advanced Study in Princeton. He has published widely on the radical press in the United States in the nineteenth and twentieth centuries and his latest book is *Talkin' Socialism.*

Index

Index

Candidus, Wilhelm, 65, 68
Carl, Conrad, 22, 214
Carnegie, Andrew, 191
Catholics, 31–32, 34, 36, 42, 63, 102, 145, 152, 185
Central Labor Union: Chicago, 88, 94–95, 97–99; Detroit, 151
Chapman-Catt, Carrie, 139
Chemnitz, 18, 20
Chicago, 3, 5, 8–9, 18, 21, 25, 29, 49–60, 66–67, 81–104, 157, 160, 203
Chicago Labor, 99–100
Chicago Tribune, 84, 104
Chicagoer Arbeiter-Zeitung, 18, 20–22, 24–25, 83–92, 94–97, 100, 103–4, 128, 168
Chicagoer Bäcker-Zeitung, 103
Christensen, Jens L., 21–23, 97, 214
Christianity, 35–36, 206
Cincinnati, 1, 9, 58
Civil War, 9, 15–17, 19, 24, 29, 49, 51, 54–56, 58–59, 65–66, 184, 203–4
Clay, Henry, 39
Cleveland, 56, 157, 160, 194
Clevelander Volksfreund, 22
Comintern, 175
Communia, Iowa, 1
Communist party (U.S.), 168, 172–78, 185–86
Communist party of Germany (KPD), 109
Conzett, Conrad, 20, 22, 25, 83, 214
Currlin, Albert, 97, 214
Czechs, 81–82, 84–85, 88, 91, 99, 102, 208

Dagslyset (Chicago), 82, 92
Daily Worker (New York), 168
Danish, 81–83, 85, 99
Darwin, Charles, 114
Davenport, Iowa, 184
Debs, Eugene, 171, 196
Declaration of Independence, 51, 190, 197
DeFord, Miriam Allen, 8, 174
Degen, Robert, 22–23, 214
DeLeon, Daniel, 170–72, 177
Dell, Floyd, 87
Democratic party, 7, 41, 53, 55, 59, 66, 88, 187, 195
Demokrat, Die (Philadelphia), 65, 68
Detroit, 9, 147, 151–54, 156–57, 159, 183
Deutsch-Amerikanische Bäckerzeitung, 22

Deutsch-Amerikanische Buchdrucker-Zeitung, 26
Deutsch-Amerikanische Typographia, 3, 90
Deutsch-Französische Jahrbücher, 33
Deutsche Arbeiter, Der (Chicago), 49, 57, 59, 82, 92
Deutsche Schnellpost (New York), 2
Dietz, Georg, 2
Dietzgen, Joseph, 21–22, 97, 103, 214
Donnersberg party, 32
Douai, Adolf, 22–23, 71, 111, 171, 188, 207, 214
Draper, Theodore, 168, 172, 175
Drescher, Martin, 22, 164, 215
Duchatel, Charles-Marie Tanneguy, 33

Echo (Cleveland), 194, 196–97
Elizabeth, New Jersey, 194
Emancipator (Cincinnati), 18
Engel, George, 85, 96, 155
Engels, Friedrich, 32–34, 170

Fackel, Die (Chicago), 82–83, 85–88, 92, 100, 103–4
Farmer-Labor party (Minnesota), 176
Ferdinand, Archduke, 195
Fincher's Trades' Review (Philadelphia), 66
Fischer, Adolf, 22, 85, 96, 155, 215
Flaubert, Gustave, 177
Fones-Wolf, Ken, 7, 204–6
Forty-eighters, 2–4, 10, 15–16, 23, 29, 49–55, 58–59, 65, 145, 147–48, 151, 169, 182–84, 204
Fourth of July, 190–91
Fraina, Louis, 172
France, 2, 34
Frankfurt, 18, 32
Franz, Jacob, 21–22, 71, 111, 215
Frauenzeitung (Milwaukee), 3
Free-Soil party, 41
Freidenker, 17, 24, 157
Freie Blätter (St. Louis), 9, 34–42
Freie Gemeinde of North St. Louis, 39–41
Freie Presse (Philadelphia), 65, 68–69
Freiheit, 85, 174
Freisinnige, Der (Philadelphia), 1
Fremonters, 34, 56–57
Fritzsche, Friedrich Wilhelm, 20–21, 215

Frölich, Paul, 174

Garfield, James A., 190
Gempp, Heinrich Wilhelm, 38
General German Workingmen's Association, 17
George, Henry, 97, 119, 170, 175
German American, 38
German-American Typographical Union: No. 10, 18; No. 9, 90
German Language Federation (CPUSA), 177
Germany, 17–18, 20, 22–25, 32, 57, 67, 108–9, 122–23, 139, 184, 187–88, 202–3
Gide, Andre, 177
Gilman, Charlotte Perkins, 124
Gleichheit (Germany), 122, 124
Glos Wolny (Chicago), 101–2, 104
Goethe, Johann Wolfgang von, 152, 161
Gompers, Samuel, 74, 203
Gorsuch, Wilhelm, 72–73
Grad'Aus (Milwaukee), 3
Greie-Cramer, Johanna, 7, 122–26, 133, 138
Grottkau, Paul, 20–21, 83, 215
Gruen, Karl, 32
Gruenhut, Josef, 83
Grunzig, Julius, 111, 215
Gundlach, Wilhelm, 114

Hall, Covington, 8, 174
Hamburg, 33
Hardman, J. B. S., 177–78
Harper, Ida Husted, 134
Harriman, Job, 112
Harriman, Mary Averell, 134
Harris, William Torrey, 40
Harzig, Christiane, 5–6, 204
Hasselmann, Wilhelm, 21–22
Haymarket Affair, 72, 79, 82–83, 96, 102–3, 148, 152–57, 162, 189, 203
Haywood, Bill, 113, 193
Heider, Ulrike, 6
Heine, Heinrich, 33, 120, 161
Heinzen, Karl, 2, 5, 17, 22, 36, 51, 215
Henderson, Edward, 55
Hepner, Adolf, 21–22, 25, 215
Herwegh, Georg, 148, 163

Hesing, Anton, 59
Hess, Moses, 32
Higham, John, 205
Highland, Illinois, 34
Hillquit, Morris, 133
Hirsch, Carl, 19
Hirth, Frank, 83
Hitler, Adolf, 115, 208
Hoerder, Dirk, 5–6, 204
Holler, Joseph, 23, 216
Holmes, Lizzie, 98
Hungarians, 137

Ibsen, Karl, 21–22
Illinois Staats-Zeitung (Chicago), 50, 52–53, 59, 87, 104
Illinois Volkszeitung, 21, 93–94, 99–100
Industrial Workers of the World, 103–13
Ingermann, Anna, 133–38
International Workers Order, 178
International Working People's Association, 82, 84–85, 88, 90–91, 95, 97–99
International Workingmen's Association, 17–18, 66, 81, 95, 97, 103
Irish, 3, 49, 55, 59, 63–64, 67, 70, 150, 170, 192, 201–2
Irish World (New York), 64, 71
Iron Molders Union, 55

Jentz, John, 5–6, 203
Jesuits, 34, 37
Jewish Daily Forward, 168
Jews, 119, 186, 208–9
Jodlbauer, Josef, 9, 146, 192–97
Jonas, Alexander, 19, 22–23, 111, 117, 119, 207, 216

Kalendar des Philadelphia Tageblatt, 110
Kamman, William Frederic, 4
Kansas-Nebraska Act, 51, 65
Kautsky, Karl, 148
Kautsky, Minna, 117
Keil, Hartmut, 5–6, 83, 191, 204–5
Keitel, August, 21, 216
Key, Ellen, 139
Kilgore, Damon, 67, 69, 71
Kirchner, John, 72
Klings, Carl, 57, 59, 82–83, 216

Index

Norris, Frank, 112
Norwegians, 81–83, 85, 208
Nye Tid, Den (Chicago), 83, 85–86, 90–92, 98

Oestreicher, Richard, 6, 8
Olson, May, 5
Omaha, 184
O'Neill, Eugene, 116
Otto-Walster, August, 21–22, 25, 217

Pankhurst, Sylvia, 174
Paris, 33–34, 89, 155
Park, Robert E., 4
Parsons, Albert, 83–84, 86, 88–89, 96–97, 155
Parsons, Lucy, 84, 87, 96, 98
Pecka, Josef Boleslav, 84, 97
Pennsylvanische Staats Courier (Philadelphia), 3
Peoria, Illinois, 52
Philadelphia, 1–2, 7–8, 29–30, 64–74, 110, 193, 206
Philadelphia Tageblatt, 22, 71–73, 110–11, 168, 193
Pinkerton detectives, 96, 189, 191
Pio, Louis, 83, 98
Pionier calendar (New York), 8, 17, 108, 110–12, 114–16, 118–20, 178
Pittsburgh, 9, 90
Polish, 32, 81, 99, 208
Poore, Carol, 6, 8
Prace (Chicago), 97–100
Progressive Age (Chicago), 94
Progressive Woman, 124
Proletarier, Der (Chicago), 81
Public Ledger (Philadelphia), 68
Pullman strike, 103

Quint, Howard, 5

Railroad strikes of 1877, 187–88
Reformed Church (German), 150–51
Reimer, Otto, 21, 25, 217
Reitzel, Robert, 4, 6, 8–9, 17, 22, 24, 26, 145, 147–57, 159–61, 162–64, 217
Republican party, 7, 41, 50–51, 53–54, 56–57, 66, 87, 187, 195
Republik der Arbeiter, Der (New York), 1, 182

Reuther brothers, 209
Revolution of 1848, 29, 52, 113
Revolutionary Socialist party, 82–83
Rischin, Moses, 2, 6
Romm, Julie. *See* Zadek-Romm, Julie
Ronge, Johannes, 31–32
Rosenberg, Wilhelm Ludwig, 21–22, 83, 217
Rowan, Steven, 6
Ruge, Arnold, 34
Ruge, Clara, 116

St. Louis, 2, 9, 18, 33–42, 149, 184
St. Louis Tageblatt, 21
Samfundet (Chicago), 98, 100
San Antonio, 184
San Francisco, 184
Sand, George, 86
Sauer, Christopher, 3
Sauk Center, Wisconsin, 160
Scandinavians, 3, 81, 83, 90–91, 98, 102, 183
Schaefer, John, 23, 218
Schewitsch, Sergius, 22, 25, 111, 113, 171, 207, 218
Schiller, Friedrich, 116, 152, 161
Schilling, Robert, 21, 218
Schlaeger, Edward, 54, 56, 58
Schlüter, Hermann, 21, 25, 111, 171, 207, 218
Schmeling, Frances, 132
Schmidt, Ernst, 24, 111
Schmidt, Franz, 9, 31–33, 35–43
Schneidermann, Rose, 138
Schwab, Michael, 21–22, 83, 96, 152, 155, 218
Second International, 173
Seifert, Ruth, 7, 204, 206
Shakespeare, William, 162
Shannon, David, 5
Shaw, Anna Howard, 134
Shea, Lawrence, 55
Sheboygan, Wisconsin, 183
Shore, Elliott, 7, 204–6
Silesia, 31
Sinovieva-Deutsch, Esther, 136
Social Democrat, 18
Social Democratic Labor party of North America, 17, 20–21
Social Democratic party of Germany

245

Index